# Cross Currents 10

N U M B E R   1 0

# Cross Currents

A   Y E A R B O O K   O F

CENTRAL   EUROPEAN   CULTURE

YALE UNIVERSITY PRESS   NEW HAVEN AND LONDON

1        9        9        1

*Editor:* Ladislav Matejka

*Associate Editors:*
Bogdana Carpenter, Irwin R. Titunik,
Jindřich Toman

*Editorial Board:*
Marianna Birnbaum, Peter Demetz, Herbert
Eagle, Emery George, George Gibian, George
Grabowicz, Michael Heim, Antonin Liehm,
John Mersereau, Jr., Ivan Sanders, Benjamin
Stolz, Roman Szporluk, Thomas G. Winner,
Harry Zohn

*Advisory Committee:*
Stanislaw Baranczak, Avigdor Dagan, György
Konrád, Milan Kundera, Adam Michnik, Czeslaw
Milosz, Jaroslav Pelikan, H. Gordon Skilling,
Josef Škvorecký, Thomas Venclova

Numbers 1–9 of *Cross Currents* were published
by the Department of Slavic Languages and
Literatures at the University of Michigan.

Articles appearing in this annual are abstracted
and indexed in *Historical Abstracts* and *America:
History and Life.*

The editorial office of *Cross Currents* is located
at 19 Garden Street, #63, Cambridge,
Massachusetts 02138.

Designed by Richard Hendel.

Set in Sabon and Gill Sans type by G & S
Typesetters, Inc.

Printed in the United States of America by
Hamilton Printing Co., Rensselaer, N.Y.

Library of Congress Catalog Number 84-643232

The paper in this book meets the guidelines for
permanence and durability of the Committee on
Production Guidelines for Book Longevity of the
Council on Library Resources.

10 9 8 7 6 5 4 3 2 1

# Contents

# Editor's Preface

Number 10 of *Cross Currents: A Yearbook of Central European Culture* is brought out by its new publisher during the startling upheaval among the former cultural and political colonies of the Soviet Empire, whose western border was determined during the Second World War at Teheran and Yalta. Since the entire political and cultural climate of Central Europe changed, the focus of *Cross Currents* has to be altered accordingly. It is no longer an outlet for an oppressed society manipulated from a power center in Moscow. Many former dissidents who used to contribute to *Cross Currents* have become political leaders and are now trying to redefine the cultural and political values in the liberated regions. The sudden freedom has brought intellectual life into a state of ferment that makes Central Europe compelling in a new way.

In the beginning, *Cross Currents* was planned as the proceedings of an East European festival organized ten years ago by the University of Michigan in Ann Arbor and inaugurated by Czeslaw Milosz, the Polish-American Nobel Prize laureate. His introductory address was chosen by the editors to preface the first issue of *Cross Currents* and to serve as a programmatic statement for the entire series. Here Central Europe was defined as a cultural unit tied together by historical awareness of a common past and maintaining its own identity even while "placed in the eastern orbit by force of arms and by pacts between superpowers."

The power of historical awareness in Central Europe and the objection of Central Europeans to the radical displacement of the millennium-old border between Eastern and Western Europe were also spelled out in the first issue of *Cross Currents* by Milan Kundera, a Czech writer who, like Czeslaw Milosz, has been a member of the yearbook's advisory committee. In Kundera's view, the transformation of Central Europe, abandoned by the West after the Second World War, was "a part of a long-lived, patient and coherent strategy designed to move a country into the sphere of another civilization." According to Kundera, all "that characterized the West since the time of the Renaissance—tolerance, a methodological doubt, a plurality"—was destined to disappear in Central Europe. But at the same time he saw the growing historical awareness as a powerful source of hope and reminded the readers that "the political regimes are ephemeral but the frontiers of civilization are traced by centuries."

In accordance with these views, the editors of *Cross Currents* felt a need to focus on the cultural underpinnings of Central Europe in spite of stubborn communist attempts to absorb it into a vast, undifferentiated Eurasia under Soviet domination. *Cross Currents* tried to implement its goal by addressing the Western indifference to the fate of Central Europe and providing a tribune for a dialogue between Western and Central Europeans in the area of culture, arts, and politics.

Today Central Europe is no longer a mere conglomerate of small nations passively accepting their destiny in an imposed political environment, but an invigorated meeting ground of cultures stretching from the Baltic to the Mediterranean and encompassing Slavic, Baltic, Germanic, Jewish, Hungarian, Romanian, and Balkan components. It is the resuscitated interaction of the diverse streams of influences that makes the Central European arena once again culturally productive and worthy of attention.

We feel that there is a need to focus on the cultural character of Central European countries and to bring to light not only their diversity but also their common cultural denominators, in particular their traditional function as a bridge between East and West.

*Cross Currents* will continue to appear as a yearbook focusing on literature, music, visual arts, theater, and film, as well as on the political themes relevant to cultural life in Central Europe. At the same time it will leave open the question of borders while entrusting their delineation to the immanent forces of the Central European cultural traditions.

# Is There a Central European Culture?

JOHN WILLETT

The subject of Central European culture became topical early in 1989, when the Western establishment, both political and intellectual, had grown seriously aware that Mikhail Gorbachev's policy of openness and reconstruction would infect all the mid-European countries that Stalin and his followers had sought to control. Each of those countries would soon have to determine its own alignments and allegiances, developing new relations (for a start) with its neighbors, the United States, and West European countries and reexamining notions of Central Europe which had prevailed in past times. Could any such Central Europe, Mitteleuropa, or Mitropa form a recognizable, self-aware entity in our changing world? Or was the whole concept hopelessly clouded by nostalgia?

The question is certainly not one that is easy to define. For the cultural patterns suggest that there are a number of differently shaped slices of Europe which could in some way be called central. What about the Alpine lands centering on Switzerland, for a start? They obviously have much that is common to them and central to Europe as a whole. Or there is the frontier belt between Germans and Latins, running roughly from Brussels to Strasbourg to Savoy; it is the setting of Nicholas Freeling's novels, with their special Middle Kingdom feel, and you need only look at the work of its artists, from the Le Nains to Courbet to Segantini—or just drive through it for that matter—to sense its coherence. Or again there is an East-West swathe from Friuli and Carinthia to the Languedoc, where such linguistic survivals of the Romans as Romansch and Provençal are still to be found. Of course none of these are directly relevant to the area we are trying to locate, but they do suggest how the whole continent is overlaid with different patterns from the past, rather like the abandoned tracks and fields one can identify from an airplane flying over the desert country.

Once we have become sensitive to these, we may start to realize that Central Europe is not a universally agreed geopolitical or geocultural expression, but very largely what we want to make it. In other words, the tangible divisions between Central and Western or Eastern Europe or the Baltic territories or even the Balkans are so unclear that the crisscrossing cultural patterns can say more than any national and political ones. Is Trieste part of Central Europe, for instance? Is Warsaw? Vilnius?

Belgrade? And which Berlin are we talking about—East, West, or both? These questions are in the first place cultural and linguistic. And because cultures and languages change and develop, the answers are different at different times.

I remember my first sight of a linguistic map of Europe. In the west and much of the center, as also round the northern periphery of the Mediterranean and in Scandinavia, the pattern coincided very roughly with present-day political frontiers. There were awkward anomalies and patches of minority languages like those of the Basques and the Celts, as well as major national exceptions to the overall division into Latin, Germanic, and Slav—that is to say, the two large areas of Magyar and Finnish which stood out by their distinctive color, bordering on the Slavic mass to the east. But once past a line running from Berlin to the top of the Adriatic the picture was very different: the great Slav area starting with Poland, Bohemia, and Slovenia and stretching away to the Urals was flecked all over with little dots and spots of German speakers, culminating (in those days) in the Volga German Republic, which existed deep within Russia from Catherine the Great's time till Joseph Stalin cleared out its people in the Second World War. Much more recently I learned just one of the practical implications of this speckled pattern—the network of German-language theaters in the old Austrian and Russian empires, whose cultural mission there appealed not only to German nationalists of mainly right-wing views but also to a man of the left like Erwin Piscator, who in the 1930s sent German theater groups to the Ukraine and even tried to establish a new communist Weimar in the plains beyond the Volga.

The search for a Central European culture therefore begins with these ancient traces of Germanic colonization. It is followed by the feudal phase, where a German-speaking aristocracy was dominant, through the beginnings of national, non-German cultures and the emergence in the nineteenth century of an ethnically mixed, German-speaking middle class, along with the impact of the great European artistic movements centering on Paris, up to the wide-ranging cultural exchanges of the 1920s, the subsequent cultural reaction propagated by Hitler and Stalin, then the confused moves toward a free modern culture in the cramping conditions of the propaganda war, with its iron curtain across Europe; finally the loosening up and speeding of communications which now seem to be taking place in a technologically interlinked world. In all this the marvelous German-Jewish culture which has managed to survive against all odds is one rich element, which must surely play a prominent part in our thoughts.

We must not forget that there have long been three main competitors for control in Central Europe, however you care to define it. These were the Hapsburg (or primarily Austrian) Empire until its fall in 1918, the German Empire as constituted by Bismarck and reestablished by Adolf Hitler after 1933, and the Russian Empire of czarism, Stalinism, and the Warsaw Pact. Two of the three profited from the widespread use of the German language—though certainly the Austrians came increasingly to respect their linguistic minorities—while the third hoped to unite the Slavs. It may be relevant to notice those intervals when their competition was less intense, as it seemed to be in the years between the fall of the Hapsburg and Hohenzollern empires and the establishment of Hitler's aggressive Third Reich. And if, as I shall argue, such a moment of reduced domination and mutual tolerance was also one of particularly active multicultural interchange, what conclusions should we be drawing for the future?

In these questions of cultural history I don't think it is possible to be very objective, for aesthetic value judgments are bound to determine the direction for the historian's interests; and unless these are personally engaged he or she might as well shut up. So I shall not try to say anything about developments in Central Europe before the mid-nineteenth century, since so many of the great landmarks—like Gluck's operas or the premiere of Don Giovanni—belong in the main Austro-Italian tradition, and even Haydn's use of Hungarian folk music had something of the same detached exoticism as the retired English nabob's taste for Indian curry. True, there were the beginnings of national theaters in Warsaw, Budapest, and Prague—cities where the popular language was being systematically developed and applied in literature and scholarship. But Rome remained Europe's recognized center for the study of the visual arts, and both Chopin and Liszt, for all their evidence of national feeling, spent their creative years and their most passionate energies outside their own countries.

What changed this still largely feudal pattern was a combination of circumstances—the rise of the middle classes and the weakening of Hapsburg autocracy after 1848, the new freedom of communication brought by cheap postage and the spread of the railways, and the artistic Realism that developed in Paris and Düsseldorf, with its initially populist and democratic flavor. As a result by the 1880s both international art movements and an identifiably ethnic artistic nationalism had been gaining ground. And a new view of Central Europe was beginning to take shape.

The modern movement in the arts is rooted in these two apparently contradictory developments of the late nineteenth century, and we still feel their effects. Symbolism (rather than the more specifically French discovery of Impressionism) was the truly international new movement or wave of feeling that struck the arts throughout all Europe as the century drew to its close, and its influence became evident in the many exhibitions, journals, and performances which now for the first time involved creative artists from a wide range of countries—the proliferating French salons and mid-European secessions from 1890 on, the Scandinavian theater and the various "free stages," the *Studio* magazine, the paintings of Gauguin, Hodler, Munch. At the same time a new interest in folk or popular art and music had begun to lend substance to the conscious nationalism already exemplified in the compositions of Smetana and Dvořák, and this seems to coincide with the beginning of serious anthropology and ethnology as well as with Champfleury's pioneering French studies in *imagerie populaire.*

Thus on the one hand Europe (*and* North America) was beginning to draw together so far as artistic innovation was concerned, while on the other hand creative artists and their public were looking more closely both at their own roots—individual via the early works of Freud, communal via Alois Riegl's examination of folk art—and at those of less-developed primitive peoples. This interest in the arts as an expression of primordial characteristics and feelings is still with us, and it underlay not only the music of the Hungarian Bartók and other powerful nationalists but also the new Nietzschean wildness of the modern movement in general, as seen in Gauguin and the Fauves and echoed in the work of the Czech Seven and the Hungarian Eight.

Looking then at Europe in the years immediately preceding the First World War, we find Berlin still a secondary center with respect to music and the official, subsidized theater; Max Reinhardt, however, is perhaps the leading European director of the time, with a repertoire ranging from the classics to Strindberg and Wedekind; Peter Behrens, working for the new electrotechnical industry in his forties, is the outstanding modern architect, with Le Corbusier as one of his pupils; while the Brücke painters, having moved from Dresden to Berlin, are assimilating the expressive violence of the Fauves to the new spatial and kinetic ideas of French Cubism and Italian Futurism, mediated by the great animator Herwarth Walden and his Sturm magazine-cum-gallery. Even madness no longer seems alien to the younger poets: witness the brilliant and tragic figure of Jacob van Hoddis, who wrote the classic "World End."

Situated less than a hundred miles from Dresden, Prague at that time is still something of an Austrian provincial city, with its German theater and opera in addition to the National and other Czech stages. It also has a budding school of notable German-language writers—Rainer Maria Rilke, Franz Werfel, Franz Kafka and his friend Max Brod. Leoš Janáček, based in Brno and already in his fifties, is an established composer in the new national tradition; unlike those of Bartók, his power and originality have not yet been internationally recognized. František Kupka, the pioneer abstractionist, has settled in Paris, and the Parisian influence is also felt on the young Czech cubist school. The great humorist Jaroslav Hašek has given a trial run to his immortal character the Good Soldier Švejk, and gone wandering round the obscure villages of sub-Carpathian Ruthenia and the other equally primitive areas of the Hapsburg Empire that figure in his short stories. In politics he is a mocking and not wholly sober anarchist.

In Vienna, the multilingual capital of that empire, Franz Josef's newly rebuilt Burgtheater has been pushed into a secondary place by Reinhardt's Berlin stages, but the music of Gustav Mahler, Richard Strauss, and the Philharmonic is still incomparable, while Arnold Schönberg has set the symbolist texts of *Erwartung* and *Pier-*

*rot lunaire* and aligned himself with Munich Expressionists of the *Blauer Reiter*. Arthur Schnitzler, Hugo von Hofmannsthal, and Karl Kraus are true Viennese writers of elegance and penetration, Adolf Loos and Otto Wagner pioneers of new design, while in Berlin and Vienna alike the young Oskar Kokoschka has shown himself to be a great modern portraitist and an individual painter outside all Isms.

This eve-of-war scene in our three mid-European cities was far from static, and in the first fifteen years of the twentieth century the trans-European cultural traffic, from north to south and from east to west, was intense. Ibsen and Bjørnson were established in Munich, Munch in Berlin and Weimar; the future Russian Constructivists—including several strikingly talented women—studying in Paris; while Frenchmen like Delaunay and Braque showed in Munich and Odessa. In 1909 Serge Diaghileff started introducing Western Europe (and later the Americas) to the brilliantly sophisticated barbarism of the new Russian ballet and its designers and composers, with Stravinsky as its counterpart to the Hungarian Bartók or the Spaniard de Falla. And while the German-Jewish writers of Central and Eastern Europe were forming their distinctive school under the Hapsburgs, a comparable wave of largely Jewish visual artists was rolling westward from those same areas to Paris, where most of them would be assimilated, along with other immigrants like Pablo Picasso and Juan Gris and the Italian Amedeo Modigliani, to make a newly mixed but identifiable group—generally figurative, yet colorfully expressive in its approach—known to dealers and critics as the Ecole de Paris.

If the Second World War would set the non-German peoples of Central Europe apart from the rest because of the appalling intensity of the suffering and slaughter inflicted on them by German racism, the war that ignited between Austria and Serbia at the end of July 1914 produced physical and psychological effects that were common throughout the whole area and brought its separate cultures closer together. The impact of this First World War on the arts was long seen in the most general terms, as if it were just a ghastly interruption in their progress and not a significant, if sometimes traumatic, contribution to it. But in fact the role of Expressionism in Germany was largely decided by that movement's growing opposition to the war, and its spirit and methods made it a model for the artists and writers in other countries, including in due course revolutionary Russia.

This can be traced back to Expressionism's prewar origins in a youthful revolt against the German establishment, with its military caste, its authoritarian fathers, and its unconscious urge to disaster, all of which now stimulated a more positive sense of activism, international brotherhood, and, in many important cases, revolutionary socialism in the cause of peace and humanity. So in November 1915 Lajos Kassák, the Hungarian artist-poet, founded his review *A Tett* on the model of Berlin's *Die Aktion,* whose title and antiwar stance it shared, then after its suppression a year later set up a similar magazine closer to Walden's *Der Sturm,* called *MA* (Today). In these journals Kassák published modernists like Apollinaire and Marinetti, who were then fighting patriotically on the other side; conversely, Walden in Berlin took to printing contributions not only from Hungary but also from the anti-Hapsburg avant-garde in Prague.

To the Czechs and Slovaks, the Poles, and the south Slavs, the wartime experience was clearly bound up with their struggles for national independence; and if the success of these meant breaking some of the older cultural ties with Germany and Austria, the result was not so much a narrow nationalism as a fresh interest in the modern movement as it filtered round via Paris or back from revolutionary Russia after 1917. The three great monarchies from which they sought freedom all fell, and the sense of revolutionary openness, with its accompanying optimism—and for a brief interval following the armistice its actual experience—gripped most of Central Europe, with often stimulating effects in the arts. Largely damped down in republican Vienna, the new climate brought wholesale changes in the official administration, direction, and application of the arts in Prussia, in Soviet Hungary, and above all in the new Soviet Russia which was still struggling for survival against a combination of former czarist forces, an independent Poland, and a somewhat halfhearted allied intervention. Like many of the other side effects of war (the shake-up of personal lives, prejudices, and values, the proximity of danger and death), these transformations gave Expressionism a relevance and a universality which it might otherwise never have enjoyed. And throughout the 1920s there was a common interest throughout Central Europe in the new cultural developments that followed.

The period identified with the Weimar Republic between the Bolshevik revolution and the national socialist takeover in Germany—which I rather tactlessly labeled "the New Sobriety" and which turns out almost exactly to coincide with the age of Prohibition in the United States—was very much what I meant when I referred to those intervals when the competition of the great powers to dominate Central Europe became less intense. And certainly it was remarkable for the comparative fluidity of its cultural exchanges and the contributions made by those former outsiders, the Magyars, the Slavs, and the Eastern Jews. The process began already during the war with the aggressively nonconformist activities of Dada in Zurich, a small multinational and polyglot movement away from Expressionism which caught the imagination of rebels both East and West. This spread throughout Europe in different ways and to different effect; thus in Berlin and Dresden it took a more committedly political form with Otto Dix and George Grosz; in Hanover it mysteriously spurned the sound poet and rubbish artist Kurt Schwitters; in Budapest it inspired the constructive abstractions of Kassák and Moholy-Nagy just as the avant-garde was being forced to emigrate through Austria to Germany; in Holland it turned the *De Stijl* artist Theo Van Doesburg briefly into a poet writing under the name I. K. Bonset; in Paris it was taken over by André Breton's Littérature group, which relaunched it as Surrealism; while in Prague the young satirists of the Liberated Theater and the left poet Vítězslav Nezval, instead of being directly infected by its German originators, followed the Parisian version and became mid-European surrealists.

Surrealism went on, thanks largely to Breton's persistence, but otherwise most of these Dada threads came to an end around 1920, to be succeeded by the influence of Russian Constructivism, first in its purely spatial and geometrical and then in its applied or productivist versions. This can be traced in the work of the Hungarian emigrés (both in Germany and after their return home) and most famously in the career of László Moholy-Nagy at the Bauhaus and elsewhere; it is also visible in the change in Schwitters and other graphic artists, and it inspired Mies van der Rohe and Hans Richter in Berlin to launch G (for *Gestaltung*), their short-lived Constructivist magazine. Probably it was the very rational, largely social and collectivist element in this new positive trend that led to the effort to form a Constructivist International, for which meetings were held in Düsseldorf and Weimar with members of MA, Dada, the Dutch De Stijl, and other avant-garde groups, as well as the Soviet-Jewish designer El Lissitzky who had been working with the major Russian abstractionist (or suprematist, as he styled himself) Kasimir Malevich at his school at Vitebsk near the Lithuanian border; this was also attended by the main Polish Constructivists. Though the planned International never really came into being, Lissitzky would remain an important link between the Germans and the brilliant Soviet avant-garde throughout the decade.

These early postwar exchanges took place when there were still all sorts of obstacles to physical movement within Central Europe. Free intercourse was scarcely possible before the summer of 1922, when the two pariah nations, defeated Germany and Bolshevik Russia, recognized each other by the Rapallo treaty—after which it was several more years before both of them became accepted by the allied powers. It was natural then that in the meantime they should turn to one another, and one of the results was a flow of influential visitors from Russia to Berlin, where the first big exhibition of the new Russian art was held that year, bringing Lissitzky, Chagall, Naum Gabo, and David Shterenberg as notable intermediaries. The Hungarians too were an important factor in this traffic thanks to the suppression of their 1919 revolution, in which most of the avant-garde had played some kind of executive or supportive role. Those who did not escape west via Vienna went to Russia, whence they too served as interpreters of the new revolutionary art—the critic Alfred Kemény, for instance, who took part in the debates on Constructivism; the Expressionist painter Béla Uitz of the old Eight group; and the theater director and aesthetician János Macza, who became a Soviet academician, then returned to Hungary after the Second World War.

With the ending of the great German inflation the following year and the failure of the last attempts at violent revolution or separatism in that country, a period of revival and reconstruction began. The important point here is that although it led to the introduction of new influences, notably that of the Americans whose loans made it possible, it did not bring any serious reaction against the modern movement in the arts: the cultural conservatism which was beginning to cramp clerical Austria and its much reduced capital city was not even very effective in restoration Hungary, let alone in a stabilized Germany or a newly prospering Czechoslovakia. It was in fact a good period for the arts throughout Central Europe, and it could only benefit from the German revival and the new consolidation of modernism to which this now led. Expressionism had run its course; Dada and Futurism were over; east of the Rhine, except in Czechoslovakia and Romania, Surrealism could not yet establish itself as a distinct school. But the new skepticism and sober practicality associated with functional architecture and the Constructivist approach to design also took over in the fine arts, both figurative and formal; and the whole process acquired its name from an art exhibition in 1925 devoted to this new matter-of-factness—*die neue Sachlichkeit.*

That phrase was not a bad description of what was now going on throughout the area and to some extent in Scandinavia and Switzerland too. The modern movement had become economical, critical, interested in coming to terms with new technologies and media and the collective approach which they demanded as well as jazz, light entertainment, the crime story, and other unpretentious means of access to a changing popular, mainly urban, audience. So the new term was extended, rather as Expressionism had been fifteen years earlier, to cover music, literature, and theater that reflected these same concerns. Reportage, documentary, photomontage, the "applied music" of Paul Hindemith's festivals, the neat light poem or song with a sting in it, the literature of fact, the topical play or revue, the jazz opera, the films of Eisenstein at one extreme and Chaplin at the other, all fell under the same dispassionate heading as the bitter war paintings of Otto Dix or the caricatures of George Grosz, and certainly the general slant sloped leftward. The link with Russia was maintained at least so long as Vladimir Mayakovsky, Sergey Tretyakov, and the great cinematographers still carried weight there; the magazine *LEF* was a good indicator of this till it collapsed in 1929. Czechoslovakia too contributed, through its avant-garde theater, its modern architecture, and Hašek's war novel, that great montage of high comedy with real episodes and individuals from a tragic, often desperate time.

One can see something like a cross section of this movement in a Czech almanac of 1927 printed without capital letters and published in Brno, which ranges across the whole field from George Antheil to Jiří Voskovec, the surrealist clown; from Iwan Goll and Tristan Tzara to the Russian formalist Yuri Tynyanov, from Lajos Kassák and Egon Erwin Kisch to Kurt Schwitters, from Walter Gropius on the Bauhaus to Alois Hába on microtones. The illustrations too put the Czech contributions in the forward-looking context of Vsevolod Meyerhold's theater, Richter's film *Rhythm,* drawings by Grosz and Schlichter, and an advance model of the Stuttgart *Weissenhofsiedlung,* which would open that year, all topped off by the Purist Ozenfant's Morgan three-wheeler with its exposed insides and the helmeted artist at the wheel. In itself this synoptic view might not seem all that unusual, for one finds it also in Le Corbusier's magazine *L'Esprit nouveau,* or the short-lived Soviet magazine which Ilya Ehrenburg and Lissitzky edited from Berlin, or Moholy-Nagy's series of Bauhaus books (which include those by Malevich, Mondrian, and Schlemmer along with planned volumes by the *MA* critic Ernö Kallai and the Czech Constructivist Karel Teige), or the semiofficial *Das neue Frankfurt,* all of which shared much the same view of the modern movement. But the point here is that the movement in question was not just a German one but was asking to be taken up by all. It was passionately believed in by its adepts yet depended on a climate of mutual tolerance. And from the Rhine eastward most of Europe could find it not only relevant but free of cultural-political strings.

The tolerance began to wear thin toward the end of the 1920s, as a result initially of Stalin's policy of "socialism in one country," which for most communists soon came to mean hostility toward socialism in all others. From then on, the new attitudes and methods of *neue Sachlichkeit* had to be turned toward this limited political end, and the corresponding artistic organizations to be split between those members who did or did not agree; all the rest of the movement was to be written off as "white socialism" or bourgeois reaction. Of course this polarization and division of the left, which went right through German politics during the run-up to Hitler, was based on a terrible misappreciation, and perhaps that is why its cultural implications had a relatively muted echo in the rest of Central Europe. This did not stop the militantly political art of the Weimar Republic's last four years from showing great originality and force, particularly where it had been initiated outside the new, ostensibly proletarian art organizations, as were such new forms as John Heartfield's political photomontage, the Brechtian *Lehrstück* or didactic cantata, the *Kampflied* or aggressive chorus for worker-singers, the high-tech documentary theater of Piscator, and the various elements of traveling agitprop. Yet although these forms later became of considerable interest to creative artists in the West (for instance in New Deal America and present-day West Berlin), they were not effectively matched in Vienna, Budapest, or Prague. Much of their importance was long-term in that they provided an alternative approach to political art to that currently maturing in the USSR.

If the years of stabilization in the mid-1920s brought the triumph of the international style of utilitarian achitecture advocated by the Bauhaus, the German Werkbund, and Le Corbusier and his CIAM, the world economic crisis which followed caused a severe reaction that seemed to be impelled by parochialism and nationalism, yet nonetheless became felt throughout Central and Eastern Europe. Much of the progress achieved since the beginning of the century was then thrown into reverse, and the effect was all the more demoralizing because the same process was experienced on both sides of the deepening political divide. The first signs of this disastrous swing-around came during the years of polarization and uncompromisingly political art, for it was just then that the Soviet leadership decided to dispense with aesthetic alternatives and group all the country's cultural forces behind the doctrine of Socialist Realism, meaning in effect the adaptation of nineteenth-century Realism to convey a message that was not so much socialist as national and socially uncritical. Within months of the abolition of the old pluralism in Russia, Hitler's national socialists came to power in Germany and started to follow a cultural policy astonishingly similar in its administrative arrangements, its critical vocabulary, and its preferred artistic styles. Under both of these outwardly opposed systems the modern movement, from the 1870s on, was rejected and the calendar put back to the time of Napoleon III.

This policy of demolition reached its twin peaks shortly before the Second World War, when on the one hand *Pravda* launched its editorial attacks on some of Russia's outstanding modernists, such as Eisenstein, Meyerhold, and Shostakovich, while on the other hand Goebbels's Chamber of Culture organized its Munich exhibition of Degenerate Art. Sandwiched between the two mutually hostile but equally philistine dictatorships, the modern movement battled on, particularly in Prague and Warsaw, though Vienna after the suppression of Austria's democracy in 1934 appeared to have little use for it, and both antimodernism and anti-Semitism were strong there. Just for a few years there was a curious communist attempt from Moscow to develop and propagate the new political art along with some of its modernist roots. This was conducted by non-Russian appointees of the Comintern secretariat—notably Piscator and Eisler, the Hungarians Uitz and Illes, the Slovak Spitzer—who in the spirit of the new Popular Front against fascism saw compatible cultural values in the radical art of such bourgeois avant-gardists as Schönberg and the French Surrealists. Such broad internationalism, however, had become politically suspect to Soviet security as well as incompatible with Socialist Realism, and it turned out that neither Stalin nor Hitler would hesitate to put a few avant-garde artists or writers to death. So Meyerhold, Koltsov, and Tretyakov died for their views in the USSR, the poet Erich Mühsam, the actor Hans Otto, and the *neue Sachlichkeit* artist Erich Ohser in the Third Reich.

National socialism was not just a political party but an all-embracing irrational creed of almost religious dimensions, whose nationalist and racist principles destined it inevitably for a policy of aggressive territorial expansion, ruthlessly and cruelly carried out. So once a Second World War broke out at the end of the dictatorial decade of the 1930s, the implications for the arts in Central Europe were very different from what they had been twenty-five years earlier. Having already moved into a not-unwilling Austria in 1938, Hitler was prepared, if not already determined, to take over any part of Central Europe—an area he regarded as having been artificially carved out of the Hapsburg Empire by the hated Versailles treaties. He himself despised its non-German populations as subhuman and hated their Jewish minorities. If these people had any choice, it was between being put under a puppet regime of more or less fascist persuasion and being governed by the Germans with ample use of the SS; alternatively they might simply become battle zones. Whatever happened, their cultural life would probably be throttled and any independent-minded artists forced to emigrate or be exterminated. On the one hand, then, there was a largely Jewish diaspora which gave the host countries a new interest in mid-European life and art; on the other were the massive cruelties which nobody considering that area would thenceforward be able to forget. All this was far beyond any injustices committed by the Hapsburgs, and at the end would come devastation much greater than that of 1914–1918. It would be supervised at first by the victorious allied armies, rather (in most cases outside Yugoslavia) than by a home-grown resistance. And those allies were generally indifferent to the modern arts—and in Russia's case positively against them.

I remember Vienna in the first winter after the war, when that city, like Berlin, was occupied by four armies—French, British, American, and Soviet—each with some kind of mission to push its own national culture rather than to revive the Viennese. A remarkable man called Norbert Bischoff, who later became the first postwar ambassador to the Soviet Union, organized what he termed the "ring" of eminent cultural figures and a few allied well-wishers who would work to make Austria once again into a center of stimulating East-West exchanges; he was unusual in not wishing himself to take sides. Some of the participants had been associated with the Nazis, some were of the left; none that I can remember (of the Austrians) had gone into emigration after 1938; the social secretary, as it were, was Egon Cäsar, Count Corti, a writer best known for his historical studies of the royal/imperial Hapsburg past. There were the composer Friedrich Wildgans, son of the poet; the eye specialist Professor Fuchs; Buschbeck the Burgtheater dramaturg; someone from the Vienna Philharmonic; Herbert Boeckl, the painter then heading the Academy; Paris Gütersloh, the fantastic painter-novelist; G. W. Pabst, the great film director of the 1920s and early 1930s; and I forget who else. All seemed keen on the objective and also on the accompanying dinner in the Rathaus cellar, which like much of the city was happily intact. But there had been too much destruction of a less tangible kind. And nobody had much to suggest in the way of concrete ideas to help cultural revival.

In the years that followed years of allied disagreement about Germany and long drawn-out Austrian peace treaty negotiations, many Central European frontiers were changed and German minorities deported, but none of the ex-Hapsburg countries was wiped off the map. They were, however, allocated to the Soviet sphere of influence (much as Greece was allocated to the British), though with assurances that their governments would include noncommunist elements and be subject to democratic elections. In this still-uncertain situation both the Russians and the three Western allies hoped to fill any cultural vacuum with their own art and the ideology which that implied, so that even before the general recognition of a state of cold war the new phenomena of government sponsorship and national cultural salesmanship largely overshadowed spontaneous efforts at indigenous cultural revival. Already the dividing line between the two sides—the communist and the economically free—ran from the Baltic down the middle of Germany and the Eastern end of Austria to Trieste; and although there were some changes, as when the occupation of Austria finished or when Yugoslavia broke ranks in 1948, the line is still more or less where it was. Despite all the changes either side of it, it is not yet all that easy to cross.

There have been new Central European developments in the arts since then, and a considerable loosening of Soviet cultural control. But except where there were threads of the prewar modern movement waiting to be picked up, and an undemoralized younger generation ready to make use of them, the cold war in the arts (or "battle for men's minds," as the new propaganda experts called it) was deeply damaging. Part of the trouble was that because the seminal innovators in the West had made their contributions half a century earlier and were now reaching the end of their lives, many of the movements now being exported—tachism, theater of the absurd, and other more or less abstract forms—were not very productive influences, and the mere fact that they were disliked by the Kremlin could not stop their adoption in Central Europe from leading to second-rate and second-hand art. Moore, Rothko, Pollock, Sartre, Anouilh, and Beckett were not Picasso and Stravinsky and the other great moderns whose work had been assimilated there before 1933, and it was quite wrong that they should be put forward as part of the democratic message and symbols of Western freedom. At the same time the remnant of the prewar left, who had once been identified with the sober, unromantic modernism of the 1920s, were inhibited from returning to it by the Soviet campaign against Formalism and the overlap between the doctrine of Socialist Realism and the Nazi view of art. This put such people in an impossible position, where they could take no initiatives of their own until that doctrine had been set aside.

In the 1950s there was an important return to the Expressionist heritage, particularly in West Berlin and the new German Federal Republic. Books, museum purchases, and exhibitions (of which some were sent abroad) all encouraged artists to look at what Germany had contributed between 1910 and 1923, and you only have to examine Polish painting since 1955 or the graphic work in a British art school today to see how widely that influence is still felt. In the visual arts, admittedly, the (East) German Democratic Republic was slower to react, thanks partly to a lack of funds; in its literature and theater, however, the official policy was to bring back important exiles, and with the new interest in the political aspects of Expressionism (as seen in the writings of the art historian Wolfgang Hütt) the validity of Socialist Realism became at least a matter for debate. By the 1960s the sequel to Expressionism too was being studied in both halves, particularly of Berlin. Brecht, the Bauhaus, photomontage, and agitprop were again accepted on the Eastern side of the divide, and in certain respects the creative results in both areas were akin—notably as seen in the work of younger poets such as Günter Kunert, Hans Magnus Enzensberger, Christoph Meckel, and the Austro-Londoner Erich Fried. In Berlin itself the scene became increasingly mixed, as East German artists absorbed the heritage of 1924–1933 in their own work, then showed, read, performed, and sold it in the West.

The greatest success in the past two decades of Central European culture appears to have been the cinema, partly no doubt because there was no aspect of exemplary Soviet art which remained so relatively immune to the aesthetic views of Stalin and his aides. Here Poland, Hungary, and Czechoslovakia have all won foreign respect. But even before that, Brecht's work was a godsend to those mid-Europeans anxious to break out of Socialist Realism: they could treat it as an extension of that essentially *passéiste* doctrine, much as they treated that of Mayakovsky, just because Brecht too was accepted by the Soviet arbiters—he even got a Stalin Prize in 1955, Stalin then being in Lenin's tomb—and cite it in justification of their own formal innovations. So in 1952 the Polish authorities had complained of Brecht's influence over their theater—from which we have since seen those of Grotowski and Kantor develop—claiming that he had undone all their cultural policy. And something similar applied to his reception in Czechoslovakia around the same time, though in that country there was one outstanding link with the prewar avant-garde in the shape of the director E. F. Burian, whom Brecht had seen as a kindred spirit since before the Second World War and tried vainly to rope into the work of his Berliner Ensemble.

During the 1960s there were signs of a new openness in Central Europe, owing much to Professor Goldstücker's Kafka conference, whose effective rehabilitation of that writer led the Austrian communist minister of education after the Second World War Ernst Fischer and the French communist Roger Garaudy to stand up for values unrecognized under Stalin. Admittedly, the climate in Czechoslovakia itself, which had been humming with new creative energy in 1967, was transformed after the Soviet invasion of 1968. In Hungary, which evolved more cautiously but in some respects further, what has most impressed me has been the song cycles of György Kurtag, the attention paid to the former Bauhaus architects, and Istvan Szabo's film *Mephisto*—whose view of the artist under national socialism is, alas, relevant to our whole theme. Finally there is Austria, which still includes a high proportion of Slavs and Hungarians—German is even now the language of only 60 percent of the population of Vienna, I believe—but has had to develop its postwar culture mainly as a single great city of the past, one deeply involved with the whole area but now largely isolated even from its own countryside. Happily, this has not killed its creativity, and the musicians and composers associated with Die Reihe, along with the poets coming from the Wiener Gruppe, have contributed something new to its once-conservative climate, while the old stodgy Burgtheater has been transformed in the last few years.

This has been a somewhat personal and patchy tour of the mid-European horizon, and I hope I have made clear the limitations which my own likes and dislikes have dictated. My interests and much of my knowledge are focused between the early years of the century and the Second World War, running well into what Brecht called "the Dark Times." I look on the establishment of the modern movement in mid-Europe after 1918 as something of a golden age, a brief renaissance of the arts in which figures like Stravinsky, Le Corbusier, Chaplin, Eisenstein,

Hašek, and Brecht stick out as great geniuses—a conjuncture exemplary in its coherence and universality, which can now however never be revived. I am also fascinated by the perversions of the arts by the German and Soviet dictatorships in the 1930s, which followed their relation to the politics of that time and to one another, and I find them ethically and aesthetically corrupt. This goes for the work of Albert Speer, Leni Riefenstahl, and Arno Breker, and I must admit to being gravely suspicious of any revival of fascist neoclassicism or gymnastic dance in the name of postmodernism, especially when it involves attacks on the modern movement, such as are currently fashionable in the West where architecture is concerned. Behind any such influence, somewhere in the distance, I smell the camps and see R. B. Kitaj's image of a train rolling across the eastern plains, set sideways and colored rose-pink on the screen print which he devoted to the White Rose Munich student group of the Scholls.

My impression is that free exchange is at present much more important to Central Europe than any common culture and that the most important common aspect of the *neue Sachlichkeit* of the 1920s was the feeling throughout the countries of the area that this movement was relevant to them. What I hope now is that as they come to terms with new communications technology and the possibilities of the new media—or more specifically with video and television and the use of reprography and the personal computer—there will again be an urge, and maybe even a need, for the same kind of exchange of ideas without strings attached. There are potential strings in Germany's traditional sense of superiority to its Eastern neighbors—seen at its worst of course in 1939–1945, as well as in Austria's nostalgia for its Hapsburg past, so like the British nostalgia for the imperial role in India. For there is life in the old nostalgias yet, and the visit of Archduke Otto to Budapest in the run-up to the new quasi-Western elections suggests that this might involve something a shade more serious than the local popularity of postcards of the Emperor Franz Josef and all that *Schrammelmusik*. The Vienna memorial celebrations for the Empress Zita must have been well worth watching, not to mention the reactions to them of Chancellor Kurt Waldheim.

It is still uncertain how the arts in Russia are going to develop under perestroika. Naturally there is a massive and in some respects stimulating interest on the part of Western dealers, critics, communicators, and collectors; but when will the artists themselves feel anything comparable to the electricity generated by the revolutions of 1917, acting on young men and women still digesting Cubism, Futurism, Expressionism, and other aspects of the international new movement? Aping the propaganda-hyped Western innovations of the 1950s and 1960s—most of them derivative in the first place, like *nouveau realisme* or minimal art—has not so far awoken the reckless genius of which that nation is capable. And good as it is that Soviet scholars and critics have rehabilitated the old avant-garde, there is even less sign of this inspiring any comparable powerhouse of new ideas for Central Europe to turn to than was the case with the German rediscovery of the arts of the Weimar Republic some forty-odd years ago.

Of course a lot has changed, and if it is true that we now live in a global village, as Marshall McLuhan used to insist, then the elements of a new Central European culture must come from even farther afield than they did before Hitler and Stalin. We certainly cannot expect them to depend on the spontaneous German-Jewish-Yiddish tradition that once seemed to link the comedian Peischachke Burstein in Vilnius with the writer Ettore Schmitz in Trieste: however unforgettable, that source is barred, buried under the masonry of the great concentration camp memorials. But the essence of mid-Europe surely is that its cultural inspiration must come from both East and West, and its role be to test ideas against one another and use the result in its own creativity. This means something more than just picking up notions and images as the new media and their owners and operators present them, for to the artist there is a world of difference between packaged reproduction and the real thing. What is needed then is the reestablishment of an open network of East-West cultural communication, into which the arts of the different countries of Central Europe can once again be plugged. The most important contacts will still be the first-hand ones, through the free circulation of performers, teachers, and creators and the direct experience of original works of art. Admittedly, neither free commerce nor political negotiation can ensure this. But at least they can see to it that the channels are not blocked.

# The Budapest Roundtable

## H. C. ARTMANN, PÉTER ESTERHÁZY, DANILO KIŠ, GYÖRGY KONRÁD, EDWARD LIMONOV, CLAUDIO MAGRIS, CZESLAW MILOSZ, PAUL-EERIK RUMMO, MIKLÓS MÉSZÖLY, AND ADAM MICHNIK

The following text is a translated transcript of a roundtable discussion among the writers who were invited by the Wheatland Foundation of New York to Budapest to the Wheatland Conference on Literature to discuss among other topics the concept of Central Europe. The meeting took place in June 1989 shortly before the dramatic events that changed the political situation not only in Central Europe but in Europe as a whole. In spite of the changes, however, the Budapest discussion has not lost its relevance. Central Europe as a cultural pattern is and will continue to be a vexed issue, as this abridged transcript of the discussion illustrates.

The panelists included Nobel Prize laureate Czeslaw Milosz; Adam Michnik, the dynamic Polish Solidarity leader and historian; three prominent Hungarian writers, György Konrád, Péter Esterházy, and Miklós Mészöly; Austrian poet H. C. Artmann; Estonian poet Paul Eerik Rummo; Italian writer and expert on Central Europe Claudio Magris; Russian novelist Edward Limonov; and Danilo Kiš from Yugoslavia, one of the most talented writers of our time, who died just a few months after the Budapest gathering. The panel was moderated by Michael Scammell, professor of Russian literature and noted biographer of Aleksander Solzhenitsyn.

### Michael Scammell

This is a rather historic moment for this part of the world. Therefore, our discussion will be quite different from what we might have expected even a few weeks ago because the context has changed so radically. There is a distinct feeling in the air that this is the end of an era, and we hope it is. It may also, therefore, be the beginning of an era. I hope the panel gathered here will discuss what this means to them, what this means for Central Europe, what this means for the literature and culture of this area. In 1988 in Lisbon, at the Wheatland Conference on Literature, Czeslaw Milosz suggested that the very concept of Central Europe was in its origins and nature mainly anti-Soviet. He is very aware of the changes that have happened since that time. In his statement he will discuss whether that idea still holds, whether Central Europe is essentially the same or a changed concept—whether in fact it will continue to exist at all as a concept in the future.

### Czeslaw Milosz

In this extraordinary year rich in political hope, it is difficult to speak of literature without speaking of politics. Let me then start with some basic questions. Here on the banks of the Danube, it is quite natural to ask oneself whether the idea of Central Europe has been just a whim of a few intellectuals or whether it will now acquire some new significance thanks to the aspirations for democracy reawakened in many countries.

The simple fact is that *our* perspective, whether we are Poles or Hungarians or Yugoslavs, is different from that of Western Europeans, Russians, or Americans. According to a frequently advanced thesis, the notion of Central Europe is artificial since the countries embraced by this name have aspired to become simply a part of Western Europe. There is some truth in this, yet the proponents of this view bypass certain facts and some durable traumas.

Fifty years ago, on August 23, 1939, an event of calamitous importance took place and became a preamble to World War II. This was the signing of the Molotov-Ribbentrop Pact, with its confidential protocols and secret clauses defining the so-called spheres of influence that divided up our part of Europe between the Soviet Union and Germany. We are separated from this event by half a century, but also by millions of deaths, by mass deportation, planned extermination of civilians, concentration camps, and slave-labor camps. And probably a basic difference between the two halves of Europe is that between memory and lack of memory. For Western Europeans the pact in question is no more than a vague recollection of a misty past. For us—I say us, for I myself experienced the consequences of that pact between superpowers—the division of Europe has been a palpable reality, as it has been for those who were born in our countries after the war. Therefore, I would risk a very simple definition of Central Europe: all the countries that in August 1939 were the real or hypothetical object of a trade between the Soviet Union and Germany. This means not only the area usually associated with the idea of centrality, but also the Baltic states—thus, the area where I was born.

A reduction to the role of an object of history creates sufficiently deep traumas and explains our wariness when we think of the two big neighbors. Independence from the Eastern Big Brother is not necessarily equated with unconditional acceptance of the West, represented by the economic power of Germany. I speak here not as a politician nor as an economist, yet a writer cannot abstain from defining a territory for his or her priorities in literature.

We are entering the last decade of the twentieth century and, taking stock, we cannot but call it a century of revolution. Even if to identify revolution in politics with revolution in art or literature would be misleading, the existence of a link bringing together artists and political revolutionaries cannot be put in doubt. The revolt of the nineteenth-century bohemians against the philistines and the bourgeoisie left a clearly visible heritage—for instance, in the history of surrealism. Now, in an era that is sometimes called postmodern, we ask ourselves whether we are thrown into a situation in which we cannot say no to the existing order of things, and whether our dislike of the bourgeois and the philistine loses all foundation. The disintegration of communist doctrine, of socialist realism, et cetera, leaves the field of art and literature submitted to the rule of offer and demand, East or West. The image of the decadent West versus the vigorous and morally healthy East has crumbled. And our countries of Central Europe are no longer protected by artificial barriers from words, sounds, and colors pouring into our area from the West.

Since I live in America and am to some extent an American writer, I should rejoice in this victory of freedom, even if it is a relative freedom only, for barriers still exist. And yet my American experience precisely reinforces my conviction that man does not live by bread alone. I would not be delighted to see us, wherever we live, enter a period when to maintain that man needs more than bread is met with ridicule. Or instead of bread put sex and violence, if you prefer. All the suffering of millions of human beings at the hands of totalitarian governments would be sentenced to oblivion were it not for something precious that was saved from disaster, namely the discovery of a clear line dividing good from evil, truth from lie. Central European countries were making this discovery while for the literati of America and Western Europe the opposition between good and evil was becoming a somewhat obsolete notion.

The critical attitude of Central European writers toward their Western colleagues is fully understandable. Those who fought against the blurring of the line between good and evil reproach, sometimes unjustly, those writers and artists who in the past eulogized the political terror of the state. I have even seen a kind of blacklist prepared by some writers in Moscow. The list encompassed all those in the West, beginning with Bernard Shaw, who dishonored themselves by making public pronouncements in praise of a system that kept millions of Soviet citizens in gulags.

Decades of pain and humiliation—that is precisely what differentiates Central European countries from their Western counterparts. Literature cannot avoid being marked by that issue, often in a quite unexpected way.

Writers in Poland (and Poland possibly can stand for several other countries) have discovered the dangers of direct involvement and participation in politics. Cowardice and sheer opportunism were not the only motivating forces behind some people's embracing the doctrine of the Communist party in the postwar period, and yet even those who were morally motivated did not escape noticing the travesty of reality and journalistic lies. Then in the 1970s Polish literature moved to the side of dissent and soon became an ally of Solidarity, both during its triumph in 1980–1981 and during its persecution under martial law. That time the moral issues were clear, and no serious writer sided with the party apparatus. Unfortunately, important pieces of writing do not necessarily result from a pure heart and good intentions. The obsessive, compulsive, monothematic poetry and prose of the last decade have been victims of their own exclusive concern with liberation from a bankrupt political system—certainly a noble task. Poetry and prose have, however, their own rules; they are bound by exigencies of form and of durability.

It is legitimate to ask what happens if a Polish, Hungarian, or Lithuanian writer decides to take a vacation from the here and now and to deal with the external subjects of love and death. Is he in the same position as a poet or novelist living in London, Paris, or New York? In my opinion, no. Here we encounter a truly difficult problem that has little to do with the political, philosophical, or religious options of a given writer. It involves rather his or her whole mentality, a mentality acquired not-quite-consciously. A specific contribution of this area of Europe to world literature may be precisely the giving of expression to that peculiar mentality, with both its weaknesses and strong points.

In translating into English and preparing for publication the erotic poems of Anna Świrszczyńska, a Polish woman poet, I noticed how different her poetry is from the work of contemporary American women poets. Instead of a confessional tone, there appears a kind of far-reaching detachment, an amused observation of herself and of a man. One is struck by a surprisingly cruel objectivity and by the absence of any attempt at psychology. This is just one example. An American friend with whom I work on translations asked me once, "Why are you and other Polish poets so interested in dealing with philosophical problems through poetry?" My answer may reflect a collective experience; that is, we share a specific sense of history that was forced on us against our will. Our participation in a historical drama and the hold of society on the individual may result in a certain objectivity, even in love poems. But such answers may not be fully satisfactory. It is also possible that a sense of proportion is involved, namely that certain ways of thinking and writing seem too frivolous in the face of the genocidal habits of mankind. Be that as it may, I have a feeling that I am touching on something real without being able to name it.

I do not intend to hide the fact that I am imbued with a dose of fanaticism that, however, is not—at least I hope not—doctrinaire. This fanaticism is directed against those tendencies in contemporary Western literature that offend my need for history—a history of values, of forms, and of styles. I have no ready-made prescriptions; I try, as I have said already, to grope empirically toward formulations simply by taking note of the common approaches in the literary works written in this part of Europe.

The term "historical imagination" escapes definition, yet without doubt some people have it and others do not. I believe a person endowed with that type of imagination is able to grasp events with precision by associating them with a proper place and time. One of the consequences of modern technology and mass education noticeable in the countries of the West is a vagueness of any notions related to history, so that the difference between the thirteenth century and the eighteenth century is blurred, languages spoken in various lands are confused, dates are mixed up.

Historical imagination is probably trained by a memory of collective suffering. If this is true, writers of Central Europe are called to make use of it in their works. Historical imagination reconstructs the past and makes us aware of its extreme durability. For example, in speaking of Central European cities it is necessary to keep in mind that they always bear traces of two different nineteenth-century empires: the czarist empire in the north, and the Hapsburg empire in the south. Similarly, the totalitarian experience will leave a permanent scar, even if, as we hope, it will not be shared by young generations.

### Edward Limonov

The concept of Central Europe is dishonest, to say the least. In 1935 Poland signed a nonaggression pact with Germany, before the Russian-German pact of 1939, you should know. In 1938 Poland took portions of Czechoslovakia. You don't remember that; you only remember the German-Russian pact of 1939.

### Miklós Mészöly

Allow me to comment briefly on Czeslaw Milosz's words. For the past century, in our part of the world, it was impossible to discuss literature without linking it to politics. Joan of Arc's statement, "When the French are in France and the English in England, then there is peace," forecasts the subdivision of Europe into states and the sharpening of national consciousnesses. But now, in various ways, some of these European states, burdened with anachronistic political arsenals and practices, have become bankrupt. The times we live in transcend the history of Central Europe because we are not alone with these problems. I think that ours is simply one version, the Central European version. Everything is the result of the struggle between empires and national states. In modern history we have had to fend off three consecutive imperialistic drives: the Hapsburg monarchy, Fascist Germany, and, most recently, Soviet messianic fanaticism. At this very moment our political and cultural future depends on our ability to take advantage of the historical opportunity presented by the Soviet Union.

To consider Central Europe as separate from Europe is unnatural, though not without historical precedent. In the various periods when Central Europe was politically isolated, it nevertheless continued to influence and nurture Europe—this common Europe that is in fact indivisible. Europe is all of us.

Speaking in broader terms, Europe has made moral, political, and cultural contributions to the history of the world. This export of civilization and technology created by the European spirit has become part of universal culture. Now, however, this export is met with ambivalence and anxiety because people feel both its blessings and its dangers. It is sad that the spiritual and cultural heritage of Eastern Europe is not a part of universal culture as well.

We cannot enter the next millennium without understanding the moral underpinnings of our culture, without identifying the political background against which literature in the Central European region developed its peculiar characteristics, without acknowledging the cultural contribution of Central Europe. Let me acquaint you with some distinguishing features of our world: the stress on philosophy in Polish literature and the pioneering aspects of the Polish theater of the absurd; the subjective metaphysics of the "little man" found in Czech writing; the richness of Croatian and Dalmatian literatures; the pathos found in the descriptions of heroic historical struggles in Serbian literature; the full and brilliant Byzantine style intertwined with Latin nostalgia in Romanian writing; finally, the bitter, tragic, existential, masochistic tone of Hungarian literature. These elements have seeped into the common European language, generally without notice.

### H. C. Artmann

What doesn't suit me is that term "Central Europe"; I only know *Mitteleuropa*. This term has been overly stretched on this panel, in fact—as far as the Baltic region. I would count Estonia among the Scandinavian countries. Being Austrian—the only Austrian here—I was not counted as Middle European, because we were lucky enough to regain our independence in 1955. Well, that is all I have to say.

### Adam Michnik

Let us speak about the phenomenon of contemporary Central European literature, because this literature is today at the center of attention, as is the entire geographical area that gave rise to it.

The strength of this part of Europe has always been the blending of religions and languages, of nationalities and cultures. This multinational, multicultural, rich mixture was able to produce a literature informed by the values of cultural pluralism and cultural tolerance. The region was characterized by multinational states, states that united within their boundaries people who spoke different languages. Living together condemned people to tolerance. They either had to learn to live with dissimilarity or fight to the death. Such indeed was the fate of the nations of this area: they either lived together or they fought one another.

Literature in Central Europe was condemned to cohabit with politics. After 1945 and the restoration of totalitarian systems, it was a cohabitation of a peculiar sort: literature was harnessed to politics and was meant to legitimize the new order. And literature did in its own way legitimize this new order—the order that invoked such values as equality, the emancipation of workers, and the universal canon of socialist utopias. Perhaps no one was able to recount so precisely the affair between the Central European intellectual and communism as did Czeslaw Milosz in his two great books, *The Captive Mind* and *Native Realm*. It is the story of an intellectual affair, a literary affair, but above all it is the story of an existential affair. The writer from our part of Europe was confronted with an especially difficult challenge. He had to come into collision with it. He was offered the position of engineer of souls, according to Joseph Stalin's unforgettable dictum. And he became the engineer of souls, meaning that he took part in the lie, in the reshaping of reality. Literature from Central Europe resembled then the shrill shouting from loudspeakers. During this time only a few managed to create a literature of whispers, a literature of conscientious dialogue with a reality so cruel, so ruthless, about a degradation so total, that only the whisper was the language of truth. In those days, people who wanted to speak the truth were condemned to whisper. But a literature of whispers was something more than literature. Shouts are appropriate at political meetings, but whispers are for the confessional. The literature was on the one hand blusterous, political agitation and on the other a confession whispered by a tormented man.

Literature from our sphere functioned in an environment characterized by a lack of civic institutions, a lack of normal intellectual and scientific reflection. It therefore had to be all those things at once. It had to take the place of sociological inquiries to record the truth about daily life. It had to take the place of political debate and function not unlike a nonexistent parliament. Finally, it had to take the place of civil education and create the moral model of a citizen who wants to live in truth amidst lies and who wants to be free amidst bondage.

The period of revolt after Stalin's death opened new possibilities for literature. The writer became an extraordinarily important catalyst in the process of social transformation. No one to this day has written the true intellectual history of the year 1956. And it is a fascinating history, for it is then that came into being the kind of thinking that later would be called the civil critique of the totalitarian state.

The fate of Central European literature is exile, to be understood literally as emigration. It is no coincidence that the greatest Polish writers from Mickiewicz and Słowacki to Milosz, Kołakowski, and Gombrowicz—as well as the Czechoslovak writers Milan Kundera and Josef Škvorecký, the Russian writers Vladimir Nabokov, Ivan Bunin, and Alexander Solzhenitsyn, and Romanian writers like Eliade and Cioran—all created in exile. The fate of this literature is also exile understood in another sense—exile from official circulation. In Poland Zbigniew Herbert, in Czechoslovakia Václav Havel and Bohumil Hrabal, in Hungary György Konrád and Miklós Haraszti, in Yugoslavia Danilo Kiš, in Russia Joseph Brodsky and Viktor Erofeev, and in Lithuania Tomas Venclova, all created outside the official structures of literary life.

Literature played an essential role when memory was at stake—the reconstruction of the continuity of national culture. But it also played an essential role when what was at stake was a revolt against that memory, the destruction of everything that seemed an anachronism and a lifeless stereotype.

Witold Gombrowicz, a great master of the word, was the one who declared war against all Polish masks, all Polish conformism. Gombrowicz and Milosz both demonstrate this unity between memory and revolt, conservation and contestation, restoration and revolution. Everything valuable that was accomplished in Poland in the past few years, that great spiritual rebirth, had its precedents in Polish literature. It was literature that first presaged and outlined the Polish victory over spiritual bondage.

When I consider the phenomenon of contemporary Central European culture, what strikes me as most significant is not at all the fact that this is an antitotalitarian literature, that it defends freedom against slavery. What is most significant is that this is a literature in which the religious question is present. In the last two decades there were two books that especially influenced people of my generation and the way of thinking in Central Europe—a selection of Simone Weil's writings and the theological reflections of Dietrich Bonhoeffer, who, condemned to death, conducted a dialogue with a silent Christ in his cell.

It is over religious questions that people were condemned to death in Auschwitz, in the gulags of the Soviet Union, and at various other times pursued, tracked down, spit upon, and shot. Nadezhda Mandelstam, the widow of the great Russian poet Osip Mandelstam, gave the world an account of the condition of the writer subjected to totalitarian pressure. It is no coincidence that the hidden light in her book is the light of religion. Simone Weil used precisely that metaphor, the metaphor of light. Describing her religious experience, she said that light is weightless, that one cannot hold light in one's hand, light cannot be measured or grasped. And blind people can live their entire lives having no awareness of light. Yet without light plants could not exist, trees would not strain upward, and the earth would not bring forth harvests.

In this sense the higher question informing contemporary Polish literature is the religious question. It is the question about the meaning of life and the meaning of artistic creation; about the meaning of courage and the meaning of opposition; about the meaning of humility and the meaning of dignity. Milosz and Herbert, Kołakowski and Konwicki, Herling Grudzinski and Baranczak, Krynicki and Adam Zagajewski—not one of them declares himself a religious writer. Yet without the question of religion their entire experience becomes incomprehensible. The return to religion is not the same as conversion. One shouldn't mechanically link the great renaissance of Catholicism in Poland, associated with the pontificate of John Paul II, with the phenomenon under discussion here. Connections do in fact exist, but they are much more subtle. Poland is a Catholic country. The Catholic Church in Poland has great power, but that Church is as divided as the nation. It is the Church that produced all that is best in Poland: the group around *Tygodnik Powszechny*, Jerzy Turowicz and Hanna Malewska, Andrzej Kijowski and Jan Błonski, are but a few examples. But the Church is not free of contamination with what is worst in Poland: chauvinism and xenophobia, hatred and intolerance, also find support, ironically, in the Catholic Church.

But that of which we speak transcends the sphere of politics. It commands us to consider what politics should be, to what values it should be subordinated. It is an attempt to confront politics with the ultimate questions. It seems that therein lies the most interesting phenomenon of Central European culture. It is a culture of ultimate questions. Or, to put it differently, between democratic and rational thought, which is the choice of a certain type of politics whose enduring characteristic is compromise, there rises the experience of Christian prophets, who pose—as do all prophets to all rulers—difficult, evangelical questions: "If I have spoken wrongly, bear witness to the wrong; but if I have spoken rightly, why do you strike me?" (John 18:23).

### György Konrád

I like Czeslaw Milosz's thesis very much—it is very convincing. Ours is a region where self-determination, in the personal, social, and national sense, was constantly disrupted because we were treated as objects—objects of imperial arrangements, peace treaties, partitions of spheres of influence. We were subjected to very different imperial arrangements from the nineteenth century on, from Vienna to Yalta, and ours was a disturbing and unpleasant part of Europe, and in fact two world wars started from disputes, conflicts, and turmoils arising in this eastern part of Europe. We say "Central Europe" because there are other more eastern parts of Europe, and indeed just now are we beginning to be aware of many other historical, political, and cultural conflicts of Europeans in the regions south of the Soviet Union that are still on the European side, as it were. So this eastern part of Europe from the Baltic to the Caucasus is beginning to be very alive; it is multinational, multicultural, multicolored, even to our eyes, which are quite accustomed to diversity, and therefore we are beginning to fear that we belong to a Central European periphery. Vanity, pride, fear, and anxiety make us wish to distance ourselves from the rest. We belong to a huge territory, to a huge continent, which is the eastern part of Europe, and which doesn't end at the Urals—because the Urals are nothing, simply mountains, and not very high ones at that. They do not represent a political border; thus we are suddenly in Asia, and Eurasia becomes more and more a visual reality to us. We are here on the anniversary of the last Wheatland Conference in Lisbon. During this year something has happened—in fact, much has happened.

First of all, it happened that in some of our countries there are now liberal democratic voices; they are very outspoken and have reached the level of policy-making. We can experience something close to the normal Western-style democratic political campaign. This is the case in Poland, in Hungary, in Slovenia, and perhaps in Croatia as well. And seeing on Moscow television Professor Sakharov, who represents the great liberal democratic opposition in the Soviet parliament, we realize that it is possible to have a kind of democratic development even in the Soviet Union. This is a historic event. But we can observe some negative developments as well. There is now the danger of other, smaller Stalinisms, independent Stalinisms, that exist without the protection of Moscow, that would like to and are able to preserve the power structure, and that use nationalistic rhetoric as a tool. And there are people who are ready to shift from communist socialist rhetoric to a national socialist rhetoric, to change from one authoritarian system to another, almost without recognizing the crossing of the borderline between communist rhetoric and nationalist rhetoric. So we look at the GDR, at Czechoslovakia, Romania, Bulgaria, and Serbia, and we notice that in Serbia, for example, people voluntarily and enthusiastically join the extremist nationalist camp and in its name support many kinds of repressive authoritarian measures. There is also a real danger that we could have a kind of coalition of nationalist Stalinisms. We Hungarians are experiencing now some first signals, some very unfriendly moves and declarations on the part of the Czechoslovakian and Romanian leaderships. This could mean the beginning of this negative process. I don't want to be a prophet of doom, but I am offering these observations for your attention because they could be significant in the near future. I guess that in a sense there are two political and philosophical alternatives for this region: a kind of democratic federalism and a kind of national socialism or national Stalinism. This can become a coalition; even the Warsaw Pact countries could become a coalition of these different dictatorships, which could count on mutual support to maintain power. Maybe the western part of Eastern Europe—I mean Poland, Hungary, Slovenia, and Croatia—may be tempted to be different, if Moscow will allow it. If not, it will be hard for us once again. I will add something that will irritate our Western colleagues. Your approach to the problem of Central Europe has been two-sided: on the one hand, there was political rhetoric, and on the other, political strategy, and there was always a schism between the two. The rhetoric supports any kind of democratization, applauds all democratic goals, and is unhappy when any democratic progress is blocked. On the other hand, counterrevolution in the Stalinist sense makes all the Western democratic leaders very unhappy.

Eastern Europeans have undergone bitter experiences not only at the hands of the East—that is obvious and known to us all—but also at the hands of the West, which was always the hope of Eastern Europeans or of East Central European nations. For instance, you may recall that when General Patton arrived with American troops and tanks in the vicinity of Prague, he stopped and waited for Marshal Konev to come and invade the city. Why? Because that was their agreement. You have the right to disagree. So, I guess we are now in a very complex geopolitical situation in which the West cannot offer any real prizes in exchange for political influence in a country of this East Central European sphere. It is almost impossible to buy—even with a substantial change in the military structure—a country such as Hungary, which is after all marginal within the Soviet bloc. Therefore, we have to stay within the Warsaw Pact framework, which is not desirable, but I see no other solution. Unilateral ways out are severely punished. We have to stay in this grouping, and we have to bear the rise of all these angry nationalisms, all these resentments against one another, whose origins are hard to understand. So perhaps the group of Central or Eastern Europeans sitting harmoniously at this table represents a utopian approach, something worthy of the age of enlightenment; but perhaps reality is something much darker.

### Péter Esterházy

Let me be faithful to this discussion and tell you the truth. The truth is that this afternoon I lost my sense of what is Central Europe. I made a last desperate effort during the break, when I turned to Susan Sontag and asked her, "Tell me, Susan, what is Central Europe?" Susan kept silent, and I did not learn the answer.

I have a problem: I seem to be a traitor moving from one extreme to another. I even agree with Joseph Brodsky and think there is no such thing as Eastern or Central Europe. To be more precise—a risky business in Danilo Kiš's presence—I could define Central Europe, say, as the Danube. But what is the Danube? Not even Claudio Magris knows that. Let's just say that the Danube defines Central Europe. But I am dead sure that there is no such thing as a Central European writer. Yet there is such a thing as an English writer, because there is such a thing as the English language. When our English colleagues want to be European writers, they fail. Or at least that is the impression one gets through translation. I think a writer belongs to a language and not to a region.

I believe that the notion of a Central European writer came about from defensive thinking, from fear. We defend ourselves against all kinds of superpowers, all kinds of ignorance, and as a result we are herded into the fences of Central European literature. This is very comfortable, very good, and very useful, but not really serious and not at all realistic. That is all I wanted to say.

### Danilo Kiš

I am interested in discussing how to *be* a Central European writer. Esterházy is free to say what he wants, but all of us at this table have something in common, a common history, with variations according to our national histories, ethnic origins, and internal conflicts. All this contributes to our various literary characteristics. Finally, I dare to mention the Jews. They have contributed and participated in this Central European history, and they represent a world that has disappeared; they represent an absence that is noticeable in our writing. This absence is a characteristic of Central European writing. And in conclusion, the experience of communism is a very important element. It is with all of these elements that I battle daily in my writing; it is the same battle that other Central European writers are engaged in; it is the battle that I am struggling with this very afternoon.

### Paul-Eerik Rummo

I am going to speak in Russian, and I beg you not to take this as yet another sign or symbol of yet another invasion of the Russian Empire into Central Europe, but rather as the opposite, as a sign that in the last fifty years, since Estonia's, Latvia's, and Lithuania's annexation by the Soviet Union, we lost considerable connection with Western Europe, with international culture. As a result, Estonians of my generation speak Russian better than we speak those languages that are still officially termed "other-land," or foreign, languages. I am sitting at this table somewhat by chance, because strictly by geography Estonia does not belong to Central Europe. We have only to look at the map to see that Estonia is not on the Danube! Nonetheless, we belong to Central Europe according to Czeslaw Milosz's definition—we are also victims of the Molotov-Ribbentrop Pact. In this sense we do in fact share the fate of Central, or Middle, Europe. But I don't really care for divisions in thought—I don't like to talk about Western or Central or Eastern Europe, and so on. I feel that when we speak in such terms, we show that we have fallen into a trap, into a closed ideology, that we consider ourselves separate from Europe as a whole. As someone already said here, we begin to see ourselves as peripheral and provincial. I think that this is very dangerous. It is dangerous to fall into the trap of superpower ideology. And I am afraid that if we talk about Central Europe, Eastern Europe, and so on, that we are reflecting a very old great-power principle, *divide et impera,* and of course it is high time that that principle die out. I want to say a few words about the role that we Estonians and other Baltic peoples, minority peoples, can play in the recently emerging political situation. I am only speaking about Estonians now—we share a common fate with Hungary, a common historical fate, especially since the Second World War, and we share with Hungary a common ethnic fate. We are Finno-Ugric people and speak a Finno-Ugric language, along with Hungary. We share a common fate with the Poles, if not earlier, then at least beginning with the Molotov-Ribbentrop Pact. And we have something else in common with the Poles—the Baltic Sea. In this way we can find many such ties and bonds between Estonia and other countries and peoples of this very large region. In addition, we are closely tied to Finland and the Finns. We are separated by the very narrow Finnish Gulf. From Tallinn, the capital of Estonia, to Helsinki, the capital of Finland, it is only eighty kilometers across the gulf. And as are the Hungarians, we are very close relatives of the Finns. But here a new concept arises, the concept of Balto-Scandinavia. We are not only the Baltics, we are part of Balto-Scandinavia, since Finland is related to the Baltic countries. Finland is already a part of Scandinavia and the northern peoples. The borders between cultures and the borders between our literatures are not very rigid. One culture flows into another. It seems to me that Estonia can now play, as a result

of its political and geographical position, the role of go-between, for example, between the region now called Central Europe and the region that is now called Scandinavia and the northern peoples.

## Claudio Magris

The boundaries of Central Europe are difficult to trace or define—in fact, not
only the boundaries. The concept *Mitteleuropa* does not merely translate into "Central Europe" but implies a certain notion of unity, of community, despite a multitude
of sharp differences and conflicts. The word *Mitteleuropa* was coined in the last century as a historicopolitical designation—a political program, in fact. It connotated
the encounter of German culture with the other cultures of the same region, but its
predominant implication was that of a German or at best German-Hungarian su-
premacy in Central Europe: List, Bruck, von Stein, and later Naumann and Srbik
supported this thesis, and with due nuances and gradations it prevailed from the
time of liberalism through National Socialism.

Today the word *Mitteleuropa* means quite the opposite. It evokes the image of
many nationalities merged, of a "hinter"-national world, as Prague writer Johannes
Urzidil said, a world "hinter"—behind—the nations (as if one did not know which
nationality one belonged to, as if one's nationality were multiple, complex, multi-
ethnic). In the history of many who are sitting at this table, and in the prehistories of
our families, we often find these mixtures of nationalities, a steady shift of identities,
a process of enrichment and loss of identity.

The complexity of its identity is certainly the most important characteristic of
Central Europe; it is one of the reasons Central Europe has produced so many great
literary works, which have explored the universal subject of individual, cultural, and
national identity. The difficulty of defining oneself sometimes leads to great literature
and sometimes to an ideological mess. In my region, in Trieste and Friuli, there are
two political movements that both call themselves Central European: one is on the
extreme left, left of the Communist party; the other is quite conservative-reactionary.
On August 18 both celebrate the birthday of Emperor Franz Josef while insulting
each other.

What are the characteristics of Central European culture, if there is such a
thing? I can only point out some elements that certainly do not constitute a unity.
There is, for example, a tendency to analyze, to defend the individual against the
totality, the fringes against the center and against every standardizing model. There
are the supranational role of Jewish culture and the debunking of big, dogmatic philosophical systems that are trying to put a straitjacket on the diversity and multifor-
mity of the world. And there is the sense that everything—history, reality—could
also be different from the way it is.

Today the Central European revival is often a flirtatious fashion or a cheap formula, but above all it is an expression of unease toward history and of resistance

against that unease. It is also a metaphor of protest—against the Soviet rule over Eastern Europe and against the American way of life in Western Europe. In Austria this revival is a medicine against the insecurity regarding the nation's identity. But primarily Central European culture is a culture that has pointed out the emptiness of the world while defying that very emptiness by refusing to accept the status quo as fate.

I believe that one cannot play at being Central European these days. Central Europe should be a part of our culture, of our sensibility, of the way we see and experience the world. At the moment Central Europe is undergoing fast and violent changes, and various countries are aspiring to achieve the structure of Western democracies. There is certainly much that Central Europe can learn from Western democracies. But it also has much to offer, to give—a human dimension, which was developed through Central Europe's tragedies and in resistance to them, a human quality that has become rarer in the West. Part of this quality is the upholding of the individual's intellectual autonomy, the refusal to identify with the way of the world. Some time ago in Łódź, Poldi Beck, a survivor of the Holocaust, gave me a manuscript, a piece of poetry, "The Book of Whistles," in which the tragedy of history is presented in the guise of a parodistic essay on the art of whistling. When invited to get in the streetcar of history, the narrator answers, "You go. I'll come a bit later or not at all." This ironical self-rejection is also Central Europe.

# Lithuania

## A Question of Identity

FRANK R. SILBAJORIS

There are bumper stickers in the American West that say, DEADWOOD: WHERE THE HELL IS IT? Everybody knows, of course: it's where they shot Wild Bill Hickok. Yet only recently did American television viewers get a fair idea of where Lithuania is, even if only few know much about who lives there and who may have been shot and for what cause. Indeed, like many other nations, the Lithuanians themselves often wonder who they are.

There are basically two written records to turn to for an answer: history, which is supposed to tell the truth, and art, the "beautiful lie." History, as written by big and hungry neighbors, has all too often lied to the Lithuanians, telling them that they are Poles, Russians, or some faceless tribe, evanescent as the smoke of their pagan altars that fell only yesterday. Art was slow in coming, for Lithuanians have not from time immemorial been a people of the book. In the thirteenth and fourteenth centuries, when Christianity, and with it the written word, were first handed to them with the iron glove of the Teutonic order, the Lithuanians did almost all of their writing with bloody swords upon the enemy. Their identity as a nation was not at issue, nor would the concept have been understood at the time. What concerned them was loyalty to their local warlord, then to the grand duke, while defending against the Germans, on the one hand, and expanding adventurously into the lands of ancient Rus', on the other.

The Lithuanians did well on both counts. In the West, increasingly close ties were developing with the kingdom of Poland, threatened by the same Teutonic enemy. Lithuania was finally baptized, under Polish auspices, in 1386, and in 1385 the Lithuanian grand duke Jogaila became the king of Poland, thus uniting the two countries under the rule of the Jagiellonian dynasty. In 1410 this union ended the Teutonic threat for a long time to come at the battle of Tannenberg. In the East, many Russian principalities fell like ripe fruit into the hands of the Lithuanians, who at that time seemed to be the only viable force to protect Rus' from the Tartars before the rise of Moscow in the fourteenth and fifteenth centuries.

Paradoxically, with these military and political gains Lithuania all but lost its chance to develop a separate national identity. When quills and parchment joined the sword, the language of government, the arts, and the church was Polish in the West and Church Slavonic of the Belorussian business-and-bureaucracy redaction in the East. Like the Scandinavians before them, the Lithuanian nobles enthroned in Russian cities quickly lost all memory of their origins, embraced the Orthodox church, and became completely Russified. Lithuanian nobility with ties to Poland became Polish in culture and language just as rapidly. The reason for this in both cases was obvious, even if paradoxical: an unlettered culture could begin to conceive of itself as an entity with a name only after that name was placed on record in the process of its absorption by the neighboring literate civilizations. From that time on, beginning late in the fourteenth century, Lithuania gradually became what the Poles and the Russians thought and wrote it was.[1]

The spirit of Lithuanian statehood found its first written expression in the *Lithuanian Statute,* a code of laws compiled in a modified Church Slavonic and first promulgated in 1529. For a long time it was the only codified system of law sanctioned in writing by a sovereign; the Russian empire repealed it in 1840.[2] Though encoding the legal norms of the state and including a number of Lithuanian customs and standard practices, it did not become a focal point of the Lithuanian national or ethnic consciousness. It applied not only to ethnic Lithuania but also to the Russian and Belorussian territories then still under the control of the grand duchy, and it did not touch the minds of the Lithuanian peasantry then submerged under the Polish- and Russian-speaking upper layers of society. Consequently, when the winds of national revival began to blow across the land near the end of the nineteenth century, they buried the statute and its Slavic idiom in the sands of time.

The earliest printed Lithuanian text was a cathechism, published in East Prussia by Martynas Mažvydas in 1547. Unlike Russia, the small, Protestant, multilingual Prussian kingdom did not deliberately seek to stifle its ethnic minorities as long as these remained loyal to the king. There was enough breathing space for the spirit to allow Kristijonas Donelaitis (1714–1780), a Lutheran pastor in the minuscule German-Lithuanian community of Tolminkiemis, to create his rural epic *Metai* (The Seasons, 1765–75).[3] It is earthy, yet lyrical, and it portrays the Lithuanians as humble, enduring peasants walking their treadmill to eternity across a sacral time and space, their land in the seasons of the year, where both the vapors of dung in springtime and the exuberant trumpet of a crane circling the sky rise to heaven in praise of the Lord.

Donelaitis's poem left little or no impression on the developing early Lithuanian letters, nor did it contribute much to the rising sense of identity as a nation, for the simple reason that it was not published until 1818. In the meantime, the Lithuanian-Polish commonwealth was divided three times among Russia, Austria, and Prussia; all that was left was for Tadeusz Kosciuszko, falling wounded from his horse in 1794, to shout, "Finis Poloniae!" In the same time span, the French Revolution shook all of Europe, and Napoleon marched in and out of Russia, leaving after him the oppressive Holy Alliance and myriad young dreams of European peoples just beginning to wake from the sleep of history.

After all this, hardly anyone, even among the Lithuanians, much noticed the return of Donelaitis's patient epic, for they were already looking elsewhere. In an important way, the Lithuanian national awakening was partially a child of Polish literature and Lithuanian history. They met in the fiery heart of Adam Mickiewicz, whose grand romantic works, *Forefathers' Eve, Grażyna, Konrad Wallenrod,* and *Pan Tadeusz,* were all placed in Lithuanian historical settings, creating a glowing legend of Lithuania's warlike past. It was precisely this romantic glory—the realization that Lithuania was a *historic* nation that had known greatness—that lit the fires of patriotism among the young Lithuanian intelligentsia, who then proceeded to build their own image of the land and, simultaneously, of its letters, abandoning all interest in Poland itself.

In 1864 the Russian authorities imposed a ban on any Lithuanian texts printed in the Latin alphabet, and the young patriots again turned to East Prussia for a permissive environment where they could publish their new journals, which were then smuggled across the border into Lithuania along with prayer books and sundry contraband. The two pillars of the patriotic movement were Jonas Basanavičius (1851–1927), founder of the journal *Aušra* (The Dawn, 1883–1886), and Vincas Kudirka (1858–1899), who established and edited *Varpas* (The Bell, 1889–1906). Both journals were full of vibrant devotion for their country and people, but neither could go much beyond an appeal to historical awareness as a basis for the contemporary identity of the nation. The much-revered poet Jonas Maironis (1862–1932), the "bard of national awakening," was in a similar predicament. Everyone pointed to the glories of the past, but there was no thread leading from Tannenberg to a present-day Lithuanian peasant hut, no continuous tradition to sustain the consciousness of historicity. The Lithuanian nobility did make its last grand historical gestures by joining the nobles of Poland in the ill-fated insurrections against the czar in 1831 and 1863. By then the nobles had already fully identified themselves with Polish language and culture and hardly deigned to cast a derisive glance at the "Lithomaniacs" who rose from the soil to claim legitimacy as a separate and civilized nation aware of itself.

Maironis and other, lesser writers did what artists could: they created a Lithuania made of words.[4] It was heroic, bucolic, and beautiful and struck a responsive chord in the people, but it remained nevertheless an *image* rather than a discovery or a practical blueprint for the future.

Most of the early patriotic intelligentsia, particularly scholars and artists, came from two walks of life: the medical profession and the clergy. These were the only avenues open to peasant children aspiring to better their lot. Basanavičius and Kudirka were both medical doctors, and Maironis was a priest. In the preceding generation the most notable names are those of Bishop Motiejus Valančius (1805–1875), a practical man who loved sobriety and diligence and preached them in his little vignettes of life, and Bishop Antanas Baranauskas (1835–1902), author of "The Pine Grove of Anykščiai," a vibrant work of painful sweetness in which the destruction of a glade becomes an extended metaphor for the destiny of the Lithuanian land. National identity at that time really amounted to such a poem. It was a myth and a memory, which, notwithstanding the readiness of spirit, could not quite configure itself into the reality of the day.[5]

Political independence came in 1918 to a nation that did not yet quite know what it was. Its medieval Orthodox past had become quite irrelevant and was long forgotten. Czarist Russia had ebbed away, leaving only scattered debris of its culture, and of the Polish Catholic tradition the country would accept only the religious, not the cultural or ethnic, ambiance.

Thus, at the beginning of independence the temporal roots of the Lithuanian middle class were very shallow, hardly comprising a single generation. Political and cultural life was in the hands of a new intelligentsia that came from the village with, so to speak, stalks of straw still sticking in its hair. Yet they were eager and energetic people, optimistic and open to all the cultural crosswinds of Europe. This was particularly true of literary movements. There were Lithuanian Symbolists, among them the brilliant poets and playwrights Vincas Mykolaitis-Putinas (1893–1966) and Balys Sruoga (1896–1947), who learned their trade in Germany and Russia. Jurgis Baltrušaitis (1883–1944), an important Russian Symbolist poet, eventually also started writing in his native Lithuanian. Futurism, in the person of Kazys Binkis (1893–1942), was only a mild, Arcadian, somewhat humorous version of the savage vigor of Mayakovsky. The literature of social commitment focused briefly around a leftist, Soviet-oriented movement called the Third Front, of which the main representative, however, was Salomėja Nėris (1904–1945), a romantic poet with a profoundly Catholic upbringing, engaged in a painful rebellion against herself in the name of her social conscience. In prose, village themes were dominant, although the territorial markers of a Lithuanian national identity were tested in such novels as *Frank Kruk*, by Petras Cvirka (1909–1947), describing the downfall of a Lithuanian American who came back home to Lithuania rich with Prohibition-era dollars only to be swindled out of them by people of true native talent, or *The Fate of the Šimonys of Aukštujai*, by Ieva Simonaitytė (1897–1967), which traces the declining destiny of a noble Lithuanian dynasty subject to Germanization in East Prussia. In the politics of independent Lithuania one could see a trend toward nationalistic authoritarianism that flirted with fascism on the Italian model. This in turn was opposed in literature by such novels as *Siegfried Immerselbe Rejuvenates Himself*, by Ignas Šeinius (1889–1959), depicting the renewed vigor of a flaccid old Nazi after an injection of hated Jewish blood.

In essence, the emerging literary outline of Lithuanian culture seemed to repeat the patterns of neighboring civilizations, only in the medium of Lithuanian language and traditional Lithuanian habits and modes of thought. There were, however, two strong forces pressing for a sense of identity nourished by the deepest roots of national consciousness. One, best represented by the intensely personal lyrics of Bernardas Brazdžionis (b. 1907), extolled the strongly felt Catholicism of the Lithuanian people, expanding it to esoteric biblical and modernistic precincts of imagery. The other, comprising such major writers as Jonas Aistis (1904–1973), Antanas Miškinis (1905–1983), Liudas Gira (1884–1946), and, in prose, Vincas Krėvė-Mickevičius (1882–1954), sought a profile of national identity emerging from the traditions of folklore and any remnants, reinforced by products of fresh imagination, of Lithuanian mythology.[6]

This particular strain of creative mythologizing has gathered considerable strength in the literature of present-day Lithuanian poets both in the homeland and in exile. During the Soviet and German occupations of 1940 through 1944, and during the subsequent harsh guerrilla war against Soviet might (1945–1952),[7] the nation found itself all alone, just as it stands today, and people were forced to look inward for some source of strength that would come from deep down in the soil and up through the ages—a knowledge of being themselves, or a knowledge of *being* that was not an echo of other, alien voices. Over the ensuing years and until the present day, through all exigencies of Soviet occupation, forced collectivization, industrialization, and a forcibly imposed new mythology of the "Great Socialist Fatherland," there were poets, playwrights, novelists, and short-story writers who carefully nurtured the perceived seed of selfhood in a sort of magic soil, translucent in the mind and sonorous with delicate vibrations of the soul in a mythical state of being evoked by the light and warmth in the native grass, in the bend of a river, in the crown of an oak tree, and in the very air that felt like a breath of ancient memory making the past and the present a single entity, one with the land.[8] Among the best poets in this vein one could mention Justinas Marcinkevičius (b. 1930), Sigitas Geda (b. 1943), Judita Vaičiūnaitė (b. 1937), Janina Degutytė (1928–1990), and many others. In prose, Romualdas Granauskas (b. 1939), Juozas Aputis (b. 1936), and particularly Vidmantė Jasukaitytė (b. 1949) have entered with care and a sort of solemn love the mythological consciousness of the nation.

In exile, the issue of national identity too often became confused with simple nostalgia for the homeland lost, gently decomposing over the years in rainbow-hued remembrance. There was, however, one poet, Algimantas Mackus (1932–1964), who made a radical break with the entire mythology of "Lithuania" as it had developed in religious and literary images and in the semantics of cultural tradition. He stood for a total darkness of dispossession, a resolute turning toward the imagery of death, a fierce challenge both to his own people and to the world to face with total honesty the tragic destruction, as he perceived it, of Western civilization.[9] In itself this sort of poetry is perhaps also a mythological gesture, an act of repeating the cycle of death and resurrection, and in that sense it does eventually contribute to the perception of Lithuanian national identity, destroyed and reborn through history.

In social and philosophical thought during the period of independence, the most articulate writer concerned with issues of national identity was Stasys Šalkauskis (1886–1941). In his view, the Lithuanian national spirit has its deepest foundations in the Far East, presumably the cradle of the Aryans.[10] This essentially mythological consciousness was later submerged as Lithuania became the arena of struggle between the Teutons and the Slavs and then between the East and West Slavs. In this conflict the country never had a chance to develop its own potential. His proposed solution was that Lithuania should now accept its historic role of developing a transcending synthesis of the three factors that shaped its character: ancient Asian racial memory, the Greek-Russian East, and the Latin-Polish West.

Except for the nebulous idea of distant Asian cultural roots,[11] Šalkauskis's notions do not seem very original or enlightening. The Russians, the Germans, and the Poles have all conceived of themselves as intermediaries between Asia and Europe, or between European East and West, in one context or another. A balancing act between different cultures cannot contribute much energy to the sense of a mission that is really the main force shaping any national identity. Lithuanian culture does not contain a statement as powerful as that of Fyodor Dostoevsky when he proclaimed a man-God relationship in Eastern Christianity that was unique to the Russian people and therefore became Russia's "own word," a universal message radiating from the Russian spirit as the source of all light for the future.[12]

But if one rejects Šalkauskis's view, then there is no semantic space for the forming of a Lithuanian national-cultural identity—no place where one can create Lithuania's own word, because all the issues that might be relevant have already been articulated by the surrounding cultures. The deep well of a mythological consciousness of the nation also will not yield any concrete agenda for living in the present with an active sense of identity oriented toward some goal.

It is of course true that a certain sense of identity has accumulated over time, even if it is difficult to describe it clearly. It consists in large part of various sets of habits, mental attitudes, encodings of sets of values, assumptions about one's own language and history, and perhaps also of some particular complexes—martyrdom as national destiny, humble endurance as national faith, even, possibly, a comforting inferiority complex that permits inaction. All this, however, will lead to stagnation.

Perhaps the problem with the Lithuanian sense of identity is that people have been talking too much to themselves about all these things. Identity can best be developed in the process of saying something to others, reaching out toward an open dialogue in the course of which one's own significant word will be born. Identity is not something that *is* and needs to be discovered; rather it is a constant becoming, a dynamic parabola to the future. A national culture can only grow as a relationship with all other cultures coming from outside. Inevitably, this is happening in Lithuania and will continue to happen, but the question is one of a conscious decision to leave the protective shell of traditions and habits misconstrued as identity and to step out boldly into the great noise of the world.

For this, of course, one needs freedom. The determined step taken by the Lithuanian people to assert their political independence in the face of all adversity could very well be the first truly new statement by the nation in a long time. This was a matter of action, not of words, but in that action itself the true Lithuanian word is encoded and is coming to fruition. It is small wonder that so many intellectuals, people that live with thoughts and letters, have actively entered the leading ranks of the independence movement. In this, the new Lithuanian identity is even better defined by similar things taking place in the rest of Eastern Europe, particularly in Czechoslovakia, but also in Poland, Hungary, and Germany. The representatives of the Lithuanian nation that stood tall and proclaimed their freedom showed by that very act that they, and the country, know who they are.

## Notes

1. Of course, they did not agree on this point, as on many others. To the Poles Lithuania was Litwa, a land of poets and soldiers, wrapped in romantic mists of history, like Scotland to the English. To the Russians it was Litva, a historical name that used to designate large tracts of their own ethnic expanse, called under the czars the Northwestern Territory of Russia proper. See R. Šilbajoris, "Jonas Maironis and the Winds of Freedom," *Lituanus* 26, no. 2 (1980): 6.

2. The *Statute* went through three editions, in 1529, 1566, and 1588. It was translated into Polish in 1614 and Russian in 1811. A Lithuanian translation, together with the original of the Russian version, first came out in Chicago in 1970. See "Lithuanian Statute," in *Encyclopedia Lituanica* (Boston, Mass., 1973), 3:404–407.

3. *Metai* has been translated into a number of languages, including English. See trans. Nadas Rastenis, *The Seasons* (Los Angeles: Lithuanian Days, 1967). A brief general discussion in English of Donelaitis and his poem is offered by R. Šilbajoris, "Kristijonas Donelaitis, A Lithuanian Classic," in *Slavic Review* 41, no. 2 (1982): 251–265.

4. Their efforts invite comparison with Bedřich Smetana, who in the years 1874 to 1879 created a Czech nation out of music in his symphonic poem *My Fatherland*.

5. The Russian poet Osip Mandelstam, equating memory with creation, once said, "An organism is for its environment a probability, a desirability, and an expectation. The environment for an organism is an inviting force. Not so much a cocoon as a challenge." "Vokrug naturalistov," in Osip Mandelstam, *Sobranie sochinenij*, ed. G. P. Struve and B. A. Filippov, (Washington, D.C.: Inter-Language Literary Associates, 1966), 2:202. This describes very well the situation with respect to Lithuanian national identity at the turn of the century. Yet the "organism" did not yet come into being at that time. Poets can be wrong at their eloquent best.

6. Unfortunately, Lithuanian folklore has no epic tradition comparable to the Russian *byliny* and entirely lacks a narrative mythology of the sort that was so abundant in ancient Greece. The entire mythological consciousness of the people resides in remnants of the most

ancient lyrical folksongs that convey an animistic pagan worldview. A recent work on Latvian folklore, Faira Vīķis-Freibergs, ed., *Linguistics and Poetics of Latvian Folk Songs* (Montreal: McGill-Queen's University Press, 1989), describes very well the kind of self-perception in relation to the world around them that is transmitted by the old Baltic folksongs.

7. The guerrilla war and other forms of anti-Soviet struggle in Lithuania are extensively described in Tomas Remeikis, *Opposition to Soviet Rule in Lithuania, 1945–1980* (Chicago: Institute of Lithuanian Studies Press, 1980).

8. For a description of this literature, see, for instance, R. Šilbajoris, "Translucent Reality in Recent Lithuanian Prose," *World Literature Today* 57, no. 1 (1983): 21–24.

9. For a discussion of Mackus's poetry, see "Algimantas Mackus—the Perfection of Exile," in R. Šilbajoris, *Perfection of Exile: Fourteen Contemporary Lithuanian Writers* (Norman, Okla.: University of Oklahoma Press, 1970), 184–217.

10. See Stasys Šalkauskis, *Lietuvių tauta ir jos ugdymas* (The Lithuanian Nation and Its Development), reprinted in *Pergalė*, no. 7 (1989): 148.

11. The Lithuanian moralist and mystic philosopher and playwright Vilius Starosta-Vydūnas (1868–1943), speaking of the principle of inner light, the perfection of self-awareness, held that its beginnings reside in the Aryan-Asian past, and that the Lithuanian people stand closer to this ancient wellspring of all wisdom than many others. This idea is most widely developed in his trilogy *Eternal Flame* (1908).

12. Dostoevsky's sense of historical mission for Russia comes through powerfully in his writings on Russian literature, where he says at one point that already Ivan III, in a little hut on a battlefield, clearly perceived the idea not only of Russia's ruling the East but also of an entirely new world to be brought about by Russia. See *F. M. Dostoevskij o russkoj literature* (Moscow: Sovremennik, 1987), 349.

# With Polish Poetry Against the World

## CZESLAW MILOSZ

Forty-four years ago I set out from this place—from Cracow, from Saint Thomas Street—and went abroad. I lived successively in America, France, again America, but during all this time I wrote exclusively in Polish. One might well ask, How did I survive as a Polish poet among foreigners? and I ask this question myself. Frankly speaking, I did not believe I would succeed, and I considered my decision to remain in the emigration as a self-destructive act. This pessimism might seem surprising today, but only if one does not remember how different was the aura of those times and how far we have moved from those situations.

The postwar emigration is already a chapter in history. Let me say that the patterns for its behavior in countries linguistically and culturally alien had features borrowed from the Great Emigration [following the defeat of the November Uprising in 1831—*Trans.*] due to the obvious analogies. On the one hand there was disappointment with the West, familiar from the *Books of Pilgrimage* [Adam Mickiewicz's *Books of the Polish Nation and of the Polish Pilgrims*, 1832—*Trans.*], a kind of pride of the pure and those initiated into misfortune. On the other hand there was a closing up within one's own world, which did not lack symbols because the main magazine of the prewar intelligentsia, *The Literary News*, continued to appear in London. As a poet I saw more than the politicians in this transposition from Warsaw to foreign lands; and the fact that the emigré reading public stopped at the poetics of the Skamander group was significant for me. I realized that my old conflict with these poetics, magnified by the experience of the war years, concealed tremendous differences in mentality. In practice it meant that my poems were absolutely incomprehensible to this milieu. I have no intention of undermining the renown of the Skamander poets, on whom I was brought up and for whom I have much admiration; but when speaking of the confrontation with the West, I must stress that the model they imposed so forcefully proved to be entirely ineffective.

In *My Age* Alexander Wat defined how the Skamander group in the first years

The address translated here was delivered by the author on October 2, 1989, at the Jagellonian University in Cracow on the occasion of his receiving a doctorate *honoris causa*.

of independence differed from others that he called "restless groups," to which he himself belonged. The first, he says, "perfectly fitted within the reality of the Polish bourgeois, professional intelligentsia, and really within Polish provincialism." On the other hand the "restless ones" understood that European civilization had already been questioned and that they were affected by "the general catastrophe of the epoch, the Great Unknown." Thus my Catastrophism from the 1930s was a variation of this intellectual crisis that extended much further than the Polish frontiers and had been seeking ways of expression ever since the end of World War I.

Once in the emigration I did not at all know what to do. I was sufficiently alert to understand that my political conflicts—both with Marxism in Poland and with the "inflexibles" in London—were only the pseudonyms for a much more basic and deeper clash but that this could not even be mentioned. When I tried to explain that my break with the Warsaw government was a result of my refusal to accept socialist realism, this met with mockery: I was a beautiful soul who egoistically worried about his writing while people were being killed.

I was either condemned to sterility or had to find a new formula for dealing with my twentieth century. Of course I am now rationalizing and simplifying. This search was carried out blindly, mostly by refusal to accept: not this, not that, so therefore what? I did not know. To express it succinctly: I did not like the West. What it was creating in art and literature I considered proper to a landscape of spiritual ruins. Before the war I had experienced the influence of Oskar Milosz, and he taught me the proud resistance to decadence.

Could it be, therefore, that as I rebelled against the inherited attitudes and principles of pilgrimage among the materialistic societies of the West, it was I who was the true emigré, only deluding himself that he could break away from his arch-Polish model? My immersion in Polish poetry, from Jan Kochanowski through the poets of the Enlightenment to the romantics, was complete; and the pro-Western snobbery of the intelligentsia that I had not escaped (in my case it was a dab of Frenchness) did not change anything. So here was a man brought up on Polish poetry, alone against the trends, schools, currents, and whatever else they may be called of postwar Europe and America, yet aware that such an education on crazy books always at the service of the single idea of national survival is quite a hump; aware, too, that this monothematic literature of an out-of-the-way region is not a very useful armor. At the same time I saw the misery of my Western partners to which I did not want to succumb; and what is more, I knew the causes of this misery, that is, the landscape of ruins other than physical that fulfilled prophecies of Friedrich Nietzsche.

The question I asked myself, and I now ask here, is whether Polish literature contains any special values that lend themselves to a new interpretation, so they could serve a poetry capable of confronting the entanglements of the twentieth century. It is because of my search for an answer to this question that I was different from the pilgrims who were enamored of the national flag.

The poetry of each language is a single estate in which the heirs till soil that has been prepared by their fathers. Unconsciously or consciously they continue the work begun centuries ago. Is it possible to name what continually renews itself in Polish literature and constitutes its very essence? It is probably its constant fusion with history, visible already in *The Dismissal of the Grecian Envoys*, by Kochanowski, and also the active participation of the individual in the fate of the collectivity, whether as bard, ironist, scoffer, or reformer. Certainly there are many other elements; nevertheless, when Stanisław Brzozowski [philosopher and literary critic, 1878–1911— *Trans.*] tried to grasp what it was that distinguished Polish literature, he spoke of Polish historicism, *storicismo polacco*. This historicism contains many dangers, among others vulnerability to what I have called the Hegelian sting, which I unfortunately experienced myself. At the same time, however, it protects from other dangers, and it is significant for me that my poetic activity of resistance to the West begins with the writings of my "Treatise on Poetry," a poem whose subject is poetry in its connections with the historical data of our century.

I am as far as possible from wanting to present the history of European and post-European civilization as a curve steadily going downward since the time of the Renaissance. Stanisław Ignacy Witkiewicz used to do this, arch-Polish in his historicism and his eschatology, although in a gloomy key and following in the footsteps of Zygmunt Krasiński, especially *The Undivine Comedy*. The dazzling and breathtaking development of science and technology in the West is inseparable from the shadow it casts upon religion, philosophy, and art. Poetry, particularly sensitive to deep transformations, loyally registers the gradual loss of faith in God and man; its history, though not the same in France, England, and America, has its own internal logic and its own dynamics, ever since Mallarmé considered the poem as a fortress erected in a void, in a great Nothing. The word "nihilism" has already lost its negative emotional connotation and is used for descriptive purposes; most likely this explains the successive follies of the theoreticians in France, of Marxists, structuralists, deconstructionists, and also in many countries the disintegration of the very texture of the poem into descriptions of purely subjective states, molecules of the broken atom of the human person.

I would risk the thesis that in these conditions one should appreciate the advantages of one's own backwardness. Already at the time of romanticism the poetry of the Western countries began to examine the validity of perceptions and put in doubt the foundations of ethics. It was, in other words, both epistemological and satanic. Polish poetry, preoccupied with public misfortune, simply did not have time for it. In this poetry the individual did not struggle directly with the difficulties of being in the universe; he remained immersed in a collectivity. Nothing is more curious than the reception of Byron in our part of Europe. The oddities of the eccentric lord—because this is what they were for his compatriots—were changed in our country into a legend of heroic deeds at the service of the freedom of nations.

Polish poetry lacks certain connecting links; that is, it did not develop according to a Western model. I must bring in here something daring that is nevertheless true. I am not alone in having a tendency to oppose to the West, overtly or covertly, our very particular kind of knowledge: "We are wiser than they." Is this arrogance? Or a compensation, as with those noblemen who found themselves in Paris after 1831? Or is it as in Mrożek, "They knocked them [teeth—*Trans.*] out, sir, they knocked them out"? Or is it a misunderstanding, as in Iwaszkiewicz's story "Flight" that was to be an answer to Camus's *The Fall?* Perhaps a little of all of these things, but not quite. For something like a historical imagination exists, nourished by the tragedies of a certain collectivity that are different from individual dramas; it is supported by the memory of innumerable details such as dates, names, places, and geographical regions. This anchoring in history counterbalances certain shortcomings just as an organism knows how to compensate for deficiencies in circulation. The imagination trained in this way can also give sureness of hand in the encounter with experiences that are stronger than the instability of history, such as love and death.

Deliberately aware of my backwardness, I took advantage of the privilege of coming from strange lands where it is difficult to escape history and where supernatural forces, diabolical and angelic, are present in a way difficult for my Western colleagues to imagine. I took advantage of this privilege not only when I wrote *The Issa Valley.* Similar to a painter who holds on to figurative painting even though his milieu thinks it is only for simpletons, I arrogantly resisted the radical subjectivization that softens sentences so they change into a mush of associations. Unfortunately, I am now watching with horror how this sickness, dragged here from abroad, destroys Polish literature.

If I had not emigrated, probably to a smaller or larger degree I would have succumbed to different fashions that find meek imitators because they are considered avant-garde or Western. Internal freedom and artistic sovereignty, once they are achieved by labor, allow us to treat the precepts of fads with a shrug of the shoulders. In my solitary place on the Pacific I did not even attempt to translate my poems into English for years. We do not sufficiently realize that scientific and technological habits continue to weigh on our thinking about art and literature. Yet their steady advances, for instance in medicine, do not mean that entire periods in the art of writing will not one day be considered as lost, mannered, and leading nowhere. Then those who resisted at such a time will be vindicated. It would be amusing if I spoke here as a defender of old-fashionedness. But there are all kinds of old-fashionedness. Justified only is the kind that opposes breaking ties with all that has preoccupied man throughout the centuries, such as philosophical reflection about existence. These ties can be broken simply by the subjectivization of languages so that it ceases to be a means of communication between people.

I started to ask myself questions about the particular values of Polish poetry as a single entity in the early 1960s, when I translated some of my contemporaries, in particular Zbigniew Herbert, Tadeusz Różewicz, Alexander Wat, and Miron Białoszewski. My anthology *Postwar Polish Poetry,* published in 1965, was of course a selection according to my own criteria. Its reception was so good that I can speak of its influence on young American poetry, and precisely because of this reception I was convinced that my criteria were correct. I was guided by a simple principle: the poem should be loaded with content, that is, it must be understandable and communicate something important. Hence an opinion arose that this poetry was oriented toward philosophy and capable of transmitting more than just emotional states. As a result, this poetry is sharp like a knife cutting butter, obtaining more or less the same position as the poems of the Greek from Alexandria, Constantine Cavafy. After this book I published volumes of Herbert, Wat, and Anna Świrszczyńska in translation. Together with the translations of my own poems as well as volumes of Różewicz, Wisława Szymborska, Adam Zagajewski, and Stanisław Barańczak done by other translators, they make it possible to speak of a Polish school in world literature. By the way, in the second edition of my anthology I also included the monologues in verse from Witold Gombrowicz's *Marriage,* translated by my student Louis Iribarne.

It is difficult to find a common denominator for such different individualities. However, I was and am forced to do it for purely practical reasons and not because of an inclination toward theory. In the most general way, one could define this poetry as completely nonpastoral, exiled from the serene earth under the protection of God the Father, ironical and sarcastic, with a considerable share of nihilistic grimace—to such a degree that one English critic proposed a rather outrageous thesis that attempted to explain why Herbert was popular in his country: England declined and became dependent on America, therefore England is self-ironical, as is oppressed Poland. Never mind the reasons; anyway, the names I mentioned mean that after the innocence of Skamander and the equal innocence of the singers of "the city, the masses, and the machine" [the Cracow avant-garde of the interwar period—*Trans.*], Polish poetry joins the demonic rituals of twentieth-century art and literature. I am inclined to add, True, it joins, but differently. Possibly the experience of history prevents Polish poetry from making the world unreal; it has preserved its volume and its weight. Every poem, even the most personal, has a subtext that relates to searing reality, which without any doubt has its own autonomous existence. One does not need to prove this is true with Alexander Wat, but in the erotic poems of Anna Świrszczyńska I also found an ability for objectivization that makes her different from the American women poets obsessed with psychoanalysis. One could add here even Gombrowicz, despite the fact that he stubbornly negated the existence of anything outside our minds, because he introduced a fundamental reservation—pain as a test of reality.

It does not seem that the familiar model of the bard has disappeared. It takes on a new shape as a nonneutral attitude toward the course of events, as a constant tendency to introduce evaluative judgments. The most simple manifestation of this is the poetry of civic duty that flourished in the nineteenth century in both Poland and Russia, a fact that later facilitated the recruitment of poets as "engineers of human souls." During the last half century we have gathered quite a few experiences in this respect: first the ample harvest of underground poetry during the German occupation, then hymns to Stalin composed by the most eminent poets, and finally the poetry of moral outrage. Probably in no other country have jeering analyses of grammar and vocabulary been used for this purpose.

The immediate obligations of the poet are usually in danger of becoming journalistic; a more interesting renewal of the pattern is when evaluative judgments are found at the very source of the poem, at its deepest layer. The crime of genocide forced poets to think of the most elementary opposition between good and evil, and one could say that all postwar Polish poetry is in this sense moralistic. It might be that this very feature gains followers in the West for the poets I have just mentioned because it satisfies a nostalgia for simple truths. Relativization of the concepts of good and evil as well as the marginal role of poetry in a technocratic civilization have rendered the poet powerless, and it seems to me that some Polish poems have elaborated a language in which the very consciousness of crimes committed by the state—returning like a stubborn phantom—can be named, at least in an indirect way. This is what the Irish poet Seamus Heaney, well known in America, has suggested in his recently published book of essays.

No, I am not trying to establish a hierarchy in which the praise of virtue has the highest place, such as the virtue of faithfulness to lost causes. I only maintain that judgments that evaluate ethically have been the right of poetry for centuries and that because of its particular condition Polish poetry has not yet renounced that right. This, together with its perhaps unwilling respect for reality, confers on it certain classical features.

To sum up, in my answer to the question of how a Polish poet can survive among foreigners, I should not skip over certain accidental factors such as a radical change in versification, thanks to which my poems and those of my friends became translatable, at least relatively speaking.

I warned at the beginning that I would touch upon problems not clear to myself. The lack of clarity comes from the fact that the diagnosis of the period in which we happen to live is usually treacherous; yet without such attempts at diagnosis one would have to remain silent. Mankind in this century has found itself in a peculiar situation indeed if it has to be reminded of universal values by the poetry of a country that has been unfortunate and crushed. We do not know what are the aims of a civilization based on acquisition and selling, growing more and more wealthy and more and more nihilistic: possibly the separation of subject and object in its art forebodes the complete disappearance of art in general and for a long time. Nor do we know whether the relative equilibrium of subject and object in Polish poetry was not, paradoxically, the indirect yet advantageous result of unbearable pressures—including pressures of doctrine—and whether this was not an exceptional, short-lived situation. If it happened because of a so-called normalization of life, only then would continuity be broken, because Polish poetry has managed in an unexpected way to give new meaning to its own heritage.

When one lives for many years abroad, it is most difficult to come to terms with one's own identity. As far as I am concerned, I never wondered who I am, because my belonging to the estate of Polish poetry has always been evident for me. This is probably why I never felt any temptation to write poems in another language, and the everyday use of French or English never disturbed my Polish. I fully appreciate my good fate, because after all I might not have lived to the moment when my books were published in Polish. In receiving here a proof that they were needed, I pay homage to Polish poetry, because it protected me from sterile despair in emigration, in solitude too difficult and painful to recommend to anyone. The sense of duty toward my predecessors and successors spared me from a disintegration of individuality that threatens men of art and literature if they have nothing to oppose to the ever more universal indeterminateness.

Translated by John Carpenter and Bogdana Carpenter

# Nationality as Choice

## Baudouin de Courtenay's Individualistic Approach

### JINDŘICH TOMAN

In March 1914 a St. Petersburg court sentenced a professor of linguistics, Baudouin de Courtenay, to two years' confinement in a fortress for "inciting sedition." In a letter to his Czech friend Adolf Černý, written in the days following the trial, Baudouin quipped, "We are still halfway in winter and we have to keep the fire going. Politically, it's also winter—and it might get even worse."[1] He was right. Several months later, the judges reviewed the case—and added two months to the original sentence. The Polish-born professor, whose pedigree is believed to reach as far back as to Baldwin, the medieval Christian king of Jerusalem, and whose full name reads Jan Ignacy Niecisław Baudouin de Courtenay, was one of the most remarkable innovators among late nineteenth-century linguists. Although he did not leave behind an all-encompassing synthesis of his scholarship, *the* book, he exercised a great influence on other participants in the emerging structuralist enterprise, mostly in the East. During his career at St. Petersburg University (1900–1917) he gathered around himself a number of outstanding disciples, such as L. V. Ščerba, E. D. Polivanov, L. P. Jakubinskij, and Max Vasmer, and indirectly contributed to the formation of OPOJAZ, the world-renowned group of Russian Formalists.

Most of Baudouin's studies were written in Polish and Russian, a fact that did not help extend his reputation to the West. (Nonetheless, he was one of the very few linguists explicitly referred to in Ferdinand de Saussure's *Cours de linguistique générale*.) Thus, the publications of anthologies of his works on linguistics, as compiled by V. P. Grigoriev and A. A. Leontiev in Russian in 1963 and by Edward Stankiewicz in English in 1972, were scholarly events of the first order.[2] Less of an event was a collection of Baudouin's journalistic writings that appeared in Warsaw in 1983.[3] This no doubt is a paradox, because it was political journalism for which Baudouin was better known to the general reader of his time than for his linguistics. And, indeed, back in 1914 Baudouin was not sentenced because of linguistics; rather, he became a target of Russian justice because of his analyses of the multinational makeup of the Russian Empire and his proposal to convert Russia into a federation.

What is forgotten about Baudouin today is that he was one of the most active thinkers concerned with ethnicity, minorities, and multinationalism, with particular reference to the Russian Empire, which around the turn of the century, and especially in the aftermath of the revolution of 1905, finally began to realize that its Slavic nature was—to use Baudouin's words—merely "a phantom."[4]

In the course of his career Baudouin wrote innumerable pamphlets, lectures, essays, and glosses on issues of nationality. In most of them he emerges as a severe social critic, a true scourge of the powers that be. His style is distinguished by self-confidence, irony, and sarcasm. He did not strive to please the reader; rather, he invited hostile reactions, and when they came, he would respond only briefly with sayings such as "Der Hund bellt und die Karawane marschiert," a German idiom close to the English "And the band plays on." His stylistic mannerisms were neither subtle nor particularly humorous. Nonetheless, he liked to play with word formation and invent new words to stun his readers; hence, presumably, his interest in the doctrines of the Russian Futurists, those proverbial inventors of new words (and, ultimately, of a new poetic language, *zaum'*). Baudouin's interest in their experiments seems to have been motivated by hopes of gaining insights into the productivity of certain suffixes. This might account for the fact that in 1914 he even presided over an apparently stormy—in any case *tierisch ernst*—Futurist evening in St. Petersburg, in which Viktor Shklovsky read his manifesto "Resurrection of the Word" and during which Baudouin got involved in a less than civil exchange with the Futurist poet Alexander Kruchenykh. The event was probably not entirely to Baudouin's liking (his evaluation of the *zaum'* experiments was rather negative), but his statements about the Futurists indicate so much personal involvement that one is left with the impression that something in their undertaking was important to him and that he felt compelled to offer his judgment.

Baudouin's intellectual style was monolithic. He by no means restricted his sarcastic nonconformism to social criticism. A good illustration of his biting wit may be taken from a collection of exercises that he put together for his students.[5] The style of the first part of this exercise book is especially noteworthy. It contains passages that he excerpted from approved textbooks recommended by academic commissions. He asked the students to search in these passages for any and all "completely absurd and indigestible rules" and other "nonsense detrimental to their reasoning." In the postscript to the book he noted that he had no problems whatsoever amassing scores of nonsensical passages from current linguistic literature.

The guiding concept of Baudouin's criticism was his appeal to common sense, to logical judgment, and ultimately to universal reason. The following passage, although from a lecture on a linguistic topic, is characteristic of his general approach. Commenting on an analysis of Russian verbs by the Russian philologist N. P. Nekrasov (1828–1913), which rendered earlier Western scholarship obsolete, he noted, "The special reason for which I am bringing this up is that I do not accept nationalization of logic—I rather assert the same laws of human thinking for everyone.

There is no European, no American, no French, no English, no German, no Russian, no Polish science; there is only one science: universal science."[6]

In 1914 Baudouin was tried because of his brochure *National and Territorial Aspects of Autonomy,* published in 1913.[7] His interest in the nationality problem, however, dates back to his student years. He did research on the dialects of the Slavs under Italian rule and later turned to the same configuration of relationships when he studied the Lusatian Serbs and the Slovaks—Slavic minorities under the Germans and Hungarians, respectively. The peak of his explicitly political interest in issues of nationality is in the years following the revolution of 1905. Under the impact of the military disaster of the Russo-Japanese War and the social turmoil, Russia attempted to move cautiously toward a constitutional monarchy. During these days of unrest, in May 1905, Baudouin surfaced as a speaker at a convention of university professors, where he addressed the Polish question, that is, the status of Poland within the Russian Empire. The question had been a focus of a meeting of Polish and Russian intellectuals not long before Baudouin's appearance at the professors' convention, and a resolution was proposed. There is little that is more telling than Baudouin's reaction to this resolution. He superseded it with his own manifesto, in which he performed a typical Baudouinian operation: in short, where the old resolution dealt with the "Polish" kingdom, "Polish" nation, and "Polish" political parties, Baudouin raised the issue to a general level and simply focused on "all non-Russian nationalities." This maneuver, as we shall soon see, was not a matter of stylistic variation. Although one might expect Baudouin to have a vested interest in the Polish cause—he was an important representative of a nation part of which was incorporated into Russia—his program of national self-determination did not single out the Poles.

Soon afterward, in the tumultuous days of early December 1905, Baudouin emerged as the chairman of a Union of Autonomist-Federalists, a group close to the Constitutional-Democratic party, the so-called Kadets.[8] The founding congress of the Union of Autonomist-Federalists brought together Armenians, Azerbaijanis, Belorussians, Estonians, Georgians, Jews, Kirghiz, Latvians, Lithuanians, Poles, Tartars, and Ukrainians. Later, ethnic Russians also joined in. One of the central goals of this group was the conversion of the empire into a federation, or, in Baudouin's words, a change involving "decentralization and autonomization of Russian power."[9] In his view, this change was possible only if the participating representatives of nationalities performed "a painful operation" on themselves, one that Baudouin had already undergone.

His opening address at the congress of the Union of Autonomist-Federalists began with these remarks:

> Before we embark upon the discussion of the questions that concern us, I propose, gentlemen, that you perform a somewhat painful operation on yourselves. You must cut off, or suppress in yourselves, a part of your ego, that part

which thrives either on the conviction that your nationality and religion are superior to others or on the desire that your own nationality and religion dominate and rule over others.

I personally find myself in the fortunate position of having no need whatsoever to remove such an organ from my psychic organism. A long time ago I lost all national and religious prejudices, and, belonging to that scorned category of people *sans foi et sans nationalité*, I do not make any distinctions between various nationalities and other social groups and treat them all completely equally and impartially.

But I do take sides with those who are unjustly harmed and persecuted. In Kazan I was on the side of Tartars when they were persecuted by the Russians. In Dorpat I defended the Estonians and Latvians against the Germans, and later all of them against the Russifiers. In Galicia I could by no means approve of violations of the rights of the Ruthenians and Ukrainians by the Poles. . . .

My nationlessness and religionlessness, or more precisely my supranationalism and suprareligiosity, and my consequent equal treatment of all nationalities and various sociocultural groups do not represent a merit of any sort. One could speak of merits only in the case of persons who have achieved a sense of justice in international matters without that painful operation mentioned above.[10]

This brief self-characterization resembles his assertion of the universal character of human reasoning. At the same time, it once again testifies to Baudouin's "supra-Polish" attitudes. Aiming at those Polish aristocrats who with visible chauvinism were asserting their patriotism—a noun that Baudouin mostly wrote in quotation marks or qualified with the expression "so-called"—he remarked with typical sarcasm that the aristocrats' peers and allies would from now on be "some" Jews, Lithuanians, Kirghiz, Buryats, etc.: "What now, fine gentlemen? A stupid time has arrived in which not a step will be made without equality."[12]

The Autonomist-Federalists brought together a number of representatives of minorities and thus temporarily became a focus for discussions about the status of minorities. This concern had of course also been visible in political thinking of other persuasions. Thus, although Baudouin repeatedly distanced himself from the left, he highly esteemed Lenin's opponent G. V. Plekhanov, who had been an outspoken critic of Russia's colonial desire to subjugate small neighbors and who had proclaimed, among other things, that he belonged with those Russians who by fighting for the liberation of Poland were defending the cause of Russian freedom.

It may surprise the contemporary reader to find out that the Autonomist-Federalists, and Baudouin himself as well, did not want Poland to secede from Russia, at least not for the moment. In fact, the first item in their program asserted the territorial inviolability of the Russian state. In the congress program of the Autonomist-Federalists Baudouin was actually not very articulate on the motives for this attitude, but his reasons may be deduced from his writings. In them he reiterated that the dismantling of the Russian Empire would harm Russian progressive parties, with whom he felt solidarity. Other of his opinions were simply rational and pragmatic—essentially, all the particularization would result, he believed, in an enormous waste of time and energy and would thus actually harm the emerging states. On the whole, it does not seem that Baudouin's "preservationist" attitude was an opportunistic maneuver intended to keep the Union of Autonomist-Federalists an enterprise within the domain of law. As late as 1925 Baudouin was not enthusiastic about the disintegration of another multinational colossus, the Hapsburg empire. He wrote to Adolf Černý, "The Slovenes were best able to develop in Austria. But the stupid Hapsburg dynasty and Austrian imperialists drove this unfortunate state to adventures and, ultimately, extinction, instead of taking Switzerland as an example, i.e., instead of practicing complete equality and peaceful coexistence. Austria, of course, was by no means alone in this attitude."[12] The passage is particularly telling because Slovenes were a Slavic community for which Baudouin had shown a great deal of affection ever since his student days. Nonetheless, Baudouin's attitude did not necessarily imply his support for Slovenian separation from Austria. Multinational federations were in order—actually desirable—provided a complete equality was their basis. As early as 1903 he wrote, "Switzerland is a perfect example of such a federation. Austria could also be such a federation if it were not for massive agitation and sowing of dissension, practiced by, among others, those who are interested in distracting attention from fundamental questions."[13] He also found in Scandinavia a good example of the fair treatment of national questions.[14]

Baudouin's most radical idea, however, concerned the very substance of national self-determination. One of the proposals he made at the 1905 congress of Autonomist-Federalists was "not to criticize anyone for conscious participation in two or even more nationalities or for conscious nonparticipation in any. And just as the right not to adhere to any religion [*Konfessionslosigkeit*] is recognized, one may also think of national neutrality [*Nationalitätslosigkeit*]."[15] This was a cornerstone of his thinking, something on which he insisted well into his late years. In 1921 he wrote to Adolf Černý, who requested his help in reviving the cause of the Lusatian Serbs, a Slavic minority in Germany: "I could only write about the Lusatian Serbs against the background of general ideas of equality and the right of individuals and all freely associated human groupings to decide their own fate and to exercise self-determination in matters of religion, nationality, and any other cultural respect."[16] Thus, while willing to speak out in support of the Lusatian Serbs, Baudouin was anxious to assert the framework within which he would do so—first, that there was no particular Slavic cause, and second, that nationality was a cultural issue on a par with religion.

In the same letter Baudouin suggested another reason for his support of federalism. He explained to Černý, "I always was an enemy of pressure in these matters [religious and national self-determination] and retain this position to this day, although I see that nations that have become states look at things differently and try to rule others."[17] Thus, Baudouin correctly understood that the complex ethnic makeup of the new nation-states would only perpetuate the relationships of dominance that had prevailed within the Russian empire. Baudouin considered the concept of "Poland for the Poles" as ill-conceived: Poland was Poland for anyone who lived in its territory. He considered the nation-state as inherently ominous because it was always in danger of turning into an instrument of nationally based oppression.

This attitude is largely consistent with Baudouin's educational ideals and his concept of the individual's rights. As Rothstein has shown in his analysis of Baudouin's usage of words such as *tresura* (drill, forced training), *stado* (herd), and *stadowość* (herd behavior), Baudouin viewed nation-states as instruments of mindless indoctrination, incompatible with the rights of the individual.[18] Thus, nationality was a matter of personal choice precisely because it had to be exempted from "herd behavior": "any herd training, whether Jewish, Catholic, or Christian in general, precludes the calm coexistence of adherents of various religions in the name of understanding and universal human solidarity."[19]

The enterprise of the Autonomist-Federalists may not have brought any perceptible results. With the exception of Baudouin's own references the Union cannot be traced after 1905.[20] Baudouin appears to be its sole historian, as is documented by the publication of his *National and Territorial Aspects of Autonomy* as late as 1913. The brochure was actually conceived in the aftermath of 1905 (it was written in 1907) and was intended for a collection of Autonomist writings, a project that did not materialize. Despite his disappointed acknowledgment of the impracticality of the project in the preface to the 1913 publication, he continued to return nostalgically to the Union as the time of his most intensive political activity. In 1915 he republished his speeches from the 1905 congress in a volume dealing with the multinational nature of the Russian empire. He explained there that a major motive for his Autonomist-Federalist engagement was the series of anti-Jewish pogroms that shook Russia from 1903 to 1906. But also here he termed his endeavor "naive." By 1915 he had recognized that given the particular time and territory, it was "ridiculous and nonsensical to talk of human rights, human dignity, the rights of nationalities, peaceful coexistence, etc. The extent to which these values are being realized is abundantly clear to us at this very minute."[21]

Not much later, after the revolution of October 1917, Baudouin left Russia. His home was vandalized, and a great part of his library and papers were destroyed. Russia as a whole was laid waste. Soon after the upheavals of 1917 Finland became independent; the Baltic countries and the Ukraine followed suit, as did the Caucasian states; the idea of a Russian federation of equals was rendered academic. Minority causes endured elsewhere, however. Baudouin, now seventy-two, began to teach at Warsaw University and continued his political activities. On taking up his new appointment at the university, he gave an inaugural address on, of all topics, the Jewish question. Such a speech, at the university of a nation that had just regained its intensely desired independence, shocked many a Polish patriot profoundly. (Nor was this the first time Baudouin had astounded Polish nationalists. At an earlier point he had demanded that Polish children learn Yiddish at school—it was a major language spoken in Poland, after all.) For Baudouin, however, there was little to be discussed: the new state was multinational, hence Poland was obliged to address the Jewish question.

Baudouin was immediately denounced as a Judeophile, but that designation, as he pointed out himself, was grossly inappropriate. He did not intend to single out the Jews. To be sure, there were many other victims of intolerance. Moreover, for Baudouin, Jewish religious ideas only contributed to the creation of anti-Semitism; in particular, he considered the idea of a "chosen nation" as "megalomania"—in fact, a pernicious prototype of all national megalomanias. Nor could Baudouin agree with the Jewish equation of ethnicity and nationality. Speaking about the question of Jewish nationality, he reiterated his key concept of a free choice of nationality: "The recognition of a particular Jewish nationality is not equal with automatic inclusion in it of persons of Jewish origin. Given the principle of equality of citizens . . . , every man should have the right to opt freely for the nationality that he regards as his own; moreover, he may opt for two or more nationalities at the same time or, equally, not opt for any at all."[22]

Over the years Baudouin's bitterness and sarcasm became more and more visible. Indeed, he did not hesitate to apply them to himself. His reminiscences of the brief blossoming of the Union of Autonomist-Federalists were acrimonious and disappointed. Nonetheless, he did not abstain from political activity in postwar Poland. In 1922 he was a candidate for the Polish presidency while also active in the movement of the Polish freethinkers. (That he was not elected is not very surprising—not many freethinkers ever have been.)

Baudouin's attitude at this time is illustrated by an episode during his visit to Czechoslovakia, where he had come to lecture as an official guest of the Czechoslovak state in 1922. Baudouin had always entertained sympathies for the Czechs and their culture; he had studied in Prague in the 1860s, and his first published work was a translation from the Czech. He and his wife, a radical feminist, were contributors to *Slovanský přehled* [*Slavic Review*], an important journal edited by Adolf Černý, Baudouin's lifelong friend. Among Baudouin's favorite authors was the Czech journalist and satirical writer Karel Havlíček Borovský—quite appropriate, since Havlíček Borovský also had little respect for romantic Pan-Slavism and idyllic Russophilia. Moreover, in the harsh persecution of Havlíček Borovský by the Viennese authorities Baudouin saw a parallel to his own fate. Writing to Černý after his trial in 1914, he confessed, "I share the fate of Havlíček and very many other people whose company one may share without shame."[23] Thus, for Baudouin, Czech culture was primarily represented by commonsense social activism rather than the subtlety, say, of the Czecho-Viennese fin de siècle. During his stay in Prague in 1922, he watched with great pleasure *The Insect Play,* by the Čapek brothers; predictably, his appreciation was not that of an aesthete. He wrote to Adolf Černý, "The third act, 'the apotheosis of communism and war' (The Ants), leaves an especially strong impression."[24] Indeed, the ant scene is a wonderful allegory in which ant generals are shown pursuing their petty dreams of authority and military domination. This rather specific reaction to Czech culture is in itself an indication that Baudouin did not come to Prague in order to admire the greatness of the Czechs—to the contrary. He listened to the speeches with which the functionaries and dignitaries of the new state welcomed him and repaid them with a typical Baudouinian scandal: just as he did not understand that the free Poles could dominate the Jews, he now could not understand that being independent, the Czechs behaved as oppressors of the Slovaks, ultimately replicating what the Germans had been doing to them. The Czech establishment was shocked, realizing too late that Baudouin was a man beyond containment, a man of principles.[25]

An adequate characterization of the social activism represented by such personalities as Baudouin's would exceed considerably the limits of this essay. Let it suffice to note that Baudouin's position was by no means unique in his time. Similar expressions of rationalism, individualism, and moralism were seen in the East, especially among the intellectually inclined liberals. Baudouin and his ideas in fact have much in common with Russian liberalism in general. His appeals to anything that was "supra" and "pan" resemble the supraclass and supraparty attitude of the Kadets (*nadklassnost', nadpartijnost'*). Like the Kadets, he did not want to dismantle Russia and thought Russian was a suitable lingua franca for its minorities. In his disillusionment he looked for a base among the notoriously esoteric freethinkers, while the liberals sought a refuge in freemasonry. Both Baudouin and the liberals lacked a genuine awareness of socioeconomic conditions.

Beyond a belief in legalism, which Baudouin shared with the liberals, it is hard to identify other clearly defined forces that would keep the future Russian, or any other, federation together. The only amalgamating force that Baudouin could propose was a feeling of solidarity with the state, a sort of "étatistic" enthusiasm: "Our ideal must be a society, a territorial community—that is, an organized union of individuals, free in matters of choice of beliefs and convictions yet united in cooperation in earthly matters at a given time. Not a herd of egoistic cattle, but a society of freethinking individuals, inspired by a sense of solidarity."[26] At an earlier point Baudouin spoke of the necessity of a "unifying decentralization, one that would develop in the population a sense and awareness of solidarity with the state [*solidarność ogólnopaństwowa*]."[27] Thoughts about enlightened brotherly love deriving from a rational commitment to the state were not entirely unparalleled in the political thinking of the time (again, mostly among liberals), but Baudouin probably succeeded in presenting them in the most abstract way. There is not much doubt that this approach had little political force; it merely defined the bottom line. In Austria the appeal to the rational nature of the Hapsburg state certainly did nothing to keep the empire together.

Baudouin remained in many ways an enlightened rationalist of the old style. His worldview was clear and simple; the world he lived in certainly was not. Was he then simply an advocate of an ultimate rationalist kitsch? Certainly not; he was too much of an individualist—and too much of a Pole. Baudouin's strength lay in the assertion of the individual's rights, and the cornerstone of his political thinking was decentralization rather than the imposition of the higher-order interests of an impersonal state. At the time in which this sentiment was expressed, there was a place and a function for Baudouin. Just as the abiding value of liberalism lay in its attempt to create a certain political style, Baudouin's role was that of an independent commentator and critic, an intellectual provocateur. At a time when the political options seemed to be narrowing to a choice between the totalities of impersonal rationality and raw nationalism, this was—at the very least—a legitimate function.

## Notes

1. To A. Černý, April 20, 1914 (new style), in *Listy Jana Baudouina de Courtenay do A. Černego*, ed. Teodor Bešta (Wrocław: Ossolineum, 1972), 199; hereafter *Listy*.

2. I. A. Baudouin de Courtenay, *Izbrannye trudy po obščemu jazykoznaniju* (Moscow: Izd. Akademii nauk SSSR, 1963); *A Baudouin de Courtenay Anthology: The Beginnings of Structural Linguistics* (Bloomington: Indiana University Press, 1972).

3. Jan Niecisław Baudouin de Courtenay, *Dzieła wybrane*, ed. J. Z. Jakubowski and J. Kulczycka-Saloni, vol. 6 (Warsaw, 1983); hereafter *Dzieła*.

4. Although Baudouin's contribution to linguistics has now been established, his social activism has rarely been written about. Notable exceptions are Robert A. Rothstein, "Baudouin as a Dissenter," in *For Wiktor Weintraub* (The Hague, 1975), 391–405, and "The Individual as Leitmotiv of J. Baudouin de Courtenay's Work," *Folia Slavica*, 6 (1983): 53–63.

5. Baudouin de Courtenay, *Sbornik zadač po "Vvedeniju v jazykoznanie . . ."* (St. Petersburg, 1912).

6. Baudouin de Courtenay, "O smešannom xaraktere . . ." (1901), in *Izbrannye trudy*, 363.

7. *Nacional'nyj i territorial'nyj priznak v avtonomii* (St. Petersburg, 1913).

8. Baudouin must have been a Kadet, at least for some time. In January 1906 he was among the St. Petersburg delegates to the congress of that party.

9. Baudouin de Courtenay, "Ze zjazdu autonomistów . . . ," *Krytyka* (1906): 240.

10. *Krytyka* (1906): 117f.

11. *Krytyka* (1906): 111.

12. To A. Černý, October 30, 1925, quoted in A. Černý, "Za J. Baudouinem de Courtenay," *Slovanský přehled* 21 (1929–30): 653.

13. Baudouin de Courtenay, *Dzieła*, 6: 115.

14. "Finland gives us a perfect example of how two nationalities linguistically as different as the Swedes and the Finns can live together in peace and maintain a whole, unified both politically and economically." Baudouin de Courtenay, "Ze zjazdu autonomistów . . . ," 199.

15. Baudouin de Courtenay, "Ze zjazdu autonomistów . . . ," 244.

16. To A. Černý, in A. Černý, "Za J. Baudouinem de Courtenay," *Slovanský přehled* 21 (1929–30): 655.

17. Ibid.

18. Rothstein, "Individual as Leitmotiv," 58 f.

19. Baudouin de Courtenay, "W sprawie 'antysemitizmu postępowego'" (1911), quoted in Rothstein, "Individual as Leitmotiv," 59.

20. One of few observers who noted the activity of the Union was Max Weber.

21. Baudouin de Courtenay, "Vozmožno-li . . . ," in *Otečestvo—puti i dostiženija nacional'nyx literatur Rossii* (Petrograd, 1915), 20.

22. Baudouin de Courtenay, *Kwestia żydowska w państwie polskim* (1923), in *Dzieła*, 6:207.

23. To A. Černý, March 16, 1914, in *Listy*, 198.

24. *Listy*, 207.

25. The episode was recalled by Roman Jakobson.

26. Baudouin de Courtenay, "Wychowanie współczesne . . ." (1912), in *Dzieła*, 6:153 f.

27. Baudouin de Courtenay, "Kwestia polska w Rosji . . ." (1905), in *Dzieła*, 6:145.

# Confessor between East and West

## JAROSLAV PELIKAN

By jet plane the journey between Istanbul and Rome now takes about two hours. Thus on the same day a traveler can (as indeed the author did, on July 29, 1986) see old Saint Sophia in New Rome at sunrise and then at sunset new Saint Sophia in Old Rome—an exquisite little adaptation of that massive basilica. The historic link connecting these two churches of Saint Sophia is the Church of Saint Sophia in Kiev, built to copy Constantinople's and represented in a mosaic on the wall of Rome's "miniature Kievan Sophia Church."[1] The third Saint Sophia, a "continuation [*prodovžennja*]" of the one in Kiev,[2] was built in Rome by Josyf Cardinal Slipyj, exiled Ukrainian archbishop and metropolitan of Kiev-Halyč, in the twentieth century; and he marked the day of its consecration on September 27, 1969.[3] The first Saint Sophia in Constantinople—the city he called the Paris of the Middle Ages—was built in its present form by Justinian the Great, emperor of the Romans, in the sixth century. Slipyj had long admired it.[4] "Having seen all the cathedrals and the greatest churches of Europe and of Asia" (including Saint Peter's in Rome, the Cologne Cathedral, Notre Dame in Paris, and Saint Paul's in London), Slipyj declared in 1966—echoing the ancient words about Hagia Sophia of the *Primary Chronicle* of Nestor,[5] whom he elsewhere called "our genial and great chronicler and historian, Nestor"[6]—"we can say that upon entering that church something sacred, holy, and mysterious envelops the human soul and incites it to prayer."[7]

The second Saint Sophia was built by Jaroslav the Wise, prince of Kiev, in the eleventh century, as "the high point of Ukrainian architecture."[8] Slipyj idealized the memory of Jaroslav, and he frequently referred to his reign as a high point of Ukrainian religious and cultural life.[9] It was a mark of the investiture of the metropolitan of Kiev when he assumed charge of Saint Sophia. To Ukrainians, therefore, it was, together with the monastery of Pečerska Lavra, a cherished symbol of "our holy tradition."[10] Slipyj came through Kiev, as a prisoner, on the morning of April 12, 1945, and he glimpsed Saint Sophia on his final visit to Kiev but was not permitted to go in.[11] Yet he was able to remind the first secretary of the Ukrainian Communist party of an icon of Pope Saint Clement I that Jaroslav the Wise had ordered to be placed there.[12] And when it came time to build a church appropriate to the situation of Ukrainians in exile, the Saint Sophia of Jaroslav the Wise served as the obvious model. The Saint Sophia in Rome would be "as though a sister" to the Saint Sophia in Kiev.[13] Of those three churches bearing the name Saint Sophia, only the little one in Rome still functions as a Christian church, instead of having been "transformed into a museum" by the state.[14] It also functions as a memorial to Josyf Slipyj, who in his "Testament" (*Zapovit*) asked that he be buried there and then eventually translated to L'viv or, God willing and the Ukrainian nation consenting, Saint Sophia in Kiev;[15] his mummified body lies in a crypt beneath the church.

In 1974, as an exile in Rome, far away from his Ukrainian homeland, and as an old man of eighty-two (although he actually still had ten more years to live, during which those parallels would continue to suggest themselves to him), Josyf Cardinal Slipyj spoke about some of the remarkable coincidences between the crucial dates in his own life and "the turning points in our church life and our national life: 1892, 1911, 1917, 1925, 1939, 1944, 1945, 1963, and 1965."[16]

Reviewing the historical atlas together with a chronological table will help to document the ways some of those dates coincided.[17] When Slipyj was born in Zazdrist', Galicia (Halyčyna), on February 17, 1892, that village was part of the Austro-Hungarian Empire; Ternopil', on the other hand, where he attended *Gymnasium* between 1903 and 1911, from age eleven to age nineteen, had for a brief time at the beginning of the nineteenth century been part of czarist Russia. With the breakup of the Austro-Hungarian Empire at the end of the First World War, when Slipyj was twenty-six, the city of L'viv (Lwów in Polish, Lemberg in German, and Leopolis in Latin), where he attended seminary and later served as professor, rector, and metropolitan, was the site of the proclamation of a West Ukrainian People's Republic on November 1, 1918; two months later that republic announced its union with the Ukrainian National Republic at Kiev, but this failed to become a stable and recognized state. Instead, in July 1919 the military forces of a newly revitalized Poland succeeded in annexing Galicia. As part of "Eastern Little Poland" (*Małopolska Wschodnia*), therefore, it had become Polish territory when the thirty-year-old Slipyj came back in 1922 from his studies at Innsbruck and Rome to serve as professor of the major seminary at L'viv; it was to remain Polish throughout the 1920s and 1930s, during most of the metropolitanate of Andrej Šeptyc'kyj.

L'viv, however, fell on the Soviet side of the line of demarcation agreed upon by Nazi Germany and Soviet Russia as part of their nonaggression pact of August 1939; this situation obtained until the German invasion of the Soviet Union on June 21, 1941, when Slipyj was forty-nine.[18] For the next three years L'viv and its Galician territory were occupied by the German armies as *Distrikt Galizien* of the *General-gouvernement* of the Third Reich. L'viv was recaptured by the Red Army on July 27, 1944, but not without continuing resistance from Ukrainian nationalists, whose principal military force was the Ukrainian Insurgent Army (*Ukrajinska povstanska armija*), led by General Roman Šuchevyč.[19] During the second half of 1944 and the first half of 1945 the political and military forces of the Ukrainian Soviet Socialist Republic, of which L'viv was now a part, were engaged in a campaign to consolidate control, one step of which was the arrest of Josyf Slipyj on Wednesday, April 11, 1945, two months after his fifty-third birthday. He was in his seventies when he was set free in 1963, and in 1965 he was made a cardinal of the Holy Roman Church by His Holiness Pope Paul VI.

"At the center of your glorious pontificate," Josyf Slipyj declared to Pope Paul in Saint Peter's on November 15, 1963, "stands the East, and above all the Slavic East."[20] As is clear from such a statement, as well as from the capsule summary just recited of external events in Ukrainian history during his lifetime, Josyf Slipyj was a confessor between East and West who presided over a church that had been positioned, both by geography and by history, between East and West. As Robert Conquest, a leading scholar of twentieth-century developments in the Soviet orbit, has put it:

> A major reason why the events we shall be describing never truly gripped the Western mind appears to be a lack of understanding or knowledge of the power of Ukrainian national feeling, of Ukrainian nationhood. In this century an independent Ukrainian state only lasted a few years, and then with interruptions, and was never able to establish itself either physically or in the world's consciousness. In fact the Ukraine, as large as France and more populous than Poland, was by far the largest nation in Europe not to emerge as an independent entity (except briefly) in the period between the two World Wars.

Conquest goes on to declare, "The Ukraine's long independent cultural tradition was little known in the West. . . . Historically the Ukrainians are an ancient nation which has persisted and survived through terrible calamities."[21]

The phrase "between East and West" is one that unavoidably comes to mind in any consideration of the Ukrainian nation, the Ukrainian church, and the Ukrainian metropolitan. Slipyj took the occasion of his appointment as a cardinal to remind the pope that the Ukrainian church stood on the crossroads "between East and West."[22] Gregor Prokoptschuk made that the title of one of the longest chapters in his informative, if somewhat hagiographic, biography of Metropolitan Andrej Šeptyc'kyj, going on later in the book to speak of "the Ukrainian minority in Poland" as "always standing, both culturally and religiously, on the boundary between East and West."[23] Hryhor Lužnyc'kyj entitled his church history of 1954 (written in Ukrainian) *The Ukrainian Church between East and West*.[24] And Johannes Madey called his highly esteemed church history of 1969 (written in German) *Church between East and West*.[25] For the Slavs, noted Slipyj, understand better than most other Europeans—and the Ukrainians understand better than most other Slavs—the price of living on both sides of that great divide, "between two world views . . . between two churches

. . . two spiritualities."[26] Josyf Slipyj was able to boast to a Communist official, and then years later to a congregation of Ukrainian faithful in Rome, that he had been persecuted by the Bolsheviks, the Poles, and the Gestapo—quite indiscriminately.[27] And during the Second World War, as Slipyj reported with a touch of irony, there were bombardments, sometimes simultaneously, "from one direction . . . and from the other," by the Nazis and the Soviets. The library of the Theological Society of L'viv was destroyed by German bombs, and then the Red Army finished the job.[28]

"Now the card of history has been turned over," wrote Metropolitan Andrej Šeptyc'kyj in an epigram,[29] and as usual the Ukrainians were caught between the players in the global card game. Like many other Slavs before him and after him, Josyf Slipyj was forced throughout his life to explain to representatives of other ethnic traditions just who the Slavs were—and, within the Slavic community between East and West, just who the Ukrainians were. The terminology of the history books and the nomenclature of the atlases did not help such explanations a great deal. Thus in many accounts, and in the practice of the Roman Catholic church, the usual name for the Ukrainians was "Ruthenians." Protesting against the use of this "ethnic terminology," a Ukrainian archbishop, writing to the pope while Metropolitan Josyf Slipyj was still in a Soviet prison, objected that in common Ukrainian pronunciation the name "Ruthenian" came out as "Russian" (*ruskyj*). Besides, "the use by the Roman curia of the antiquated appellation 'Ruthenian, Ruthenians' makes it very difficult for Ukrainian Catholics to achieve any rapprochement or understanding with the Ukrainian Orthodox."[30]

While the name "Ruthenian" was, therefore, objectionable and highly charged, the Old Church Slavonic name *Rus'* was extremely confusing, and its translation as "Russia" was even more objectionable. As a recent study has observed, "Seventeenth-century ancestors of the modern Ukrainians, Belorussians and Russians all used variants of the term *Rus'*" when referring to themselves. . . . Both Ukrainians and Belorussians called themselves 'Ruthenians' (*rusyny*)."[31] *Rus'* is the term that appears in the ancient chronicles, including *The Primary Chronicle* bearing the name of Nestor. There it is usually translated into English and other Western languages as "Russia," so that Nestor becomes (as, for example, in the standard English version) *The Russian Primary Chronicle*.[32] Slipyj was determined not to surrender the name to the Muscovites.[33] Seeking to explain the meaning of *Rus'* to Eugène Cardinal Tisserant of the Sacred Congregation for the Eastern Church, Slipyj cited a number of the ancient chronicles to prove that in those documents *Rus'* was synonymous with what was called "Ukraine." The term "Russia," he went on to explain, was a neologism that had come into usage only with the rise of Muscovite Russia many centuries later.[34] Presumably on the basis of Slipyj's explanation, that understanding of the name was often reflected thereafter in Vatican usage. An interesting example of such usage can be found in two letters written to Josyf Slipyj on March 19, 1979, by Pope John Paul II, who before his election as pope had been Karol Cardinal

Wojtyła, archbishop of Kraków. In the first letter the term *Rus'* appears in quotation marks throughout, but the second letter consistently refers to *Rus' (Ucraina).*[35]

In their various letters,[36] as well as in the pope's memorial tribute of September 16, 1984, a week after Slipyj's death, Karol Wojtyła/John Paul II and Josyf Slipyj wrote to each other in Polish, Ukrainian, Italian, or Latin. Indeed, Slipyj took obvious glee in being able to append a postscript in Polish to an official letter for the pope that he had written "in the language of the members of the Roman curia," that is, in Italian.[37] On other occasions he would write to the pope in Ukrainian and then send along an official Italian version for the files.[38] Such polyglotism is interesting and important not only because each of them was an accomplished linguist—though that is, of course, eminently true—but because each of them belonged to what Slipyj called "the great family of Slavic nations" and had a Slavic language as his mother tongue.[39] As John Paul II wrote to Cardinal Slipyj in March 1979, "Through the inscrutable design of Providence, the Holy See is occupied for the first time by a Slavic pope."[40] Or, as he declared at Gniezno three months later, on the Sunday of Pentecost, June 3, 1979, during his first visit to his homeland after being elected pope:

> These languages fail to be heard especially by the first Slav Pope in the history of the Church. Perhaps that is why Christ has chosen him, perhaps that is why the Holy Spirit has led him. . . . Is it not Christ's will, is it not what the Holy Spirit disposes, that this Polish Pope, this Slav Pope, should at this precise moment manifest the spiritual unity of Christian Europe? Although there are two great traditions, that of the West and that of the East . . . , our lands were hospitable [also] to those wonderful traditions which have their origin in the new Rome, at Constantinople.[41]

The Slavs are the only European people to have received both of those "two great traditions" as a permanent heritage, but that means that they are also the only people for whom conversion to the Christian faith has meant cultural division rather than cultural unification and who have therefore lived between East and West throughout their history. For whereas over the centuries the gospel has been responsible for giving many nations their alphabet, to the Slavs it has given three—the Glagolitic, the Cyrillic, and the Latin. Even a Soviet historian of Kiev was obliged to acknowledge that "the adoption of Christianity was unquestionably a fact of primary importance." "Christianity, as the generally accepted religion in Europe," he adds, "served to draw the state of Ancient Rus closer to the rest of Europe," while at the same time "the efforts of the Byzantine Church to draw Rus into the sphere of age-long Byzantine culture serves to raise her cultural level."[42]

It is well known that in addition to doctrinal and theological emphases, the two most immediately striking of the distinctive features of Eastern Christianity that the Byzantine missions brought to the Slavs lay in the areas of polity and liturgy. Many observers, Eastern as well as Western, have suggested that the differences of doctrine between East and West, including even the celebrated *Filioque* doctrine, could probably have been worked out if the differences in the area of polity had been resolved; and many of these observers would also agree that the differences in liturgy became as decisive as they did primarily because they illustrated and exacerbated the differences of polity. Certainly to the common people these were the decisive differences of both method and outcome between the Byzantine and the Western (usually German) missionaries, and historically that assessment has been vindicated over and over. Differences in polity and differences in liturgy, moreover, have been closely related to each other, as Eastern rite Catholics of various traditions have had to discover when they have sought to combine a polity that tied them to the Holy See with a liturgy that set them apart from the vast majority of those who were also in communion with Rome; for that combination Josyf Slipyj found justification in the legacy of Cyril and Methodius.[43]

An oversimplified formula for the description of Byzantine mission policy, but a formula that correctly identifies the central issue, is to say that although it was the purpose of Western missionaries during the Middle Ages to convert a new people by incorporating it into the *corpus Christianum* of which the pope was the visible head, it was the intention—or, at any rate, the result—of Byzantine missions to convert a new people by calling into being a new church that would have its life and its administrative structure within that people and would establish fraternal and federative relations with other churches. Nevertheless, despite this feature of Byzantine mission strategy, there have not been many scholarly studies that would coordinate missiology and foreign policy in the Byzantine empire, as that policy expressed itself not only in the Christianization of the Slavic peoples but in the military conquest of others and in the establishment of diplomatic relations with yet others.[44]

This difference in missionary policy precluded not only the imposition of a single pyramidal structure in polity but also the program of a single *Kultsprache* in liturgy. For the Slavs to whom the Byzantine missions came, the principle of autocephaly found its most cherished symbol in the Church Slavonic liturgy, to which bishops from various Slavic lands could go on pointing, even at the Council of Trent in the sixteenth century and again at the Second Vatican Council in the twentieth, as evidence that Catholicity and Latinity were not to be equated. In the cultures that have been shaped by *pravoslavie* (Orthodoxy), the linguistic inheritance of the Byzantine missions has been transmitted through the special role that Church Slavonic has played in relation to the various individual Slavic vernaculars, the vocabulary it has bequeathed to them, and the link it has sometimes formed among them. As the history of the *raskol* (schism) in Russian Orthodoxy makes clear, attachment to the forms of the Church Slavonic liturgy, even to certain pronunciations of individual sacred words, could become a divisive issue whenever attempts were made at liturgical reform. Less drastic in their outcome, but often more far-reaching in their implications, have been those reform movements within *pravoslavie* that have pointed out the anomaly of resisting the imposition of Latin but retained in the name of "the language of the people" a language that is in fact used only in the liturgy. Campaigns for the vernacular—if not those of the Protestant Reformation, then those of the liturgical reformations coming out of the Second Vatican Council—have heightened that anomaly in Western Slavic lands; and the liturgical evolution of *pravoslavie* in North America calls attention once more to this distinctive feature of the Byzantine missions.

There is another linguistic consequence coming out of this distinctive liturgical philosophy. The cultural superiority of Byzantium to the West throughout the Middle Ages, which spokesmen for the East had to recognize even when they defensively refused to acknowledge it, was based on a fortunate combination of various economic, political, even military factors. Yet beneath and beyond all these factors it was the consequence of one factor—the Greek language. Byzantium felt entitled to the Christian culture of Athanasius and the Cappadocian fathers, to the text of the New Testament, to Plato and Aristotle, Aeschylus and Sophocles, and to Homer, as a single, though not uniform, inheritance that was bound together by the simple and powerful fact of its having been written in Greek. Nevertheless, although the heritage of Latin culture could not be compared with all of this, and the Latin of the Mass, the Vulgate, and of Augustine was not classical, the fact remains that by teaching the nations Latin and imposing it upon them as a condition of their becoming Catholic Christians, Western missionaries did give them at least some access to the language and the culture of Rome, pre-Christian as well as Christian, to Roman jurisprudence and to Virgil, to Roman rhetoric and to Horace. The Eastern Orthodox heirs of Byzantine culture who lived in Constantinople or in Athens did indeed receive the treasures of Greek culture, but the Slavic peoples did not; for, as Slipyj pointed out, Greek never became as dominant in the East as Latin did in the West.[45] The indigenous Christian culture and language of the Eastern Slavs were no doubt often the richer for it, but they did not have in that culture the point of contact for a renaissance in the way that both Byzantium itself and the Latin West did.

As part of the heritage of Josyf Slipyj, Byzantine missions also carried deep implications for the unity of Christendom. The historical contemporaneity of the Byzantine missions of Cyril and Methodius with the alienation between Constantinople and Old Rome made the battle in the Moravian mission field, a battle that was waged over both polity and liturgy, the first and in some ways the most dramatic of a series of conflicts that have torn the Slavs apart. The question came to be seen as a choice between following Cyril and Methodius in maintaining a Slavonic liturgy and a national church or following Cyril and Methodius in preserving the unity of Christendom by affiliation with the Apostolic See. In the history of *Rus'*/Ukraine the question has been not only its political relation to Poland, toward the west, and Russia, toward the east and north, but also its ecclesiastical relation between Old Rome and New Rome. The missions to the Slavs came *from* New Rome; in a sense, even those to Poland were the Western heirs of a Byzantine mission. But Cyril and Methodius went *to* Old Rome, and repeatedly the implications of that move have formed the agenda for Slavic Christians in various lands. As became evident at the Second Vatican Council, this duality in the legacy of Cyril and Methodius has continued to be a central component of the ecumenical agenda for the Slavs, whether Eastern Orthodox or Catholic, in the twentieth century.[46]

These issues received further clarification, during the generation that preceded Josyf Slipyj, in the thought of Vladimir Soloviev. His ecclesiological vision, grounded as it was in his cosmological speculation and incarnationist metaphysics, is an undeniable descendant of the Christian philosophy of Byzantium. And yet it is a vision that carried beyond Byzantium to the universality of the church, which is what the Byzantine mission of Cyril and Methodius itself had done. But if, according to Josyf Slipyj, Cyril and Methodius had manifested "the true Catholicity of the Church" and were at the same time "the precursors of authentic ecumenism,"[47] the search for Catholicity among the Slavs and the patterns of ecumenical reconciliation between East and West were fundamental to any understanding of their legacy.

## Notes

The text is an abridged version based on the first two sections of Jaroslav Pelikan's book *Confessor between East and West* (Grand Rapids, Mich.: Wm. B. Eerdmans, 1990).

© 1989 by Wm. B. Eerdmans Publishing Co. Published with permission.

1. Slipyj to Joseph Frings, June 7, 1964, *Archivum Patriarchale Sanctae Sophiae* (Rome: Università Catholica Ucraina, 1964), 30:290.

2. Slipyj, *Tvory Kard. Josyfa Verchovnogo Archyjepiskopa (Opera omnia Card. Josephi [Slipyj Kobernyckyj-Dyčkovskyj] archiepiscopi maioris)* (Rome: Universitas Ucrainorum a S. Clemente Papa, 1968–), 14:175.

3. Slipyj, *Tvory*, 10/11:143 (144).

4. Slipyj, *Tvory*, 2:107, 114.

5. "The Russes were astonished, and in their wonder praised the Greek ceremonial. . . . 'We knew not whether we were in heaven or on earth. For on earth there is no such splendor or such beauty, and we are at a loss how to describe it. We only know that God dwells there among men, and their service is fairer than the ceremonies of other nations. For we cannot forget that beauty.'" Samuel Cross, ed., *The Russian Primary Chronicle: Laurentian Text* (Cambridge, Mass.: The Medieval Academy of America, 1953), 111.

6. Slipyj, *Tvory*, 12:19.

7. Slipyj, *Tvory*, 12:227.

8. Slipyj, *Tvory*, 13:17.

9. See, for example, Slipyj, *Tvory*, 13:233, 237–238.

10. Slipyj, *Tvory*, 12:120 (125), 13:29 (30).

11. Josyf Slipyj, *Spomyny* (unpublished memoirs), colophon dated "Napysano pid čas ferij 1963 i 1964 r. v monastyri Otciv Pasionistiv v Nettuno" (Written during vacation time, 1963 and 1964, in the monastery of the Passionist Fathers at Nettuno), 111, 193.

12. Slipyj to N. V. Podgorny, January 1961, *Arch. Pat.*, 28:35.

13. Slipyj, *Tvory*, 13:24–25, 14:196.

14. Slipyj, *Tvory*, 12:227.

15. Slipyj, *Tvory*, 14:487.

16. Slipyj, *Tvory* 14:139 (at eighty-five), 14:80–81 (at ninety-two), 9:230.

17. Paul Robert Magocsi, ed., *Ukraine: A Historical Atlas* (Toronto: University of Toronto Press, 1985); Stephan M. Horak, *Ukraine in der internationalen Politik, 1917–1953* (Munich: Verlag Ukraine, 1957). In maps 20–24 Magocsi has geographically presented this evolution; Horak provides a detailed chronology.

18. Myroslav Prokop, *Ukraina i ukrajins'ka polityka Moskvy* (Ukraine and the Ukrainian politics of Moscow), 2d ed., 2 vols. (Munich: Sucastnist', 1981), 1:94–147.

19. See Slipyj's tribute to him, in *Tvory*, 14:225.

20. Slipyj, *Tvory*, 12:112.

21. Robert Conquest, *Harvest of Sorrow: Soviet Collectivization and the Terror-Famine* (New York: Oxford University Press, 1986), 25–26.

22. Slipyj, *Tvory*, 12:176.

23. Gregor Prokoptschuk, *Metropolit Graf Scheytyckyj: Leben und Wirken des grossen Förderers der Kirchenunion*, 2d ed. (Munich: Verlag Ukraine, 1967), 179–197, 214.

24. Hryhor Lužnyc'kyj, *Ukrajins'ka Cerkva miž schodom i zachodom: Narys istoriji Ukrajins'koji Cerkvy* (The Ukrainian Church between East and West: Outline of the history of the Ukrainian Church) (Philadelphia: Providence Association of Ukrainian Catholics, 1954).

25. Johannes Madey, *Kirche zwischen Ost und West: Beitrage zur Geschichte der Ukrainischen und Weissruthenischen Kirche* (Munich: Ukrainische Freie Universität, 1969); for praise of Madey's work, see Volodymyr Janiv, ed., *Cerkva i relihija v Ukraini: 50 lit pislja zovtnevoji revoluciji (1917–1967)* (The church and religion in the Ukraine fifty years after the October revolution) (Munich: Ukrainische Freie Universität, 1984), xvii.

26. Slipyj, *Tvory*, 14:260.

27. Slipyj to N. V. Podgorny, February 17, 1961, *Arch. Pat.*, 28:89; Slipyj, *Tvory*, 13:151.

28. Slipyj, *Spomyny*, 100, 70.

29. Slipyj, *Spomyny*, 83.

30. Ivan Bučko to John XXIII, September 30, 1959, *Arch. Pat.*, 28:4–7.

31. Frank E. Sysyn, *Between Poland and the Ukraine: The Dilemma of Adam Kysil, 1600–1653* (Cambridge, Mass.: Harvard Ukrainian Research Institute, 1985), 27.

32. Cross (1953).

33. Slipyj, *Tvory*, 14:139.

34. Slipyj to Eugène Tisserant, June 12, 1963, *Arch. Pat.*, 28:395–398.

35. John Paul II to Slipyj, March 19, 1979, *Arch. Pat.*, 118:75–86.

36. The first of these, from one Slavic cardinal to another, seems to have been a Christmas greeting: Slipyj to Karol Wojtyła, December 23, 1967, *Arch. Pat.*, 36:402.

37. Slipyj to John Paul II, November 23, 1983, *Arch. Pat.*, 118:292–293.

38. Slipyj to John Paul II, June 3, 1979, *Arch. Pat.*, 118:99–100 (Ukrainian); Slipyj to John Paul II, June 15, 1979, *Arch. Pat.*, 118:99–100 (Ukrainian); Slipyj to John Paul II, June 15, 1979, *Arch. Pat.*, 118:102–105 (Italian).

39. Slipyj to Władysław Rubin, June 15, 1979, in Slipyj, *Tvory*, 14:374.

40. John Paul II to Slipyj, March 19, 1979, *Arch. Pat.*, 118:83.

41. Virgilio Levi, ed., *The Common Christian Roots of the European Nations: An International Colloquium in the Vaticans*, 2 vols. (Florence: Le Monnier, 1982), 1:4–5.

42. B. Grekov, *Kievan Rus*, trans. Y. Sdobnikov (Moscow: Foreign Languages Publishing House, 1959), 636, 639.

43. Slipyj, *Tvory*, 13:270.

44. In the first of the six Andrew W. Mellon Lectures that I delivered at the National Gallery of Art in Washington in the autumn of 1987 under the general title "Imago Dei: The Byzantine Apologia for Icons," to observe the twelve hundredth anniversary of the restoration of the icons by the Second Council of Nicaea in 787, I discussed "Realpolitik and Religion Byzantine-Style" as this affected both the abolition of images and their recovery.

45. Slipyj, *Tvory*, 2:111.

46. Ivan Hryn'och, "Vidhomin Kyrylo-Methodijivs'koji ideji na II Vatykans'komu Sobori" (Echo of the Cyrillo-Methodian ideal at the Second Vatican Council), *Bohoslovija* 44 (1980): 181–187.

47. Slipyj to John Paul II, February 10, 1981, *Arch. Pat.*, 118:200–201.

# The Snows of Yesteryear

## JOHN-PAUL HIMKA

As he tells us in his *Memoirs of an Anti-Semite*, Gregor von Rezzori hails from "an almost astronomically remote province in southeastern Europe."[1] This is Bukovina, one of those tiny, historically convoluted and culturally variegated lands of East Central Europe that has nurtured a disproportionate number of geniuses, some forgotten and some still celebrated. Among the celebrated are Paul Celan, Mihai Eminescu and Olha Kobylianska, major voices in German, Romanian, and Ukrainian literature respectively. Rezzori is understating the case somewhat when he writes of Bukovina's "half a dozen nationalities" and "half a dozen religions" (36).[2] The bulk of the population (about two-thirds at the beginning of this century) was of the Orthodox faith and fairly evenly divided between the Ukrainian and Romanian nationalities. But there was also a substantial German minority who were Roman Catholics and Lutherans. There were about as many Jews as Germans, and on the outskirts of Bukovina's capital one could find the luxurious court of the famous Hassidic rabbi of Sadagura. There were Russians, the so-called Lippovanians, who were Old Believers. They played a distinguished role in the modern history of the Old Belief because it was they who revived the Old Believer hierarchy in their settlement at Bila Krynytsia in 1846; to this day the Bila Krynytsia hierarchy presides over the majority of Old Believers in the Soviet Union. There were Armenians, Polish-speaking and Uniate in the north, Kipchak-speaking and Apostolic in the south. There were Ukrainian Greek Catholics and Polish Roman Catholics as well as a small population of Hungarian Calvinists. All this diversity—the product, of course, of a tangled but absorbing history—was to be found in a small land in the Carpathians, just a little more than ten thousand square kilometers in area and with a population barely exceeding eight hundred thousand when Rezzori was born in 1914.

In his latest volume of autobiography, *The Snows of Yesteryear*, as in his earlier *Memoirs of an Anti-Semite* and indeed as in most of his fiction, Rezzori has a lot to say about his native province. Although the main concern of his autobiographical writings is psychological portraiture, Bukovina figures in them as much more than exotic background. Rezzori often feels that Bukovinian situations form his charac-

67

ters in a profound way. The lives and personalities of his father, mother, and sister, to each of whom he devotes a chapter of *The Snows of Yesteryear,* are terribly flawed because Bukovina passed from Austrian to Romanian rule in 1918–1919. His books are peopled by specimens of humanity improbable outside of Bukovina or other parts of what Karl Emil Franzos termed *Halb-Asien,* such as the Lippovanian who suddenly leaps out of an apple tree in *The Snows of Yesteryear* (252) or the Sephardic Jewess raised as an Armenian Uniate in *Memoirs of an Anti-Semite.*[3] Rezzori's attitude toward his Carpathian homeland is ambivalent, to be sure, but above all it is obsessive.

Rezzori is obsessed with Bukovina the place—his hometown of Czernowitz and the forests where his father hunted—but much, much more so with Bukovina the congeries of peoples. In *Memoirs of an Anti-Semite* Jews figure most prominently; in *The Snows of Yesteryear* Germans (or should we call them Austrians?) occupy center stage. In both books Rezzori also speaks of an ardent attraction to the Romanians and their culture, although Romanian characters do not stand out in either. In *The Snows of Yesteryear* one of the chapters, the first, is devoted to a Ukrainian, and references to that character reappear in later chapters. I find the treatment of this particular Ukrainian and of all people and things Ukrainian in this book disturbing and worthy of more extended commentary.

The first of the five "portraits" offered by Rezzori in *The Snows of Yesteryear* is that of his nursemaid, called Cassandra. He describes her in a most singular manner. In the very first sentence introducing her, Rezzori tells us that when she came to his family household, she was "hardly more than a beast" (5). Later on, too, she was perceived to be "not fully human" (14). Rezzori remembers her as akin to his dog, his magpie, his rabbit, his stuffed bear, and his toy elephant (23–24). He thinks of her mainly as an animal, although he cannot seem to decide precisely what kind. Most of the time he describes her as "simian." She is "a female gorilla" (12) with "simian ugliness" (14), a "chimpanzee face" (22), "monkey's eyes" (35) and "monkey teeth" (46), "wrinkled simian cheeks" (47), and "long simian arms" (43). At other times she is compared to a dog (13, 48, 247–248). In one memorable passage Cassandra is caught "romping with the dogs . . . bare-assed, a beast among beasts" (22). Yet at still other times Rezzori likens her to a sow (14, 19). (When Rezzori compares his mother to an animal, it is to a swan [30]). At times he recognizes Cassandra's humanity, but it is of a "primitive" and "savage" sort. She is a "Stone Age female" (50), a "Cro-Magnon female" (53); she is an Eskimo (47, 52), a Samoyed (47).

This Cassandra, as Rezzori remembers her, spoke a "higgledy-piggledy garble of incomprehensible foreign idioms" (14); more precisely, she "spoke no language correctly, [but] expressed herself in snatches of Romanian, Ruthenian, Polish and Hungarian, as well as Turkish and Yiddish, assisted by a grotesque, grimacing mimicry and a primitive, graphic body language" (8); or even more precisely, "the main component [of her language] was a German, never learned correctly or completely, the gaps in which were filled with words and phrases from all the other tongues spoken in the Bukovina—so that each second or third word was either Ruthenian, Romanian, Polish, Russian, Armenian or Yiddish, not to forget Hungarian and Turkish" (44).[4] As a young man, encouraged by his former governess, a German from Pomerania, Rezzori imitated Cassandra's "linguistic blossoms" to amuse some visitors; thus he "entertained an audience who knew how to appreciate them: well-educated Jews seem to me to have a remarkable feel for language" (263). The reader, unfortunately, is not let in on the full joke. When Rezzori actually quotes examples of Cassandra's speech (51–52), these are much tamer than he describes—merely German sentences with a Ukrainian word tossed in.

Rezzori's Cassandra is not just any kind of Ukrainian, but a Hutsul (43), that is, a representative of the distinctive Ukrainian mountain folk. Hutsuls and their folkways have often been romanticized, such as in *Shadows of Forgotten Ancestors*, both Serhii Paradzhanov's film and Mykhailo Kotsiubynsky's novel,[5] and in the work of the Polish anthropologist and litterateur Stanisław Vincenz.[6] But Rezzori doesn't romanticize the Hutsuls. No, to him they are "dim-witted" (33), barely touched by the hand of progress. Their noses have been eroded by syphilis. And, in contrast to Rezzori's father, who hunts, they poach (222–223).

Almost until the end of the book Rezzori refers to the Ukrainians not by their modern name but by their former designation, "Ruthenian," as in "an old Ruthenian hag, Mrs. Daniljuk" (121). By the interwar era, however, the term "Ruthenian" was already an anachronism in Bukovina, and it carried a certain connotation of condescension. Also almost until the end of the book (and the same is true of *Memoirs of an Anti-Semite*), the Ukraine does not exist in Rezzori's geography. There is Romania on one side of the border and "Russia" on the other (17, 136, 175). When a Bukovinian, not an American, exhibits this sort of geographical conceptualization, it is not a case of ignorance or convenience but one of refusing to recognize that Ukrainians constitute a nation.

In the epilogue to *The Snows of Yesteryear* Rezzori returns to his hometown after more than half a century's absence. He tells us that the town's name "underwent several changes—from Czernowitz to Cernăuți to the present Chernovtsy" (275). The Ukrainian name of the city, Chernivtsi, does not figure in Rezzori's list. But Ukrainians, finally called such, do figure in Rezzori's account. What he has to say about them is worth quoting at length:

> What now moved through the streets before my confused and astonished eyes was utterly uniform and obviously homogeneous, nothing provoking any particularizing pride. . . . The faces were—as the saying goes—all of the same stamp: of Slavic broadness and angularity with coarse skin and light-colored hair. These were Ukrainians. In the old days we called them Ruthenians, one of the many minorities in a place where there was no majority. . . . Now they were

the only ones left, those people's comrades of the Soviet Republic of the Ukraine, which, as the former "Little Russia" enlarged by the annexation of Galicia and the northern Bukovina, now accounts for more than half the European territory of the Soviet Union. Nor were these people different from other Russians. The women were almost without exception plump, the men stocky and puffy, a people of cabbage eaters, not in dire want, not dissatisfied but inclined to submit resignedly to God's will, serious and well behaved. (284)

These are very strange impressions for 1989, the year when Rezzori visited Chernivtsi. In that year much of the world press was writing about the Ukrainian nation's distinctiveness, in connection with the founding congress of the Popular Movement of the Ukraine (Rukh). But Rezzori could only see a people no different from "other Russians." In that same year Chernivtsi itself was host to Chervona Ruta, a huge Ukrainian rock and folk music festival in which hundreds of bands participated. I can just imagine the *metalisty* nibbling on cabbage as their electric guitars blasted the Carpathians.

So what does all this mean and why do I bring it up? For one thing, I find Rezzori's view of Ukrainians to be historically quite resonant. Polish landlords and Austrian officials in the eighteenth and nineteenth centuries frequently thought of the Ukrainian peasants as beasts.[7] Could Rezzori have inherited this view of Ukrainians from his father, who had served as an Austrian state official? The view of Slavs in general and Ukrainians in particular as in some sense subhuman and at best extremely primitive was quite common in virulent forms of German chauvinism, not just in the Nazi variety. Could Rezzori also have picked this up from the family milieu? His father, as Rezzori points out time and again, was convinced of the Germans' innate superiority to all the other peoples of Bukovina, particularly to the Jews, whom he despised.

Rezzori pays special attention to the Jews. He dwells on them lovingly in *Memoirs of an Anti-Semite,* and all the Jews in *The Snows of Yesteryear* are positive and colorful characters. Yet we know from the *Memoirs* that Rezzori had once been an anti-Semite, quite unthinkingly, simply because his father and so many others of his place and station were. In the end Rezzori overcame this particular set of prejudices, and the *Memoirs* can be understood at least in part as a chronicle of how his attitudes toward Jews evolved. It seems, however, that the ethnic prejudices in Rezzori's milieu extended beyond the Jews to the Ukrainians, but that Rezzori has not yet worked out that set of prejudices. Anti-Semitism is a notorious and easily diagnosed mental disease; anti-Ukrainian prejudice often escapes attention, but I think it can be diagnosed clearly in Rezzori's writing.

In raising these points, my intent is not to single out Rezzori for censure. Rather, I seek to call attention to the existence of an ethnic prejudice that seems to be fairly easily tolerated by otherwise cultured and sensitive people. I doubt very much that any other reviewer will be bothered by the image Rezzori projects of Ukrainians as dim-witted talkers of gibberish or just another species of dull Russian—"stolid cabbage-eating Ukrainians," as one of Rezzori's previous reviewers has called them.[8] Yet could a white American author write about blacks the way Rezzori does about Ukrainians without provoking indignation? I think not.

Rezzori is very sad that "the only ones left" in Bukovina are Ukrainians. Although he mixes his deplorable prejudices in with this sentiment, I have to agree with the main point he is making. Bukovina was once a land of crosscurrents, a lush garden of cultures. It was the commingling of German and Jew, Romanian and Ukrainian, Armenian and Pole that produced this little land's cultural geniuses, including Rezzori. But this cross-cultural world has well nigh vanished, like the snows of yesteryear. The first blows came down on it in the interwar period, when the extreme nationalisms deliberately barred the way to cross-fertilization. The Second World War removed the political and even biological bases for cultural interaction. The borders were redrawn so that largely Ukrainian northern Bukovina was incorporated into the Ukrainian SSR, whereas the largely Romanian south remained part of Romania. By mutual agreement of Hitler and Stalin the German population of Bukovina was evacuated. Most of Bukovina's Jews were murdered by the Nazis.[9] This once multilingual, multicultural region was reduced to a largely Ukrainian-Russian, *Soviet* homogeneity in the north (and a largely Romanian homogeneity in the south).[10] The Soviet government has until recently done all in its power to isolate Ukrainian culture in Bukovina from its traditional East, Central, and West European influences and to substitute for this cosmopolitan context a strictly enforced Russian orientation. The crossroads of East and West has been, as Rezzori feared, swallowed by the East. We have all been somewhat impoverished as a result.

## Notes

1. Gregor von Rezzori, *Memoirs of an Anti-Semite,* (New York: Viking Press, 1981), 1.

2. Page numbers in parentheses refer to Gregor von Rezzori, *The Snows of Yesteryear: Portraits for an Autobiography* (New York: Alfred A. Knopf, 1989).

3. This was Miss Bianca Alvaro, born in neighboring Bessarabia, not in Bukovina, who figures in the chapter "Löwinger's Rooming House."

4. Rezzori himself is said to write "im Bukowiner Idiom, Deutsch mit rumänischen, ukrainischen und jiddischen Ausdrücken vermengt." Amy Colin, "An den Schnittpunkten der Traditionen—Deutsch in der Bukowina u.a.," *Neue deutsche Hefte* 30, no. 4 (180): 764–765. This article is an excellent introduction to Bukovina's cultural legacy.

5. The novel is available in an English translation by Marco Carynnyk (Littleton, Colo.: Ukrainian Academic Press, 1981).

6. *On the High Uplands: Sagas, Songs, Tales and Legends of the Carpathians* (New York: Roy Publishers, n.d.).

7. In fact, about Hutsuls in particular one official said that in their case "those features that distinguish people from animals are but little developed." John-Paul Himka, *Galician Villagers and the Ukrainian National Movement in the Nineteenth Century* (New York: St. Martin's Press, 1988), 14.

8. Michael Ignatieff, "The Old Country," *New York Review of Books,* February 15, 1990, 4.

9. Chernivtsi was once an important center of Jewish, particularly Yiddish, culture. In 1908, for example, the city hosted an international Yiddish conference that sought to make Yiddish the exclusive Jewish national language. But by 1985 there was only one Yiddish writer left in Chernivtsi.

10. In 1970 the population of Chernivtsi Oblast, which includes part of the former Bessarabia as well as northern Bukovina, was 69 percent Ukrainian, 19 percent Romanian and Moldavian, and 6 percent Russian, with Jews and others accounting for the remaining 6 percent.

# A Tragic Love for German

## Holocaust Poetry from the Bukovina

AMY COLIN

Poetry of the Holocaust written in German uncovers a deep fissure between the language it uses and the experience it attempts to convey. To respond to the Holocaust in the language of those who murdered the Jewish people is a dilemma. In trying to solve it, Paul Celan destroys the traditional syntactic and semantic structures of his native German tongue. Out of the residues he creates an innovative poetic idiom that bears his testimony of the Jewish persecution as an urn bears ashes. But Celan's Bukovinian contemporaries—Alfred Margul-Sperber, Moses Rosenkranz, David Goldfeld, Isaac Schreyer, Alfred Kittner, Rose Ausländer, Immanuel Weissglas, and Alfred Gong—often used traditional poetic devices and a classicist German style to utter the unspeakable.

These poets were part of a multifarious Jewish culture that emerged and flourished in the Bukovina, a region located between the northeast Carpathian Mountains, the river Dniester, and the Bessarabian steppe. During its tumultuous history the Bukovina belonged to a variety of countries and spheres of influence from the neighboring Kiev Empire, the dukedom of Halicz, and the Moldavian duchy, which in turn became a vassal state of Poland as well as of the Ottoman Empire, to the Austro-Hungarian monarchy, the Kingdom of Romania, and last but not least the Soviet Union. In this distant "land of the beech trees," as the Slavs called it, Romanians, Ukrainians, Germans, Jews, Magyars, Poles, Hutzuls, Russian Old Believers (known as Lippovanians), and Armenians coexisted for many decades. As a crossroad of heterogeneous traditions, the Bukovina became a model for a united Europe, a kind of United States of Eastern Europe. Karl Emil Franzos, in his popular but controversial cultural sketches from "Half-Asia," depicts his homeland as a fortress of civilization in the Eastern European "wilderness."[1] A representative of Austrian Enlightenment, Franzos regards the Bukovina as embodying an ideal way in which German culture could harmoniously merge with regional traditions so as to offset the negative "Asiatic" influence in Eastern Europe. Franzos, a middle-class German Jewish writer, held Asia responsible for all social, economic, and political problems in the world. Time and again the memory of Moses Rosenkranz, Alfred Kittner, Rose Ausländer, Alfred Gong, Immanuel Weissglas, and Paul Celan—all modern poets from that region—returns to their homeland as a peaceful haven of multi-lingual people. "Bukovina, sweet country, / shrine of many languages / and various manners," writes Georg Drozdowski in a nostalgic poem from the late 1960s.[2] Even Gregor von Rezzori, whose *Memoirs of an Anti-Semite* (1981) uncovers the growing tensions and discrepancies between Germans and Jews in the Bukovina, is so intrigued by the fusion of Western European and Oriental cultures that he feels forced to admit that in the Bukovina everybody, the liberals as well as the fanatics, peacefully coexisted in the mutual consent of cynicism.[3]

In his well-known speech "The Meridian" Paul Celan suggests that the Bukovina was a "region where books and people lived,"[4] for it produced a variegated German, Romanian, Ukrainian, and Yiddish literature as well as, many years after its downfall, a Hebrew literature by expatriate writers living in Israel. Among the representatives of Bukovinian writing are the foremost Romanian poet Mihai Eminescu, the leading Ukrainian writers Osip Fedkovič and Olha Kobylianska, Yiddish poets Itzig Manger and Eliezer Steinberg, Hebrew authors Aharon Appelfeld, Dan Pagis, Manfred Winkler, and numerous German writers from Karl Emil Franzos to Edgar Hilsenrath. It was characteristic for the Bukovina that Ukrainian, Romanian, and even Yiddish poets wrote their first literary texts in German; under the impact of growing nationalism some of them turned to their native language, but they still integrated German literary tradition into their works. Yet others, including leading Romanian and Jewish poets, continued to write in German despite all political and historical changes. Nowhere does the unusual Bukovinian bond to the German tradition become more evident than in an address to the Viennese parliament by the Bukovinian politician Dr. Konstantin Tomaszczuk, a half Ruthenian, half Romanian, who promoted the idea of a German university in Czernowitz: "German *Wissenschaft* has universal validity. It is only because German culture has universal significance that the non-German sons of Bukovina establish a German university. We are not just Poles, Germans, Romanians; we are primarily human beings who are rooted in the same soil from which we derive our strength. I mean Austria."[5]

There were historical reasons for such fascination with German culture. For almost a hundred and fifty years (1774–1918) the Bukovina was a part of the Austro-Hungarian Empire. Its bureaucracy was relatively tolerant of all ethnic groups in that region, admitting Romanians and Ruthenians into the civil service and thus facilitating their assimilation into German culture. The Bukovinians, who had greatly suffered under the Ottoman Empire, welcomed the Austrian regime. In the late eighteenth century, when the Austrian government put the Bukovina under Galician administration, discontent and opposition arose among the Bukovinians, leading to the first nationalist movements in that region. But in 1949 Romanian politicians, stimulated by growing liberalism and nationalism during the 1948 revolution, suc-

ceeded in acquiring for the Bukovina the status of an "independent crown land" with
its privileges of partial self-government and freedom of the press.[6]

The relative political freedom fostered the economic and cultural prosperity of
all ethnic groups, but had a special impact on the Jewish population, deepening its
receptivity to the German tradition. In the nineteenth and early twentieth centuries
European Jews were often discriminated against and regarded merely as a religious
group, but Jews living in the Bukovina enjoyed a relatively privileged status and in
1910 were officially recognized as an ethnic nationality. Such an improved social and
political situation nourished their deep loyalty to the Hapsburg monarchy, which in
turn motivated Austrian officials to see the Jews as representatives of the Hapsburg
Empire.

The Jewish population had indeed a crucial part in the emergence and develop-
ment of the Bukovina's German literature and culture: in the nineteenth and early
twentieth centuries most German writers from the Bukovina, including Franzos,
Ausländer, Kittner, Alfred Margul-Sperber, and Victor Wittner perceived themselves
as Austrian rather than Jewish poets. Yet even Orthodox Jews, such as Rabbi Eliazar
Ladier, wrote in German; in fact, the Bukovinian Karl Korn was the first and only
Jewish poet ever to write in a German dialect, the Svabian idiom of the Bukovina.
Whether assimilated or religious, these different poets considered themselves German cultural mediators, aware that they translated a considerable number of literary,
historical, and religious texts from various languages into German.[7]

Despite the downfall of the Austro-Hungarian Empire and the integration of
the Bukovina into the Romanian Kingdom, the Bukovinian Jewish love for Austria
persisted. At the October 4, 1918, session of the Viennese parliament the Bukovinian
Jewish delegate Dr. Benno Straucher voted for the joining of his homeland to Austria. In 1919, when Bukovinian citizens were granted the right to choose between
Romanian and Austrian citizenship, many Jews opted for Austria. (Their decision
was fatal, however, because during World War II the Soviets classified Bukovinian
Jews with Austrian passports as German citizens and deported them to Siberia.) As
late as 1928 a Zionist leader from Czernowitz was still praising the Jewish love for
the German people and language:

> For no other people in this world did the Jews preserve so much love and faith-
> fulness as for the Germans. . . . They carried the German language with them
> into exile; they cherished and protected it and turned it into the Jewish people's
> tongue; and these Jews made out of German a universal language, and nine-
> tenths of all Jews in this world speak German, and even the poorest "caftan-
> Jew" in Barnow loves and admires Schiller, as if he were part of the cannon of
> biblical writings.[8]

Despite the rise of Nazi Germany, poets such as Victor Wittner clung to their
German identity. In a letter to Alfred Kittner, Wittner, already an exile in Swit-

zerland, emphasized that he considered himself an Austrian and an Austrian poet as well:

> It is illogical to assume that one's place of residence or work is "accidental" but not one's birthplace. Quite the opposite is true—after all, I have been able to choose my place of residence but not my place of birth! One chooses precisely according to one's affinity for a language, a country, a people. If it had drawn me toward the Bukovina, I would have gone there. . . . Or I would have left Berlin in 1933 for London or Paris rather than for Vienna. The fact that I now still reside in Zurich has mostly to do with the German language, which I will not willingly give up.[9]

In the late 1930s, Wittner still placed hope in the reemergence of a "beautiful Germany." His letter reveals, however, that his bond to the German tradition was deeply rooted in ambivalence toward the Jewish legacy, for Wittner explicitly disregards his Jewishness, forbidding Kittner to include him in an anthology of Jewish writing. But despite his alienation from Judaism, Wittner also wrote powerful Holocaust poems, which signal a change in his relationship to both German and Jewish identity. Wittner's "In Beautiful Order" documents the sadism of the Nazis in Auschwitz, ironically exposing how the German sense for "beautiful order" became the motor of a machinery that systematically exterminated millions of victims.[10]

Wittner's change in attitude was characteristic of other Bukovinian authors who first insisted on their Austrian identity but later rediscovered their bond to Judaism. Their deep affinity for German is one of the reasons why the German Jewish component of Bukovinian literature paradoxically reached its culmination precisely at the time when the final catastrophe was looming. In the 1920s and early 1930s, however, the still relatively liberal political situation in Romania may have nourished the illusions and false hopes of the Bukovinian poets of Jewish descent, thus indirectly stimulating their literary endeavors. Although Romanian was declared the official language of the Bukovina, the Romanian officials tolerated the existing German and Ukrainian schools and a private Hebrew institution. But in the late 1930s, the rapidly growing chauvinism and racism undermined the peaceful coexistence of the multilingual people in the Bukovina and deeply affected Jewish life in that region.

In the late summer of 1941 German and Romanian fascists occupied the Bukovina. Within the first forty-eight hours they murdered between two thousand to three thousand Jews. By the beginning of September they had forced all Jews living in Czernowitz to move into a ghetto. During the following few weeks thirty thousand Jews were deported to the death camps of Transnistria in the western Ukraine. Although the mayor of Czernowitz attempted to stop these deportations, in June 1942 new deportations began, and only a few deportees survived.[11]

In the ghetto and the concentration camps Bukovinian intellectuals, writers, and artists continued their literary and artistic endeavors, defiantly persisting in writing German verse. They chose to create poems rather than prose texts, for verse can be composed on small pieces of paper and can be hidden easily. The integrity of poetry, set against the chaos and cruelty of reality, gave these deportees strength and purpose. Some of their texts speak of love, making few direct references to the war and the camps, whereas other poems describe the murders and are significant as historical documents. Yet most of these poets believed in the indestructibility of language and in the possibility of restoring the pure meaning of words by clearing away negative connotations. Some of them (Rosenkranz and Weissglas) assumed the existence of a pure, holy realm within language, a kind of "Goethe-language," which neither history nor political events could ever affect. Others (Kittner and Ausländer) hoped to create this realm within their own work.

It is characteristic of these authors that they displayed a strong preference for traditional poetic devices and images. But their traditionalism was not simply a lack of innovative power. Rather, it was rooted in their unusual situation as German poets in multilingual surroundings. Their growing isolation under Romanian rule produced an insecurity about their native tongue that resulted in a strong attachment to established poetic values and an even deeper concern with language. Unlike most Bukovinians, who spoke a German mixed with Ukrainian, Romanian, and Yiddish expressions, these poets and writers were particularly proud of their High German. As did Bukovinian writers living in the time of the Hapsburg monarchy, they followed fin-de-siècle movements in Austrian and German art, literature, and philosophy. Karl Kraus, along with Stephan George, provided Bukovinian poets with linguistic theories that justified and reinforced their attachment to traditions of German. Like Kraus, these authors considered themselves epigones living in the ancient house of language. Alfred Margul-Sperberg, the mentor of the Bukovinian Jewish poets of his time, explicitly refused to be included among modern poets: "Spare me with your labels, please / I am no poet of the mid-centuries / I save my golden freight of future days / faithfully from the forgotten yesterdays." [12] These verses could well serve as an epigram to his generation of writers and poets.

But there were also crucial political reasons for such traditionalism. As early as the 1920s and 1930s many avant-garde artists were playing with residues of the classicist tradition from sonnets to Greek and Roman columns, lending them a postmodern dimension. As a reaction to these artistic experiments as well as to the avant-garde in general, Nazi artists and poets laid claim to the classicist tradition to propagate their perverted belief that nazism was the only true heir to German culture. Seen against this background, the attempt of Holocaust poets from the Bukovina to write German sonnets in the midst of the ghetto, the war, and the death camps is a political act. It is the conscious endeavor to rescue a tradition misused by the Nazis, a desperate struggle to show that there could still be other heirs to German culture. The most powerful document of these beliefs and endeavors is included in Weissglas's unpublished volume of poems, "Gottes Mühlen in Berlin" (1947), written during and shortly after his deportation to a quarry in Transinistria. The motto of this collection reads as follows:

> The author of this book has never seen Germany face to face but has lived and suffered long. The German lament that we have harvested here, of love and death instilled by centuries past and by generations sung into grave, is as old as language: it needed only an urgent poet. During the years of the clash of arms 1940–1947, not without play on God's mills, which grind slowly but certainly, it was written down in a German-speaking foreign land.[13]

Weissglas, who had never been in Germany, considered himself not only an indispensable instrument but a legitimate heir to German culture and literature. In his verse, which continues the German tradition of elegies, Weissglas—similar to other Jewish poets from his homeland—creates a memorial to the Jewish dead, conveying the poet's confidence in the lasting validity of his mother tongue, German, as well as in divine justice, which, according to him, ultimately resulted in the downfall of the Nazi Germany.

Among the Bukovinian poets of the Holocaust who shared such love for German was the talented Sigi Laufer, whose poems were praised by Stefan Zweig and Hermann Hesse as an important contribution to German literature. Laufer committed suicide when Hitler came to power. Isaac Schreyer, whose verses collected in *Psalm eines einfachen Mannes* (Psalm of a Poor Man) were published and introduced by Ernst Waldinger in the 1920s, also saw his life and work come to an abrupt end. An exile in London and the United States, Schreyer wrote poems that resonate with bitterness, conveying, in "Requiem" and "Scenery of the Hanged,"[14] the destruction of his homeland. Shortly after the war Schreyer died embittered by the hardships of emigrant life. But the fate of those poets who remained in the Bukovina is even more heart-wrenching.

In the ghetto Selma Meerbaum-Eisinger, Paul Celan's cousin, translated Romanian, Yiddish, and French poetry into German and wrote romantic love poems that read like a counterpart to Anne Frank's diary. The sorrow and tragedy of Selma's life is reflected in her near identification with nature: "I am the rain and I wander barefoot from land to land. The wind's slim brown hand plays with my hair. / My thin dress made of spider web is grayer than the grayest sorrow" (August, 1941).[15] Selma was deported first to a quarry in Transnistria and then to the German zone beyond the river Bug, where she died of typhus at the age of seventeen.

In the midst of the war Moses Rosenkranz, who was deported to a Romanian labor camp, wrote classicist poems insisting on the sanctity of the German language. For him, Goethe's German remained a free and holy linguistic realm that could not be affected by the hostile Nazi "yelling": "To him all are succumbing / Only you remain still free / Hostile to his yelling / O language, you, holy."[16] Rosenkranz's poetry is particularly unusual in that it captures the perspective of those Germans who had been driven into the murderous war. In poems such as "Fatal Repetition" and "What remains"[17] Rosenkranz evokes the suffering of German soldiers bleeding to death in battle. By giving soldiers a voice in his poems, he hoped to make them rethink the outcome of the violence and recognize the significance of life.

While living in the ghetto, Rose Ausländer wrote German poems that invoke a pure linguistic space of mystical visions and romantic images: "Where the purest words ripen, / Springtimes gleam as fresh as roses, / . . . the one invisible genius reigns / as solitary witness."[18] It is in this language of spring, dreams, and purity that Ausländer inscribed her *Ghettomotifs* (1942–1944). Her collection of verses from Czernowitz alternates reminiscences of happier times with expressionist metaphors of suffering: "Threads stretched out in nothingness: we lie wounded / woven into the material of pain / a pattern of a gray background / as a black will has commanded it," writes Ausländer in one of her bitter poems from that time.[19] But in such sonnets as "Love for Beauty" and "Beauty," Ausländer derives strength and meaning precisely by setting the poetic reality she creates against the violence and destruction she experiences.[20] Unlike most other Bukovinian poets of her generation, Ausländer later realized that what "descended upon us was without rhyme or reason, so nightmarishly oppressive that it was not until the aftereffect that the rhyme broke apart."[21] In the 1960s and 1970s Ausländer, who followed Celan's model, started to destroy the syntactic structures of language, embedding in them both unusual metaphors and neoromantic images. Such language of the past and the present conveyed an innovative idiom in which she still inscribed her memories of the Bukovina.

During his deportation to a deserted quarry in Transnistria and later to a ghetto, Alfred Kittner engraved his testimony of the Jewish destruction into the language of his persecutors. His volume of poems *Hungermarsch und Stacheldraht* (Starvation march and barbed wire) is a requiem for the Jewish dead but also the testimony of a survivor who believes in the continuing validity of the German language and poetic devices he uses. Kittner's "Ballad of Kossoutz Forest," written in the extermination camp Obodowka on February 13, 1943, renders his terrifying experiences as a deportee.[22] As the subsequent poetic fragment conveys, his verses acquire the significance of historical documents:

> On our march the soldiers made us
> Wade through slime up to our knees;
> If one of us so much as bent over,
> Blows rained down on his head and back.
> In this way we were clubbed for days,
> Driven through the rain-drenched land.
>
> You couldn't miss the path to Dniester:
> There was no need to choose the road
> Or ask anyone the destination

> For we saw corpses heaped everywhere,
> Most of them decayed and half
> consumed by the dogs ripping at their flesh.

Kittner's later poems, such as "Requiem 1944," written in July 1971, transgress the language of his early work, for they no longer capture his traumatic experiences in a kind of "report": "Snow, a knife, pulled / to slaughter a Christ in the ice frost of the steppe . . . streaks in the stream of blood."[23] As these verses reveal, Kittner's metaphorical constellations still draw on literary traditions to invoke the persecution of the Jews but attain an innovative poetic voice, transforming poetry into a tombstone for the unburied dead.

Immanuel Weissglas was so fascinated by the German language that life without a German *Sprachbrockhaus* dictionary was inconceivable to him. "A German poet cannot exist without a *Sprachbrockhaus*," remarked Weissglas who included a *Sprachbrockhaus* among the few things he was allowed to take to Transnistria.[24] In his poems written during the deportation, Weissglas places the Holocaust into a broad historical context, identifying the *shoah* not only with Jewish suffering throughout history but also with the fate of all victims of violence and war: "We sat by the waters of Babel / By the waters of the Bug and lamented, / Thousands and thousands and twenty years ago, / And rooted history / Out of water and wind," writes Weissglas in his "Babylonian Lament," from the volume *Nobiskrug*.[25] In other poems he compares the Jews, a people "lost in nowhere and never," with the troops of mercenaries during the Thirty Years' War who wandered until their death. Yet as "Inscription on a Mass Grave" suggests, his Holocaust poems are a desperate attempt to inscribe a tombstone for all victims of violence in the language of those who murdered the Jewish people: "Who lived here? Who suffered here? / . . . And this coffin is the measure of your heaven, death: / All that broad field full of wind and death."[26] As these lines suggest, Weissglas envisions death as an all encompassing force as well as the only refuge from the violence and destruction.

Though many Holocaust poets have argued with God, Alfred Gong, who was a classmate of both Celan and Weissglas, is the first German poet of Jewish descent who uses the Job motif and the structure of the psalm to capture the last words and thoughts of victims in the gas chambers. In "Israel's Last Psalm" the victims' prayers to God gradually turn into doubts in His existence and mercy.[27] As the gas comes out of the pipes, they cry out for justice:

> Soon we will be yours alone . . .
> Death hums in the pipes.
> Out of flues the greasy smoke will rise . . .
> O Yahwe, can you hear our voices?
>
> This is the last Psalm
> and our voices tremble.

There is great fear in us. We sing
to shake the faith of the blond knights of death.

Are we your people?
Were our sins greater than those of the others?
Will our peace blossom in Eden?
Will there be an end to the suffering and the wandering?

As this fragment of Gong's poem suggests, the poet's bitter irony resonates in the victims' questions as to whether being God's chosen people ultimately means being doomed to experience the Holocaust. Unlike Weissglas, Gong does not view death as a refuge from violence and suffering. In lines such as "Lord! . . . Let us live here in this Hell on Earth!" his poem pleads for life and the right to live, rejecting Jewish self-abnegation, in particular the understanding of the Holocaust as God's punishment.

Tragic love for German is a link connecting the Bukovinian authors to other German Jewish writers who considered themselves sons and daughters of "the German language alone," as the Austrian Jew Ernst Waldinger noted about himself.[28] Many years after World War II Frederike Maria Zweig, for instance, asserted, "Language is a region from where I cannot be expelled."[29] Martin Buber, in a letter of 1949 from Jerusalem, emphasized, "A love relationship like mine with the German language is an objective fact."[30] Even Hannah Arendt, in her book *Die verborgene Tradition* (The hidden tradition), admitted: "Today, it is not easy for a Jew, even for a German speaking Jew, to publish in Germany. Considering what happened, the seduction to write in the native tongue does not really count, though this is the only true homecoming from exile which one can never quite ban from one's dreams."[31]

The notion of language as a constituent of human identity, which underlies these various reflections, draws on Herder, Humboldt, and Fichte, who were the first to stress the inextricable link between language and the speaker's "self."[32] In the Age of Enlightenment, when the Jews in German-speaking areas were given the opportunity to integrate into surrounding societies, they developed the same close bond to the German language as did the Germans themselves. Jews identified Lessing, Humboldt, and Schiller, who stood up against anti-Semitism and pleaded for Jewish rights, with German culture per se, refusing to see another, deeply anti-Semitic, anti-human bias also inherent in German thought. As a response to the rise of Nazi barbarism, Jews thus called on these writers to question the legitimacy of the Nazi murderers. Expelled from German-speaking areas and persecuted, the German poets of Jewish descent clung to their mother tongue as their only remaining homeland. In a desperate attempt to protect it from destruction, they incessantly insisted on its holiness.

In contrast to his German Jewish contemporaries from the Bukovina, Paul Celan, as early as 1946–1947 in his poem "Nähe der Gräber" (Nearness to the graves), unsettles the idea of a valid and pure German. "And mother, you bear it, as once, oh, at home, / the quiet, the German, the heart-wrenching rhyme?" writes Celan in the last stanza, which could well be the motto of his later work.[33] The words "as once, oh, at home" evoke a time in the past when German was entirely accepted as a valid means of expression. It was a time when the speaker was still at home, when he felt secure and sheltered. It was a time when he wrote neoromantic verse— configurations of love, flowers, and suffering—a time when he created powerful but still traditional metaphors of night and darkness, metaphors evoking the death of his parents in the extermination camps of Transnistria as well as his own suffering in the ghetto and in a Romanian labor camp. It is the time of his "Death Fugue," which speaks of the Holocaust in the language of German tradition from medieval German poetry to Rilke's and Trakl's verse. The loss of such a home within his native language itself motivated Celan's quest for new means of poetic expression. In 1948, when "Nähe der Gräber" appeared, Celan also published his introduction to *Edgar Jené and the Dreams about Dreams,* which underscores that any attempt to write in a traditional poetic language is a hypocrisy, for it seeks to restore the original, innocent meaning of words. "What could be more dishonest than to claim that words have somehow, at bottom, remained the same?" wrote Celan, who believed that World War II had radically transformed words and images, leaving ineffaceable testimonies of the destruction.[34]

At first glance, Celan's poetry thus appears to be a total rejection of the Holocaust literature from his homeland—a rejection of the mother tongue. But his poetry actually continues in a different and unusual way the literary aspirations of other poets from the Bukovina. Like them, Celan does not abandon the German language. Rather, he consciously tries to make it vibrate so as to uncover the wounds that words and even letters bear. In his late poem "Leuchtstäbe,"[35] for instance, Celan's linguistic game embeds "ZK" (the abbreviation for Central Committee), which when reversed as "KZ" refers to concentration camps. In its multiplicity of potential meanings his powerful poem shows that the political and historical connotations of "ZK" ultimately overshadow even the most innocent linguistic configuration, revealing the impact of history on language. Celan's "Leuchtstäbe" thus ultimately testifies to his continuing belief in the strength and power of language. In "The Meridian" Celan argues, "Yes, language. In spite of everything, it remained secure against loss. But it had to go through its own lack of answers, through terrifying silence, through the thousand darknesses of murderous speech. It went through. It gave me no words for what was happening, but went through it. Went through and could resurface, 'enriched' by it all."[36]

Although language, according to Celan, provided no words to name what happened, no image to reveal the horrors of the war and the tragedy of the Jewish persecution, it did not lose its significance but still testifies to the impact of violence and destruction. Celan's belief in the indestructibility of words gave him the strength to write poems in German despite the incompatibility of his native tongue with his task.

"In this language I tried, during those years and the years after, to write poems," Celan stresses in his Bremen speech. Indeed, his volumes of poems from his *Die Niemandsrose* to *Schneepart,* written in Paris many years after the war, realized in a mysterious and uncanny way his dream of dreams. Through a fusion of innovative metaphors that subverts the German tradition of lyric poetry as well as familiar syntactic and semantic structures, Celan's texts uncover the impact of the war upon words, uttering the unspeakable, the horror of the Holocaust, without naming it. As his poems radically transform poetic language, they reveal that in Celan's case the tragic love for German that motivated Jewish poets from the Bukovina turned into a traumatic love. Its last message was silence. In the spring of 1970, in Paris, Celan committed suicide.

## Notes

1. Karl Emil Franzos, *Aus Halb-Asien: Culturbilder aus Galizien, Bukowina, Südrussland und Rumanien* (1876). His *Kulturbilder* include humorous sketches and detailed descriptions of Galicia, Poland, and Romania.

2. Georg Drozdowski, *Sand im Getriebe des Sanduhr: Gedichte,* trans. Joanna Sheldon (Klagenfurt: Carinthia, 1965), 77.

3. See Gregor von Rezzori, *Maghrebinische Geschichten* (Hamburg: Rowolt, 1959).

4. Paul Celan, *Collected Prose,* trans. Rosmarie Waldrop (Manchester: Carcanet Press, 1986), 33.

5. Cited in Franz H. Riedl, "Die Universität Czernowitz als völkerverbindende Institution 1875–1919," *Der Donauraum* 15, nos. 3–4 (1971): 220.

6. The Romanian politician Eudoxiu Hurmuzaki (1812–1874) was the leading figure of the Romanian national movement at that time; Ruthenians and Jews supported his endeavors.

7. Margul-Sperber, for instance, made German translations of Robert Frost, Wallace Stevens, and e. e. cummings; he was the first to translate T. S. Eliot's *The Waste Land* and Apollinaire's *Calligrammes* into German. Kittner, Weissglas, and Celan also made a name for themselves as translators of poetry.

8. Cited in Wolfdieter Bihl, "Die Juden," *Die Habsburgermonarchie 1848–1918* (Vienna: Verlag der österreichischen Akademie der Wissenschaften, 1980), 3:934–935.

9. Victor Wittner to Alfred Kittner, September 18, 1939, collection of Alfred Kittner.

10. Victor Wittner, "In Beautiful Order," unpublished poem, collection of Kittner.

11. *Geschichte der Juden in der Bukovina,* ed. Hugo Gold (Tel Aviv: Olamenu, 1958).

12. Alfred Margul-Sperber, *Das verzauberte Wort* (Bucharest: Jugenverlag, 1969), 351.

13. Immanuel Weissglas, *Gottes Mühlen in Berlin,* unpublished poems, trans. J. Sheldon, collection of Kittner.

14. Isaac Schreyer, *Das Gold der Väter* (Vienna: Bergland, 1969), 34, 35.

15. Selma Meerbaum-Eisinger, *Blütenlese: Gedichte,* ed. A. Rauchwerger (Tel Aviv: Tel Aviv University, 1979), 44. After Selma's death these poems were handed from friend to friend until they reached Israel, where they were deciphered by Hersch Segal.

16. Moses Rosenkranz, unpublished poem, collection of Kittner.

17. Moses Rosenkranz, *Im Untergang* (Munich: Süddeutsches Kulturwerk, 1986), 59, 62.

18. Rose Ausländer, *Die Erde war ein atlasweisses Feld: Gedichte 1927–56* (Frankfurt am Main: Fischer, 1985), 208.

19. Ibid., 152.

20. Ibid., 166, 171.

21. Rose Ausländer, *Hügel aus Äther unwiderruflich: Gedichte und Prosa 1966–75* (Frankfurt am Main: Fischer, 1984), 61.

22. Alfred Kittner, *Schattenschrift* (Aachen: Rimbaud, 1988), 47.

23. Ibid., 74.

24. Information from Edith Horowitz-Silbermann.

25. Immanuel Weissglas, *Nobiskrug* (Bucharest: Kriterion, 1972), 29.

26. Immanuel Weissglas, unpublished poem, collection of Kittner.

27. Alfred Gong, "Israels letzter Psalm," in *Welch Wort in die Kälte gerufen: Die Judenverfolgung des Dritten Reiches im deutschen Gedicht,* ed. Heinz Seydel, trans. J. Scheldon (Berlin: Verlag der Nation Berlin, 1968), 307.

28. Cited in Harry Zohn, . . . *ich bin ein Sohn der deutschen Sprache nur* . . . (Munich: Amalthea, 1986), 159.

29. Ibid., 10.

30. Ibid., 15.

31. Hannah Arendt, *Die Verborgene Tradition* (Frankfurt-am-Main: Suhrkamp, 1976), 7.

32. See Kurt Mueller-Vollmer, "Der Transzendentale Gedanke," *Die geganwärtige Darstellung der Philosophie Fichtes,* ed. Klaus Hammacher (Hamburg: Felix Meiner Verlag, 1981).

33. Celan, "Nähe der Gräber," *Gesammelte Werke,* trans. A. Colin (Frankfurt am Main: Suhrkamp, 1983), 3:20.

34. Celan, *Collected Prose,* 6.

35. Celan, *Gesammelte Werke,* 2:42.

36. Celan, *Collected Prose,* 34.

# Between Dada and Marxism

## Tristan Tzara and the Politics of Position

ALINA CLEJ

*What we call dada is a farce of nothingness in which all higher questions are involved; a gladiator's gesture, a play with shabby leftovers, the death warrant of posturing morality and abundance.*
– *Hugo Ball,* Flight Out of Time

The Romanian-born poet Tristan Tzara had the good fortune, one might say, to achieve an international reputation at the age of twenty-one. This early recognition, which turned out to be his most enduring claim to fame, stemmed from Tzara's contribution to the Dada movement, which he helped kindle and disseminate. The name "Dada" itself is said to have been found by Tristan Tzara as he opened at random the pages of a dictionary. "Dada" can mean, according to Tzara, a wide variety of things: "the tail of a sacred cow" among the Kru people of Africa, "the cube or mother" in certain parts of Italy, "a wooden horse, a wet nurse, [or] the double affirmation in Russian and Romanian"; but ultimately, as Tzara insists, "Dada means nothing."[1] This all-inclusive and yet empty name came to designate a loose association of European (and, occasionally, American) artists. Through their bold manifestos and irreverent productions in the second decade of this century, these artists from all domains began to challenge the institution of art itself. What started as an improvised, spontaneous activity in Zurich in 1916, and took shape largely owing to Tzara's inventive genius and organizing talents, soon became an international phenomenon branching out to New York, Paris, Berlin, Cologne, and Hanover. Although Tzara "officially" buried Dada at the Bauhaus festival in Weimar in 1922, its spirit never quite died out. For one thing, it persisted in the works of some of the onetime Dada artists like Marcel Duchamp, Francis Picabia, Max Ernst, and Kurt Schwitters, but it also inspired at least one direction of the Romanian avant-garde between the wars, represented by the journals *Integral* and *Unu*. After the war the Dada spirit reemerged in *lettriste* poetry in France—an invention of Isidore Isou (another Romanian-born writer)—and in various neo-Dada manifestations in Europe

Tristan Tzara. Photograph by Helena Kolda.

and the United States. A Dada affinity can be recognized in the works of Robert Rauschenberg, George Segal, Claes Oldenburg, Yves Klein, Jean Tinguely, and, more recently, Christo, not to mention the ephemeral products of urban pop culture.[2] Ironically enough, however, the movement that brought Tzara to fame also obscured his figure. Tzara became just another name for Dada.

There is one side of Tzara's generally ignored personality that I would like to explore in this essay, namely his political involvement in his later life, an aspect that at first sight may seem totally unrelated to his well-known and much-celebrated Dada identity. Indeed, nothing could be more unlike the Dada insolence and anarchist defiance that Tzara vaunted in his precocious youth than the communist image of conformity that he adopted in his adult life. He chose to become a member of the French Communist party in 1935.[3] It is not that Dada and communism could not meet, but when they did—as in the case of the Berlin Dadas—it was almost by mistake. One may describe this accidental convergence as an optical illusion, which by straining, as it were, the field of the ideological apparatus, allowed for the political and the poetic, pragmatic reason and imaginative freedom, to appear in the same frame. In Tzara's case the optical illusion works in reverse: it creates a double image where in fact there may be only one. Beyond the troubled, uneven surface of Tzara's life and work one can detect, I think, a nebulous consistency, which brings his apolitical Dada and politicized communist phases into a disturbing approximation. Behind all the shifts and the changing political stances lurks a restless (but oddly immobile) politics of position and context. I choose to call it a politics of position because it seems to me that ideological moves, in Tzara's case, have no substantial value but are subsumed instead to a highly personal oppositional practice. Charting some of the surface variations and deep resonances of Tzara's political engagements will be the aim of what follows.

Tzara's embrace of communism, although by no means uncommon among European intellectuals in the late 1920s and early 1930s, remains somewhat of a surprise insofar as it comes from one of the most fiercely independent spirits among the Dadas. No matter how much one would wish to excuse him, and in spite of a mostly discreet and possibly guarded allegiance, the fact remains that Tzara maintained his Communist party membership with equanimity, if not enthusiasm, through the Stalinist purges, the Nazi-Soviet pact, and the cold war period until the very end of his life, in 1963. Although he did not go as far as to change his poetic style to suit the ideology, as Louis Aragon did, Tzara's was nonetheless a long-standing fidelity, which the French Communist party duly acknowledged by claiming Tzara in the hour of his death, as its own.[4]

And yet Tzara was anything but politically dishonest or naive. There is from the very beginning a kind of implacable rigor, an almost abrasive lucidity in his judgments of situations and events, which could hardly accommodate an unreflective form of ideological infatuation, let alone delusion. Moreover, the very idea of an inconsistency or of an irrational break between different moments of his life would have been infinitely displeasing to his sense of cogency. When his early poems in Romanian were being collected for publication, Tzara objected, for instance, to the title *Poèmes d'avant-dada* suggested by the editor, Saşa Pană. According to Tzara, such a title "would imply some kind of rift in [his] poetic personality," when in fact there had been, in his own words, "a continuity by fits and starts more or less violent and potent, if you wish, but continuity and interpenetration nonetheless, related in the highest degree to a *latent necessity*" (OC, 1:632).

On the face of it there seems to be as little connection between Tzara's early poetic exercises inspired by symbolism and his Dada experiments with language as there is, at another level, between his Dada credo and his Communist party loyalty. And yet I would argue that the same invisible, spasmodic continuity, which Tzara himself claimed for his poetic development, may apply to his political career. In that case both the Dada and the communist phases could reflect the same "latent necessity" to which Tzara alluded in relation to his poetry. It is this latent necessity, its literally hidden, unsuspected character, that provides, I believe, the key to understanding Tzara's uneven trajectory.

## From Dada Anarchism to Communist Orthodoxy

Tristan Tzara (Samuel Rosenstock) was born in Moineşti, in the Romanian province of Bacău, in 1896, the son of a prosperous forest administrator. Judging by his unfinished autobiography *Faites vos jeux* (Place your bets), it seems that from early on Tzara was a difficult, wayward youth embattled against his traditional family, his father in particular. Whether there was any link between Tzara's revolt against his bourgeois father and his precocious interest in socialism must be a matter of speculation. Be that as it may, it appears, however, that at the age of ten Tzara knew already about "profit, surplus value, capitalist exploitation, socialism, and revolution" through the good services of a typographer who provided him with popularizing pamphlets on the life and thought of Jean Jaurès and the doctrines of Russian and French socialist thinkers.[5] For Tzara, socialism was, I suspect, not only a discourse of resistance (in relation to his bourgeois milieu), but also one of seduction, by virtue of its exotic appeal. The image of the proletarian (the undernourished, sickly worker, the ragpicker, or the prostitute) was already part of the symbolist landscape and must have been familiar to Tzara from his youthful readings of French and Romanian symbolist poets.

It is this symbolist landscape that only fleetingly appears in Tzara's early poems, which otherwise bear no trace of his socialist readings. The image in question is worth mentioning, however, for what I believe to be its symptomatic nature. In a variant to "Cântec de război" (Song of war) the siren "calling the workers to the factory" is said to "echo faintly, [like] a shepherd's horn in faraway hills."[6] The implicit simile that brings together the rural, untrammeled ground of the shepherd's world and the industrial, grimy landscape of a suburban factory is, I think, more than a poetic conceit. It evokes a figure of double estrangement, from both past and present, an uncertain space stretched in two directions between which desire and resistance can shuttle back and forth. It seems that the image of the distant call, which makes the shepherd and the worker equally remote, contains *in nuce* the script of Tzara's poetic itinerary and its ceaseless play between impossible limits.

The siren's plaintive call (probably suggested by Emil Isac's poem "Sirena fabricii" [The factory siren]) reappeared as the title of a journal published by Tristan Tzara and Ion Vinea in 1915, *Chemarea* (The call), which after the uninspired title of their first journal, *Simbolul* (1912), seemed to indicate a shift toward a more militant position. Whether, in Tzara's case, this choice of title was an intimation of a real political engagement is hard to determine. The young poet, not yet twenty, was soon to leave Romania for Zurich, where he started a literary "insurrection" that became a landmark in modern literary history.

In spite of its antibourgeois claims and its occasional outbursts against the war, Dada in its Zurich phase (1916–1919) displayed little overt interest in political commitments or affiliations. Without discounting the revolutionary potential of Dada as a reservoir of imaginary destruction, slogans, and battle cries, the fact remains that in 1916 in Zurich political action was not an issue. The founding group, which included—besides Tzara—Hugo Ball, Emmy Hennings, Marcel Janco, Richard Huelsenbeck, and Hans Arp, had little in common with the various socialists and pacifists that were then operating in Switzerland. Lenin was preparing for the Russian revolution in his study, across from the Cabaret Voltaire, where the Dadas were carrying on with their boisterous performances, and yet the two sides never came together, except in Tom Stoppard's *Travesties*. It is only in its last stages that Dada attempted to orient itself toward a more constructive revolutionary program, and this was owing mainly to the efforts of Marcel Janco, who in 1919 created, together with Arp and Hans Richter, an Alliance of Revolutionary Artists to express the Dadas' support for the popular uprisings in Munich and Budapest. But in this late development Tzara, curiously enough, did not participate, and rumor has it that he even tried to sabotage Janco's initiative.

On the other hand, the implicit political value of the Dada offensive on language should by no means be underestimated, and most critics, in fact, do recognize the ideological significance of Dada and of Tzara's destructive enterprise. But in this "poetic revolution" Tzara's master was not Marx but Nietzsche, whom he appears to have known already from Romania.[7] And the value that the Dadas attached to the overhaul of language outweighed the importance of social reform. Their concern for the masses, such as it was, is indistinguishable from a poetic interest in naive, infantile, or primitive art, which represented, in their eyes, a source of untainted creative energies. In this respect the child, the madman, the Zulu, and the worker were on an equal footing. One should add, however, that by stripping language of its privileged aura, Dada was implicitly granting the masses the right to creativity, following in this respect Lautréamont's famous injunction, "Poetry should be made by everybody, not by one alone." Implementing this desideratum was another story. The educational programs that Dada envisaged, most certainly inspired by the Dada "educators" Ball and Janco, did not go very far. The Galerie Dada, which opened on March 1917, organized events for schoolchildren and workers as well as for upper-class women and art dealers, having more success with the latter than with the former. All in all, during the "Zurich insurrection" Tzara's outward behavior was more that of an eccentric dandy than that of a committed revolutionary.

The Dadas in fact made no secret of their lack of interest in political action. As Hugo Ball put it, "Politics and art are two different things."[8] But their rejection of politics was motivated less by political indifference than by a high sense of moral righteousness and by the desire to avoid contamination with what they saw as the general corruption of public life. One may understand why the word "disgust" (*Ekel*) is perhaps the best expression of their ontopolitical stand, very much the way *nausée* distilled the underlying spirit of existentialism. The Dadas' revulsion for political concepts and manifestations derived, however, from a specific historical context, that is to say, from the grievous compromise of the very notion of political discourse, which, in the form of nationalism, was responsible for the outbreak of World War I. As Tzara put it, "This war was not our war. We suffered it through its false emotions and petty excuses. . . . Dada was born of a moral imperative, of an implacable will to achieve a moral absolute. . . . Honor, Fatherland, Morality, Family, Art, Religion, Liberty, Fraternity . . . all these notions that had once answered to human needs had been reduced to skeletal conventions" (*OC*, 5:65)." It is true that this is a late assessment (1947) and that in the meantime Tzara had given a more deliberately political coloring to the Dada gesture of absolute defiance. Yet it is hard not to see behind Dada's wild grimaces and verbal stunts a desperate search for "a moral absolute" that entailed a radical purge of linguistically coded values. And in this sense Dada could be seen as the effective realization of Nietzsche's project of a "transvaluation of all values."[9]

From this perspective, anarchism, rather than communism, was the only legitimate political position. In his rejection of all ideological systems (including Dada itself), and in his lack of interest in the Bolshevik revolution, Tzara shared Ball's anarchist credo, inspired by Bakunin, and maintained it even after moving to Paris in 1920. In an interview with Ilarie Voronca published in the Romanian avant-garde journal *Integral* (no. 12, April 1927), Tzara reveals political opinions that echo closely Ball's reflexions in *Flight Out of Time*, especially in the attack on the reductive, philistine nature of communist ideology: "To recognize dialectical materialism, to formulate in clear sentences, even with a revolutionary goal in mind, this can only be the profession of faith of a shrewd politician." Like Ball, Tzara had few illusions

Tristan Tzara, by M. H. Maxy (1924).

about the promises of the Bolshevik enterprise: "Communism is a new bourgeoisie started from scratch; the communist revolution is a bourgeois form of revolution. It is not a state of mind but a 'sad necessity.' After it, order begins. And what order! Bureaucracy, hierarchy, Chamber of Deputies, French Academy" (*OC*, 2:418). Communism, in other words, was a travesty of the old regime, in a more ruthless form.

Dada was supposed to be precisely the opposite of all this, "a perpetual revolution . . . of the spirit," and it was only an irony, as Tzara saw it, if Dada turned into a movement, with himself as its leader. Many avant-garde scholars take Tzara at his word, but it is quite obvious, judging by the historical evidence, that one of Tzara's driving motives *was* the creation of a movement. He was the one who, among the Dadas, was the most interested in giving a formal sanction to the disruptive activities of the Cabaret Voltaire by transforming it into a Voltaire Society with an international audience. Not unlike "a shrewd politician," he initiated an extensive press campaign, advertising Dada (as well as himself) in all the important avant-garde journals of Europe and New York. As Huelsenbeck remarked in *En avant Dada,* perhaps not without a grudge, "Tzara was devoured by ambition to move in international artistic circles as an equal or even a 'leader.'"[10] Janco himself, Tzara's fellow countryman and at first a close friend, described Tzara as the "strategist and later [the] publicity manager" of the Cabaret Voltaire (*Dada Créateur*).[11] It was indeed Tzara's organizing talents that launched Dada in Paris in 1920 and prepared the audience for the surrealist adventure, from which, however, he would be left out.

And yet it seems unfair to ascribe to ambition alone Tzara's pressing desire to found a movement and his later disputes with André Breton over "the direction and defense of the modern spirit" or the politics of the surrealist group.[12] Tzara's contradictory manifestations and political maneuverings, both for and against organizing the avant-garde, were motivated, I believe, by psychological needs that happened to coincide with a more widespread pattern among European intellectuals at the time. This could be described as a dynamics of exclusion and inclusion, in which Tzara was easily absorbed, for personal as well as political reasons.

Tzara had already experienced, in more than one way, the effects of exclusion. His exile from Romania is perhaps the most conspicuous instance, although one should note that it was an exclusion that was provoked as much as suffered. (Tzara was sent—one might say "banished"—to Zurich by his parents, who were anxious to keep him away from the "decadent" milieus of Bucharest, a city known at the time as the Paris of the Balkans). To counteract this expulsion, Tzara seems to have sought a different form of integration in the collective spirit of Dada, which made art or anti-art the abode of those without a country: the founding Dadas were all exiles. One should also mention, in Tzara's case, a different, more subtle kind of exclusion, which he must have experienced already in his native country and which seems to haunt his works. Under the name of Samuel Rosenstock, Tzara was labeled, as was the custom at the time, as an ethnically alien subject, "of Israelite nationality." And to compound this estrangement, Tzara seems to have been fairly removed from his Jewish heritage, which left him hovering between equally distant cultures.

But Tzara's sense of exclusion and isolation, which pervades his work in all its various phases, was by no means a singular phenomenon. Most European intellectuals between the wars seem to have suffered from some form of *horror vacui,* a nagging fear of being left out, which appears to have been both existential and social in nature and which explains, I think, much of the tiresome wranglings over formal affiliations that went on within artistic communities at the time. It is in this general context of defensive strategies, which overdetermines, in Tzara's case, a personal configuration, that I would like to situate Tzara's ideological shifts and political reactions.

During and after World War I, internationalism represented both a form of subversion and a political defense for the European intelligentsia, modeled, in that respect, on the Workers' International. It is remarkable, in fact, to what extent the opposition between nationalism and internationalism shaped the ideological battles that raged during the 1920s and 1930s. Through its association with the disasters of the war, nationalism had come to be viewed by left-wing intellectuals as an immediate threat not only to their freedom of expression and to the idea of a universal heritage but also to their biological existence. Young intellectuals represented one of the heaviest casualties of the war. Intellectual vigilance and panic naturally grew with the rise of fascism. A critical point was reached in the late 1930s when it became clear that communism, in its Stalinist form, was no longer a safeguard or a model to imitate. This dark realization threw many intellectuals into despair or made them embrace the right-wing alternative. It is at this moment of mounting tension, in 1935, that Tzara decided to become a member of the French Communist party, a move that coincided with his definitive break with the surrealist group.

This is how the former enemy of the establishment came to don official roles and pose as intellectual spokesman for the *Maison de la culture*, a propaganda platform established by the French Communist party. Tzara also acted as cultural ambassador to the Spanish Republic on behalf of the Writers' Association for the Defense of Culture, an intellectual coalition controlled by the communists, which made him, even unwittingly perhaps, a representative of Stalinist policy in the area.[13]

Can the need for a political stronghold alone explain Tzara's allegiance to communism? The threat of fascism was no doubt very much on Tzara's mind at the time, and other political alternatives, like Trotskyism or different forms of socialism, were far less well equipped to deal with its perils. Tzara's reluctance to return to his native country, even for a visit, may have had something to do with his anxiety, especially in the late 1930s, when a wave of belligerent nationalism gained momentum in Romania, provoking a campaign against modernist art and against what was called the "Judaization of Romanian literature," one of whose main targets was Tzara himself.[14]

Tzara's antifascist commitment took shape in his active participation in the French Resistance and in his postwar initiatives, among which was a lecture tour through a number of Central and Eastern European countries, including Romania (which he visited for the second and last time in his life). Tzara undertook this journey, in the autumn of 1946, with the full confidence of a man who had seen the defeat of fascism and who took some pride in his personal contribution to the Resistance.[15] He offered his services to the French Ministry of Foreign Affairs and financed his own trip in order to have the opportunity of expressing his support for the "emancipation movements" under way in Eastern Europe.[16] In retrospect, Tzara's upbeat mood appears sadly out of place. In heralding what he saw as the noble continuation of the French revolution in those recently liberated territories, Tzara was clearly unaware of the sinister turn that events were about to take. Eastern Europe was still in a state of political turmoil, and few were those in the West who could, or were willing to, predict the brutal suppression of democratic forces that was to ensue. At that juncture Tzara may well be excused for his lack of political insight.

And yet the threat of fascism alone cannot explain Tzara's political moves. In examining the interpersonal dynamics of the French intelligentsia between the wars, one could easily see how Tzara's position may have varied according to that of his main rival, André Breton. It seems that when Breton was in, Tzara was out, and vice versa. At the time of the dispute over the Congress of Paris masterminded by Breton, in the spring of 1922, Breton was warning the public against "the agitations of a personage known as the promoter of a movement coming from Zurich," which in those days was synonymous with the German enemy.[17] The fact that Tzara was Jewish only added to the irony. Tzara was subsequently excluded (with only a brief reinstatement) from the surrealist group dominated by Breton and, in a more discreet way, marginalized in the history of French poetry (he was already a marginal figure in Romanian literary history).

In the 1920s the Surrealists' attempts to collaborate with the Communist party left Tzara, who was still an anarchist at the time, even further adrift. When, later on, the surrealist group no longer had a chance to win the communists' confidence, the roles were reversed. On the occasion of the International Congress of Writers for the Defense of Culture, it was Tzara, by then a member of the French Communist party, who was on the program and Breton who was denied access to the proceedings. While Tzara went to Spain during the Spanish civil war, on behalf of the same forum, Breton stayed in Paris, allegedly to tend to his recent paternal duties. While Tzara was directing the literary broadcast of the Resistance in the south of France, Breton was socializing in New York, broadcasting for the Voice of America and editing the largely apolitical journal *VVV*.[18]

This antagonistic play, which was as much the result of circumstances as it was of deliberate intentions, finally came to a climax on the occasion of Tzara's lecture at the Sorbonne entitled *Le surréalisme et l'après-guerre* (Surrealism and the postwar period [1947]), in which Tzara did not fail to remark upon Breton's absence during the Occupation. In an ironic reversal from his previous Dada performances, Tzara played the serious orator on the stage, whereas Breton was vociferating from the audience; and it was Tzara's communist bodyguards who strove to impose order. One could almost say that Tzara became and remained a communist in part because Breton happened to occupy the other alternative positions in the spectrum of the left, namely those of a Trotskyist and of a libertarian.

Tzara's lecture at the Sorbonne, following his tour in Eastern Europe, was one of his last memorable public appearances. After this final attempt to reclaim his position as the legitimate leader of the European avant-garde and to secure the place of Dada in the Western tradition of poetry (a very non-Dada gesture), Tzara was obliged to retreat to less exposed ground. He became more and more of a recluse and spent the last ten years of his life in Paris, decrypting anagrams in the works of Rabelais and Villon. It was three scholars who brought the Romanian-born poet back into the consciousness of the general public: Michel Sanouillet, with his impressive volume *Dada in Paris* (1965); Claude Sernet (Mihail Cosma), with his translation of Tzara's Romanian poems, published the same year; and Henri Béhar, the editor of Tzara's complete works. Even now, however, there remain large segments of Tzara's writings that are still draped in silence.

In retrospect, the main drift of Tzara's Sorbonne lecture, namely the idea of placing poetry "in the service of the Revolution," in contrast with the mystic, retrograde position of the surrealist group dominated by Breton, seems astonishingly fragile. At the time, Tzara was consciously searching, as he had been since the early 1930s, for a "dialectical solution" to the general condition of literature (and the "stagnation" of surrealism, in particular), which would allow poetry, "without surrendering any of its essential virtues, to play an active part in the revolutionary becoming [of the world]" (*OC*, 5:638). This "dialectical solution" may have also been meant as a cure to the "stagnation" in the poet's own life. The question remains, however, how Tzara's revolutionary conception of poetry as "an activity of the mind" went beyond the fanciful theories invented by Breton, that is, beyond the "amusing game" of "creating myths out of one's own study" (*OC*, 5:638). How did it retain its historical relevance?

## The Poet as Lonely Wolf

It is clear that in spite of his political alliance with the communists—motivated, as I have tried to show, by strategic rather than purely ideological reasons—Tzara was very much a lonely poet, wary of organized groups that represented, in his eyes, a threat to the freedom of the individual. On the occasion of the Congress of Paris, in 1922, he warned that "the current state of dejection," resulting, among other things, from "the substitution of groups in the place of individuals, could be more dangerous than the reaction itself," adding that he had personally suffered from a similar backlash.[19] This somewhat enigmatic allusion seems to refer not only to his exclusion from the congress but also to a deeper feeling of alienation, which may explain why Tzara both sought and avoided political and literary organizations. Even more intriguing, perhaps, is that his marginality appears to have been as much the result of external factors as it was a matter of personal choice. In *Faites vos jeux* Tzara describes his writing as a form of opposition and at the same time as a curious form of therapy: "I began writing in my first youth . . . from a sense of contradiction. I was writing poems 'against' my family, on the sly, and in order to mitigate a state of imbalance in my mind." This habit of "transcribing a psychological malaise" became for Tzara a "therapy of mental release" and eventually "turned into a kind of latent vice, by virtue of the pleasure that it procured" (*OC*, 1:260). One may compare this notion of "latent vice" to that of the "latent necessity" connecting Tzara's early Romanian poems to his later Dada output. What is hidden or latent seems to be precisely the torment and pleasure of resistance at the heart of writing, which the subject both produces and attempts to overcome.

This self-generated exclusion created by a conscious oppositional act (writing "against" the family and then later the audience) combines, to the point of becoming indistinguishable, with a sense of enforced exclusion or banishment.[20] The resulting feeling is one of haunting sorrow, which resonates throughout Tzara's poetry. Affliction is present in unexpected ways, even in his mischievously funny Dada poems, like "The First Celestial Adventure of M. Antipyrine," where the sorrow appears as a distorted echo of metaphysical despair ("grief without a church come on come on coal camel") or as the blunt expression of a lack of human community ("closed door without brotherhood we are grieving" [*OC*, 1:78]). There are moments, however, when sorrow is specifically related to Tzara's feeling of exile and separation from home: "I am without soul waterfall without friends and talents lord / and I don't often receive letters from my mother" ("The Great Lament of My Obscurity One" [*OC*, 1:90]). It is certainly surprising to discover, under the detritus of the Dada's language, a persistent lyrical residue or at times even the remnant of a traditional lament.[21] The Romanian words "nu mai plânge nu mai plânge veux-tu" (don't cry anymore don't cry anymore will you), at the end of "The Great Lament of My Obscurity One," bring, moreover, a distant echo of nursery rhymes, Romanian folk lyrics (*doine*), and Romanian mourning songs (*bocete*).

Images of isolation and separation, departure and estrangement, are all too frequent in Tzara's poetry, recalling, to a certain extent, the obsessive themes of another exiled Romanian poet, Paul Celan. Tzara's best known poetic work, *Approximate Man* (1931), is a lengthy meditation on man's loneliness and uncertainty in a hostile world and expands his earlier "laments" to universal proportions. It is perhaps no accident that the poet's pseudonym, Tristan Tzara, carries with it a double load of sorrow since it means "sad" in Romanian (*trist*) and "trouble" in Hebrew (*tzara*).[22]

If, as I have tried to suggest, Tzara's exile is self-induced as much as suffered, it is perhaps less surprising to discover a valedictory sorrow in the Romanian poems, which predate his actual departure from his native country. In fact, Tzara's pseudonym in Romanian can mean "sad in his country," a meaning that the poet himself acknowledged.[23] Leaving and traveling are perhaps the two most frequent activities in Tzara's early Romanian poetry. Even in his later work endless journeys appear, often by train, as the title of one of his collections of poems suggests (*The Railway Timetable of the Heart* [1928]), or else images of flight (*fuite*), which gives the title to one of his later plays (*La fuite* [1940]). This poetic obsession materialized into a very real and traumatic experience when Tzara had to flee for his life from Paris to the south of France during the war.

The motif of exile is conveyed on a different register, by the image of the lonely animal (horse, dog, or wolf) running away or hunted down in the closed space of a poem. It is the circular image of the howling wolf or wind that creates in its vortex the movement of many of Tzara's poems, as if the force of an original expulsion were converted into poetic energy. A whole page of the *Seven Dada Manifestos* is covered with the word *hurle* ("howls") arranged in parallel columns, in a mounting crescendo of maddening reverberation (the page itself seems to vibrate), broken at the end by the innocuous description "Qui se trouve encore très sympathique" (who still finds himself quite pleasant) which introduces the subject, Tristan Tzara.[24]

The wolf is not only a recurrent image in Tzara's poetry (a whole poetic cycle is entitled *Where the Wolves Drink*) but also a principle of poetic production, which Tzara names "lycanthropy" (a term borrowed from Petrus Borel). The originally magical practice of assuming a wolf's shape becomes, in Tzara's case, a theory of oppositionality *avant la lettre*. As a solitary wolf, the poet refuses his society, being a traitor to his own social class; and yet it is precisely this distance that allows him to integrate poetry and life, or rather to transform life into a mode of poetic activity. Lycanthropy acquires, at the same time, a therapeutic value in Tzara's writing, which harks back to its old magical function. It is as if being "against," in opposition to a certain social environment, parallels the state of imbalance in the poet's mind and serves to channel and release a certain amount of pent-up energy. The poem becomes the site of an antagonistic conflict followed by a momentary resolution, the result of an action and reaction. In a similar way one could say that Tzara himself creates the conditions for his own nostalgia, a space of exile in which blank energy can become meaningfully oriented in the form of sorrow and longing (*dor*).

Lycanthropy can be seen to function, moreover, as a form of mythical or utopian integration. It is perhaps not without significance that Tzara chose the symbol that he did; according to Mircea Eliade, the wolf may have given the name to the Romanians' ancestors. Ancient authors called the Dacians *Dahae,* a word probably derived from the Iranian *dahae* (wolf) and which may allude to both their religious and military rituals. But the wolf was also the symbol of the outcast, the exile, or the fugitive protected by Apollon Lykeios, a meaning that may have been assimilated to the original name of the Dacians.[25] Such an explanation eminently suits the dynamics of exclusion and inclusion that informs not only Tzara's historical experience but also his poetic practice.

## Dialectical Materialism as a Transgressive Practice

Tzara was not content, however, with a mere subjective form of opposition-ality and attempted, especially in his later life, to both historicize and politicize this notion. In the early 1930s he turned toward dialectics (historical materialism) in order to use it as an instrument for analyzing poetry in everyday life. The result of Tzara's extensive readings in this area was his *Essay on the Situation of Poetry* (1931), which marked his transition to a new form of poetic discourse. Tzara's de-parture from his previous views is considerable: in his interview with *Integral* Tzara had spoken disparagingly of dialectical materialism in the name of that to which it was opposed—"the perpetual revolution," "the revolution of the spirit, the *only* revolution that I envisage, and for which I would be willing to pay with my life, be-cause it does not exclude the Sacredness of the self, because it is *my* revolution" (*OC*, 2:418). In 1931, however, dialectical materialism became for Tzara the only valid scientific method that could allow for the definition of "living poetry."

Given the dynamics of Tzara's life and poetic thought, the switch is not surpris-ing. Dialectical materialism obviously offered him a way of creating a sense of mean-ingful continuity, by which negations could be reintegrated at a higher level, a method of throwing "bridges" and forging "links" between things and events that were far apart. At the same time, the oppositionality (lycanthropy) characteristic of the avant-garde poet could be interpreted as the propelling force in the history of poetry, a source of revolutionary energy. Moreover, dialectical materialism also provided an unexpected model for poetry, which Tzara developed in his *Essay on the Situation of Poetry.*

As a material activity bearing on language, poetry is here said to function as a superstructure (Tzara applies Marx's terms of political economy to poetic theory); but it is a refractory superstructure, one that does not always reflect its material and economic base. For, according to Tzara, poetry is not only the result of certain socio-economic conditions but also of their refusal, which thus prepares the ideological conditions for a new social formation. In this sense it has a superior, independent power as a "superstructure of a psychic order imposed on the existing mass of living civilization" (*OC*, 5:22) and may become the equivalent of a "dictatorship of the spirit" (*OC*, 5:12). This particular interpretation recalls Nietzsche's superman as much as Marx's superstructure and proletarian dictatorship, but Tzara himself was by no means a purist in his use of Marxism. Besides, he was well aware that poetry and revolution are incommensurable.

Even as a communist, Tzara had little faith in the poet's ability to carry on practical political work. The task of the poet could only be of a conceptual order, that of changing the sensibility, mental patterns, and linguistic habits of the masses in order to prepare them for the society of the future. Since the poet can be of little use in an actual revolution, his revolutionary role can only be envisaged in a postrevolutionary society, in which, as Marx's utopia goes, all practical problems will have been solved. This is how Tzara can claim that the main function of the poet is that of organizing "the activity of dreaming, idleness, leisure, in view of the communist society" and then declare in all seriousness that this is "the most immediate task of poetry" (*OC*, 5 : 27). Tzara's investment in the establishment of the communist society is in this sense very close to Georges Bataille's, who, taking for granted the success of the Soviet revolution, saw in it the end of history and of dialectical struggle and hence the possibility of using the liberated negativity in unproductive forms of "expenditure": festivals, sacrifices, and so on.[26]

Ultimately it is the revolution that is said to serve the poet, by giving him a utopian ground on which to play out his fantasies and allowing him to "pass," at least in imagination, from the individual to the collective. Like the barley grain, which is both negated and multiplied in the plant (Engels's example from *Anti-Dühring*), the poet's identity is both annihilated and enhanced in the communist society, in which poetry is no longer a "quality" reserved for the happy few but is transformed into a "quantity" destined for the use of the masses (*OC*, 5 : 27).

What seems to fascinate Tzara in the dialectical process of conversion from a quantitative change to a qualitative one and back is less the result than the "passage," the rapture that comes with the change. It is difficult not to see in the poet's obsession with passages and nodal points of transformation as they appear in dialectical materialism (via Hegel) Tzara's old fascination with trains and junctures. Dada itself challenged the "static" notion of beauty through the idea that art is a "state of mind" that is able to prove that "everything is movement, constant alignment along the flight of time" (*OC*, 1 : 18). It seems indeed that with dialectical materialism Tzara had found a way of scientifically aligning his life along the flight of time.

*Grains et issues* (Grains and issues), published in 1935, offers a poetic realization of the utopian project already sketched out in the *Essay on the Situation of Poetry* and is the most telling illustration of Tzara's use of dialectical materialism. It is this text that offers perhaps one of the most important sources for understanding Tzara's commitment to a certain form of Marxism and his relationship to the Communist party, which he joined the same year, as the dangers of fascism were growing. *Grains and Issues* is not only a personal poetic document; it is also one of his most original, and least appreciated, efforts to combine Marxist ideology, psychoanalysis, and poetic theory. The closest equivalent at the time may be in Bataille's antiphilosophical essays. Tzara's experiment in poetic theory, arguably, anticipates the "revolution in poetic language" initiated by the critics of *Tel Quel* in the late 1960s.

And yet this essay, never reprinted until 1979, remains—for all its richness, and possibly because of it—a source of vexation rather than of enlightenment. The text is formless, with countless pages of dense prose, in which lyrical passages, oneiric scenes, and philosophical reflections are hopelessly mingled in disconcerting patterns. These intricate reflections, distributed into three sections—"Grains and Issues" (subtitled "Experimental Dream"), "On Nocturnal and Diurnal Realities," and "From Top to Bottom Clarity"—taper off in a concluding series of theoretical notes, seven in all, which attempt to explain the poet's enterprise. Tzara's sources are eclectic, ranging across Marxist and Freudian terrains as well as anthropology, and his tangled argument echoes the polemics surrounding the development of Freudo-Marxism in the early and mid-1930s and the new explorations in anthropology initiated by Bataille and his group. Tzara's own ideological motives, however, recede into a zone of approximation that befits what he called "the approximate man."

*Grains and Issues* is in many respects a utopian text, offering the vision of a postrevolutionary society in which the poet can freely indulge his imagination in order to organize and direct the crowds in their pursuit of happiness. The text is in this sense a perfect demonstration of what Tzara had curiously defined as "the most immediate task of poetry": "organizing the use of dream, idleness, and leisure in view of the communist society" (*OC*, 5:27).[27] This "new culture of joy," over which the poet presides as a master of ceremonies and which evokes in more than one way Bataille's image of the festival, is a blend between a Rabelaisian paradise and a Hollywood superproduction, combining rural, earthy pleasures with technological excitement. "Piles of fruit will be staked at crossroads," "eggs of light will be gathered on the breast of buildings," and the whole city will be flooded with florescent lights (*OC*, 3:10). This wild expenditure often suggests a massacre scene (reminiscent of the last war) that has turned into a sacrificial feast of unbridled consumption. Amid the "mountains of lamb" and "veal heads hanging from the trees," "tons of honey will pour through the mouths of military cannon," and chandeliers will hang amid the "remnants of planes built out of mangroves and carrots" (*OC*, 3:23).

There is an undeniable cruelty in Tzara's vision, in which the artist plays the role of a mad scientist (Caligari), an "exquisite being" whose "scattered madness" infuses the "propriety of the crowd." Tzara imagines a city in which "undergrounds are transformed into laboratories of suffering and cruelty" (*OC*, 3:16), in which "dogs gorged with gasoline and set on fire will be roused against naked women, the most beautiful, of course. Bowls containing the tongues of aristocrats will be exhibited in shop windows amid pots of mustard and jam. Fast cars provided on their front with steel prongs could impale long queues of people waiting in front of a cinema, for instance" (*OC*, 3:14).

One might well wonder at the hidden sources of this delirious vision, in which pleasure and cruelty are so closely fused. What is the meaning of the invention of new rituals, based on the principles of "osmosis and contagion" (*OC*, 3:59) and which recall Antonia Artaud's theater of cruelty? Tzara is ostensibly offering a drastic cure for various forms of psychological repression, "war neuroses," and so forth, on which fascism thrives, by advocating a poetic release of inhibitions and aggressive fantasies. What is odd in all this is that the release in turn resembles the disease itself (that is, fascism). Bataille's essay "The Psychological Structure of Fascism," written in 1933, turns on the same paradox. Tzara's proposal of sadomasochism as a synthesis between masochism and sadism, meant to channel the aggressive instincts in man, combines a Swiftian sense of enormity with the most extreme forms of science fiction. And yet Tzara appears to be striving to make the valid point that uncured repression may lead to the most violent explosions. His solution for the "reduction of the monstrous antagonisms" of bourgeois society (which, in his view, are psychological rather than social) is in fact a libidinal liberation of man, in retrospect something far more radical than the sexual liberation of the 1960s since Tzara's involves the release of all ambivalences and even perversions.

On the other hand, "vice" or violence serves as a "solvent" or subversive element in the destruction of the "conventional image of the world," which may explain some of the macabre visions in *Grains and Issues,* not to mention his explicit praise of Sade. Tzara's attempt to dislocate or undermine the old ideology is very much like a practical application of Nietzsche's project of a "transvaluation of all values"; it consists in the transformation of matter into a "non-Euclidean" space that resists authority (*OC,* 3:19). By creating a system of imaginary resistances, Tzara's utopian vision acquires a manifest oppositional value. The poet speaks of a "utopian will that obsesses him; the desire to set across the roads obvious propositions and so solid that people stumble and can no longer recover from the mental deformation that these emerald obstacles have imprinted on them" (*OC,* 3:59). In Tzara's oppositional project, deformation serves as a principle of construction. In the same way, negative conditions, like melancholia, are turned into positive energy (*OC,* 3:59), suggesting the possibility of recycling nonproductive forces to create productive meaning (*OC,* 3:63).

Negativity, however, like opposition itself, functions in a closed, inert field, where movement can only occur through a deliberate act of transgression or acceleration. Writing operates like "the rapid successions of lightning produced by a feathery wheel . . . whose stopping creates a deep gash . . . in the amorphous flow of memory" (*OC,* 3:56). It is only by sudden leaps, by "transgressing barriers," that the poet can attain "the indefinite terrains of roaming and even those of confusion," where memory is reactivated in the "psychic residues of instincts" (*OC,* 3:60). It is finally unclear, however, whether the ultimate aim of Tzara's utopia is to achieve release and oblivion, as he repeatedly claims, or, on the contrary, to create an effect of memory, a semblance of recollection that would shake his state of numbness produced by what he calls the "absence of filial local maternal paternal love" (*OC,* 3:24).

This ambiguity becomes apparent in the notion of the "birth traumatism," which occupies a significant place in *Grains and Issues.* The term, borrowed from Otto Rank, implies in Tzara's case both an ontological threshold and the prohibition of incest. One may assume that the desire to return to the mother's womb parallels the nostalgia for the lost homeland, whereas the possibility of return is censored by the incest taboo or, in Rank's understanding, by the birth traumatism, the painful memory of the original expulsion, which preempts the return. Not only does the maternal world represent simultaneously the ultimate recovery and final loss of memory, but this ambiguous construct is itself the object of ambivalent feelings, being at once coveted and abhorred. And yet these bewildering paradoxes do not stop at the level of personal history. Through a curious twist the threshold represented by the incest taboo is, in *Grains and Issues,* further identified with the historical break created by a revolution, the breach against and beyond which Tzara's utopia is set. In this double scenario the past and the future, incest and social transgression, expulsion and return, are collapsed in the same figure. The moment of rupture itself can only be thought of, however, from a utopian perspective, that adopted by *Grains and Issues,* and can only be experienced through the successive shocks and ripples that the text produces, artificially as it were, within its movement. As the revolutionary trauma can only be envisaged from a point of beyondness, so too the threshold of birth or the return to the native land, the going back in time to the point where memory is ultimately regained and extinguished.

It may well be that what Tzara is really combatting through his images of cruelty is both pain and anesthesia—not only memory but also its absence. It is this tension between the will to remember and the desire to forget, between the urgency of memory and its inertia, that underlies, I believe, the particular dynamics of Tzara's poetry. In a vivid image from *Grains and Issues* Tzara describes himself as living "half immersed in total absence and half in the torment of electromagnetic nostalgia," which creates "the axial ruptures of the roots" (*OC,* 3:86–88).

Tzara's poetry represents this spasmodic movement, which creates its own resistance and, through resistance, perpetuates itself, not so much as movement but as an illusion of movement. Life appears as a "perpetual flight of contorsions of verses that nudge each other . . . looking for a tortuous solution to oppositions and obstacles produced by the movement itself" (*OC,* 3:49). It is this friction, this endless convulsion, that creates a lyrical residue, a trail or trace suggesting a positive presence, the tangible shadow of memory, which the poet both pursues and rejects: "As the materialized cloud raised behind the desperate flight of the cuttlefish, which conceals it, clears off and then quietly settles down when the subterfuge is devalued at its basis, so will I chase away the now-futile smoke, under which the exaltation of the senses was installed" (*OC,* 3:90). Like the ink of the cuttlefish, the poet's writing conceals the aimless flight, the painful realization that there is nothing to conceal, and prompts in turn a new desire for erasure and inscription.

Through its inner turmoil Tzara's work ultimately communicates an image of Heraclitean flux, a migratory pattern that, like the shuttling movement of a train in his earlier poems, translates into the motility of images. In this respect, however, Tzara's poetry may evoke in a strange and unexpected way what Lucian Blaga called the "mioritic space," an "unconscious spatial horizon" modeled after the Romanian landscape of hilly pastures, where shepherds drive their herds back and forth with the changing seasons.[28] Tzara's use of a veiled image of transhumance in his utopia suggests seasonal movement and shifting positions—"cultures of gyratory worlds" where "the wind shakes the almonds," "regions of transhumance where the staff breaks . . . toward the crippled landscape the cohesion of steps" (*OC*, 3 : 83 – 84). And in this distant landscape resounds—never completed—a prophecy, a clamor, as remote as the factory siren in his early poem "Song of War," the "hour of the shepherds," Tzara's dim vision of a mythic, utopian community, from which he was forever barred by "the traumatism of birth" (*OC*, 3 : 10).

Facing this never-fulfilled destination, one is left with an endless "traversing of signs," signals, milestones, indices of a passage in continuous transformation in which both the flight and the positions taken form part of a simulacral economy whose center is fixed but absent ("the axial rupture at the roots"). Tzara's very definition of poetry follows this line of "flight": Dada was described, in contrast with static notions of beauty, as a "*state of mind* in which all is in movement, a constant alignment along the flight of time" (*OC*, 5 : 18). Dialectical materialism proved to be but an explanation, a justification of this "state of mind" and of this endless movement, giving a semblance of meaning and stability to its "provisional" moments. "I will have to insist," Tzara writes, "upon a principle that I hold dear, 'the provisional,' but a provisional solidly rooted in a development that can no longer escape our consciousness . . . , a provisional state conscious of its objective value. . . . I can give facts no other importance . . . than that which derives from their value as signs, witnesses, milestones in a perpetual transformation, and which is only measurable against the scale of their future" (*OC*, 5 : 7 – 8).

Tzara's constant attempts at politicizing his personal experience, and then depoliticizing, proves in fact the extent to which the political and the poetic are enmeshed in a common web of desires and phantasms, which only action can briefly separate, the way a fish line passes through the water, an act that has to be constantly renewed in order to keep apart the closing folds of the real and the imaginary. And yet if Tzara, unlike Breton, was fully aware of the dangers of confusing politics and poetry, he nonetheless found it hard to maintain his lucidity without falling back into the silent pain of reality. Tzara's restlessness and anxious shifting of positions was but a measure of his will to retain his wakefulness and the right to resist, which Tzara learned to assert even at the cost of self-contradiction.

## Notes

1. Tristan Tzara, *Oeuvres complètes*, 5 vols., ed. Henri Béhar (Paris: Flammarion, 1975 – 1982), 1 : 360. All further references to Tzara's works (*OC*) are to this edition and are included in the text. Translations are mine.

2. For the aftermath of Dada, see Matei Călinescu, "Avangarda literară in România," in

*Viaţa românească*, no. 11 (November 1967): 106–117; Elmer Peterson, *Tristan Tzara* (New Brunswick, N.J.: Rutgers University Press, 1971), xi–xx; John D. Erickson, *Dada: Performance, Poetry, and Art* (Boston: Twayne Publishers, 1984), 119; Greil Marcus, *Lipstick Traces: A Secret History of the Twentieth Century* (Cambridge: Harvard University Press, 1989).

3. This is the most likely date for Tzara's adherence to the Communist party, as it appears in the chronology published by Jacques Gaucheron and Henri Béhar in the commemorative issue of *Europe*, no. 555–556 (July–August 1975). There is, however, a discrepancy with Henri Béhar's chronology included in the first volume of *OC*, where the date is given as 1947.

4. Isidore Isou, the *lettriste* poet, had to brave "the insults, threats and provocations of the Stalinists" in order to read his "Epistle to Tristan Tzara" at the poet's funeral (Maurice Lemaître, *Le lettrisme devant dada* [Paris: Centre de Créativité, 1967], 17), and it was Louis Aragon who delivered Tzara's funeral oration over French radio.

5. Claude Sernet (Mihail Cosma), Introduction to Tristan Tzara, *Les premiers poèmes* (Paris: Seghers, 1965), 17–18.

6. In Saşa Pană, *Primele Poeme ale lui Tristan Tzara* (Bucharest: Editura Cartea Românească, 1971), 19. The volume is followed by a postface entitled "The Zurich Insurrection."

7. Tzara and his friend Ion Vinea had been reading Nietzsche together during the summer vacation of 1915, before Tzara left for Zurich. Cf. Ion Vinea's poem "Dintr-o vară" ("From a Summer") and Simion Mioc, *Opera lui Ion Vinea* (Bucharest: Editura Minerva, 1972), 219.

8. Hugo Ball, *Flight Out of Time: A Dada Diary*, ed. John Elderfield (New York: Viking Press, 1974), 114.

9. For the connection between Nietzsche and Dada, see Rudolf E. Kuenzli, "The Semiotics of Dada Poetry," in *Dada Spectrum: The Dialectics of Revolt*, ed. Stephen C. Foster and Rudolf E. Kuenzli (Iowa City: University of Iowa Press, 1979), 51–71.

10. Richard Huelsenbeck, *En avant Dada*, in *The Dada Painters and Poets*, ed. Robert Motherwell (New York, 1951), 26.

11. Marcel Janco, *Dada: Monograph of a Movement* (New York: St. Martin's Press, 1975), 30.

12. For the polemics between Breton and Tzara over the Congress of Paris, designed by Breton as "The International Congress for the Determination of the Directives and the Defence of the Modern Spirit" (1922), see Emil Manu, "Insurecţia de la Paris din 1922 (Polemica Breton-Tzara)," *Revista de istorie si teorie literară* 26, no. 2 (1977): 271–288.

13. Most of the details regarding Tzara's political activities between the wars come from Helena Lewis, *The Politics of Surrealism* (New York: Paragon House Publishers, 1988).

14. See Tristan Tzara's correspondence with Saşa Pană, documented by Henri Béhar, in *Manuscriptum*, 1982, no. 4: 158.

15. This contribution was mainly literary and consisted in Tzara's direction of the cultural broadcast of the French Resistance in the south of France (1943–1944).

16. See "Interview with Tristan Tzara across the Balkans" (*OC*, 5:381–387) and "Conversation with Tristan Tzara" (*OC*, 5:388–392), which was first published in *Cahiers France-Roumanie*, no. 7 (February–April 1947): 62–68. See also the interview that Tzara gave for the Romanian journal *Rampa*, no. 27 (1946).

17. See the exchange between Breton and Tzara in Emil Manu, "Insurecţia," 277.

18. See Lewis, *Politics of Surrealism*.

19. See note 17.

20. On the question of literary opposition, see Ross Chambers, *Mélancolie et opposition: Les débuts du modernism en France* (Paris: Librairie José Corti, 1987).

21. Tzara's *Great Lament of My Obscurity Three* evokes through its incipit ("chez nous les fleurs des pendules s'allument") a "classical" elegy by Octavian Goga, "La noi."

22. I would like to thank Rudolf Kuenzli for bringing this latter meaning to my attention and Sandor Goodheart for additional clarification of the meaning of the word.

23. See Colomba Voronca's testimony in Serge Fauchereau, ed., Tristan Tzara, *Poèmes roumains* (Paris: La Quinzaine littéraire, 1974), 17.

24. Both the scream and the image of the lonely wolf become theorized later as the very conditions of poetic expression and productivity (see *Note sur le comte de Lautréamont ou le cri* and *Tristan Corbière ou les limites du cri*).

25. See the chapter entitled "The Dacians and the Wolves" in *De la Zalmoxis la Genghis-Han* (Bucharest: Editura științifică si enciclopedică, 1980).

26. See Allan Stoekl, "The Avant-Garde Embraces Science," in *A New History of French Literature*, ed. Denis Hollier (Cambridge: Harvard University Press, 1989), 933.

27. This view perhaps explains Tzara's enthusiasm over the artistic activities that were going on in Romania in 1946—the newly organized proletarian theater in Bucharest and the proselytizing tours organized by poets and writers through the Romanian countryside. Tzara failed to realize to what extent these activities were ideologically programmed and compared them instead to Federico García Lorca's popular theatrical representations in Spain (*OC*, 5:383–384).

28. See Lucian Blaga's description of the mioritic space in his essay "Horizon and Style" (1935), in *Trilogia Culturii* (Bucharest: ELU, 1969), 48–49.

# Three Hungarian Interviews

## MARIANNA D. BIRNBAUM

György Spiró (b. 1946) studied Hungarian, Russian, and Serbo-Croatian at Budapest University. Subsequently, he held jobs at Hungarian Radio and at various publishing houses. In 1981 he became professor of world literature at Budapest University, and he is active in the Kaposvár Theater. Among his best-known works are *Kerengö* (The Cloister, 1974) and *Ikszek* (The X's, 1981). Perhaps his most popular play, *Csirkefej* (Chickenhead), was also staged in England. As a scholar, Spiró is known for his monograph on Miroslav Krleža (1981) and for his work on East European drama (1986). His latest novel, *A jöveveny* (The Newcomer), was published in 1990.

MDB: Is there a chance for the theater in Hungary or in the West?

GS: Of course there is. There has been a chance for some thousands of years, and I also think that the theater is something that doesn't need writers or directors, only actors and an audience, and there will be actors and there will be an audience as long as human culture exists. I don't believe in the death of the theater.

MDB: The way you describe it, the theater is closer to the ritual drama than to anything else, and the ritual drama probably will survive. But would you say that there are many good plays nowadays in Hungary or in the West?

GS: No, I wouldn't. I wouldn't say that there are many good plays, but I don't agree with this term, what you call a modern play. There is comedy and there is tragedy, and there is something in between. There is also musical theater, what we call opera or operetta or musical comedy. These forms are very strong.

MDB: And permanent.

GS: And permanent, absolutely. I consider myself neither a traditional writer nor a modern writer because I write the same things as our ancestors wrote some hundreds of years ago. I don't see anything new in theater in this century.

MDB: The educational purpose of modern theater is of course very clear, I mean from Brecht to Thomas Bernhard.

GS: Yes, the Schiller-type theater is very well known in Eastern Europe. But I oppose this. I would like to let everyone cry and laugh. That's all I want.

MDB: Does literature have a purpose?

GS: No, literature has no purpose at all.

MDB: Let's put it on the record: literature has no purpose, okay?

GS: It has no purpose. It's deeply human. And our life has no purpose at all.

MDB: Nonetheless, we have a changing culture. Given this changing culture, have you written anything differently in the past twenty years just because of the cultural context in which you wrote it, or have you not written things precisely because of the cultural context?

GS: I don't see major changes in European history and European life for some two hundred years, since the Enlightenment, and I think that the limits of our lives and possibilities have been the same since the end of the Napoleonic Wars.

MDB: Is this featured in your last novel?

GS: I think so, yes.

MDB: Could you tell me about it?

GS: My latest novel is about an interesting movement after a revolution in Poland that took place in 1830 and 1831, after which many Polish intellectuals went to Paris. They formed a mystical circle with a living Jesus Christ. One man considered himself an incarnation of Jesus Christ, and the entire group acted as "the chosen people." I think they lived the whole Christian movement over again, and they experienced everything that happened after both world wars. They experienced, in advance, the entire twentieth century. That's why I try to understand their acts, their deeds, and their thoughts. It was the last moment when people involved in politics had the attachments to the ancient religious thoughts and ideas. To me, it was a very interesting moment in the nineteenth century.

MDB: We always say that very important things are born at moments of crisis and transition, you know, like Shakespeare and all that; but in Eastern Europe, I have a feeling that we always have a crisis. We always have a transition.

GS: That's right.

MDB: So this is a frozen moment. Hungarian history is nothing but a series of frozen moments, and very often they have very little to do with each other. Do you use the genre of the classical narrative? I mean, in a Solzhenitsyn style—nineteenth-century prose in the twentieth century?

GS: I use a lot of literary forms in this novel. I use some romantic forms. The position of the narrator might be called postmodern, but I would call it romantic.

MDB: A narrator with a distance?

GS: Well, the narrator is important in the whole story but he has a certain role of irony. For me, it was a very interesting situation to be in and to be out of. I'm not religious, but religion is very important for me. I try to understand the lives of the religious people because all my heroes were religious people.

MDB: Does your work as a playwright come in? Is this also a drama?

GS: No, I was not a dramatist in this novel. I used to be in my previous novels, but in this case all my heroes really lived, and I didn't add anything to their lives and souls. Truly, I tried to understand their deeds and their thoughts. I tried to understand them like a historian or like a philologist.

MDB: Yes, but that's also judgmental because both selection and organization are, *eo ipso*, judgments. Is the narrator a peripheral figure or a nonexistent figure?

GS: The narrator is me. So there is certain information from my life.

MDB: Now I understand what you said about stepping in and out of the piece. And what do you think the reception of this novel will be in Hungary and in Poland?

GS: There will be certain difficulties with the reception. There will be a lot of critics who won't like this novel.

MDB: Will they find it offensive?

GS: Yes. I think this is a very provocative book.

MDB: So were your other pieces.

GS: No, no. This is much more provocative because certain Catholics and a lot of Jews and a lot of Poles won't like this novel. Believers, real believers, won't like this novel. And the Hungarians won't like this novel because it's not about Hungary.

MDB: What are you working on now?

GS: There are certain themes that I would like to write about, one of which is national hatred, a big problem in Eastern Europe and the Soviet Union.

MDB: Do you have anything in your drawer that you have kept for many years but haven't published, that you want to go back to, or that you simply couldn't write or just didn't write?

GS: Unfortunately, there is nothing in my cupboard.

MDB: But your next concentration will be on the theater?

GS: Yes, of course.

MDB: Has your visit to America benefited your writing?

GS: Absolutely.

MDB: In what way?

GS: I started gathering the materials for this last novel in America because they have fantastic libraries there. And I realized there that from an American point of view European culture no longer exists. The whole issue of European culture is nonexisting. There is no need for European cultures and languages, and this became clear to me. This happened in America. So I'm very, very thankful to America.

MDB: Coming back to the situation in Hungary: there are a plethora of journals and literary magazines here, and I try to keep up with some of them, and I look for your name, and I don't find it. Why?

GS: Well, you know, these periodicals and monthlies and weeklies are full of articles written by those people who now want to create a new image about themselves. They are so-called ex-Marxists and ex-Stalinists, and I don't know what other kind of people want to show up now, in the new regime. I have no reason to change my image.

MDB: If somebody asked you to define yourself, who are you? What is the first thing that comes to your mind? What does it mean to be Central European?

GS: I am not Central European; I am European of course. And I'm European because my native culture is European.

MDB: I said Central European and you extended this to European. Why?

GS: I don't believe in the terms Central Europe or Eastern Europe.

MDB: Why?

GS: I think that national cultures, such as Polish, Czech, Slovak, Serbian, Croatian, and so on, are European cultures. These cultures were created by free men, writers who were *European* fighters. Because their mother tongue was not German, French, or English, they're not known in the West.

MDB: But then what is that? The Judeo-Christian tradition.

GS: That's right, with certain Greek elements.

MDB: And how about America?

GS: America still belongs to Europe.

MDB: As opposed to—

GS: As opposed to nothing—

MDB: To the Soviet Union?

GS: No, no. As opposed to Asia, but Asia doesn't necessarily mean the Soviet Union.

MDB: I agree with that.

GS: I think that Russian culture, Russian literature, is deeply European. Culturally, there is no other culture in this huge territory from Normandy to the Urals or to Siberia than European literature and European culture. But from the inside, these relatively small cultures or literatures are very different, and this is what made a big impression on me because I learned almost all these languages and all these cultures. The richness of these small cultures is really fantastic and all these small cultures belong to European culture. So I wouldn't make a political question of this term.

MDB: Do you consider yourself a Jew?

GS: First of all I am a European. My mother tongue is Hungarian. My culture is Hungarian, making me a Hungarian writer and then, if you want, I am a Jew.

MDB: I don't want it, I'm asking you about it.

GS: Well, I didn't care for a very long time about being or not being a Jew. With these new waves of anti-Semitism in Hungary and in the whole territory, I had to think about everything. I don't think that all those people who were killed in Auschwitz, the so-called Hungarian Jews, were Jews. I think that they were primarily Hungarians. They felt Hungarian, but nobody asked them of course.

In the Hungarian press you can see the number of Jews living now in Hungary. It's an estimated eighty thousand or hundred thousand. Nobody asked them if they feel like Jews or not.

MDB: Are you planning to come back to America?

GS: Sometime.

MDB: What would you do there?

GS: Well, first of all I'd sit in Chinese restaurants. Second, I'd sit in libraries, and third, I'd meet people. I have a lot of friends in America, emigré's from Eastern Europe, and I need some good conversations with them.

> Miklós Vámos (b. 1950) is the author of several novels, including *Elöszó az ABC-hez* (Foreword to the Alphabet, 1972), *Jelenleg 13-ik a listán* (Currently No. 12 on the List, 1973), *Borgisz* (1975), *Váltás* (Exchange, 1977), *En es en* (I and I, 1979), *Valaki mas* (Someone Else, 1981), *Zenga zenek* (Sing Song, 1983), *Jaj* (Oh, No, 1988). His story "Cédulák" (Slips of Paper) was made into a film, *Csok, Anyu* (Love, Mom). Vamos has taught writing at several universities in the United States.

MDB: What can a Central European dramatist teach the students at Yale? What is the special approach, the special point of view, you represent?

MV: Well, there are two different questions here. The first and the more important of the two is: what can the field of European literature and drama contribute to the American audience and professionals? I think we know something that is generally not known in this country. This something is a consequence of the turbulence of our history. A writer, actor, director, or stage manager in Europe is more sensitive to the situation created by history and life, and somehow this approach is totally missing in the American theater, literature, and film. But my special approach is a little bit different because somehow, for me, the fact that I am a European is not as important as the fact that I am from a small country. I believe this to be true for literature. As novelists, I think, we have two main concerns. The first is time, and the second is space, or "room." In big countries it's rather easy for the writers to feel both. In small countries you can't really feel the room, the size, the magnitude. Here is one example: the writing of a novel that unfolds in a small town with a river. In Hungary, it can only be one town, and everyone knows which town you are talking about. Therefore, in my lectures I always try to present this approach, which I wouldn't call a European approach because I'm positive that neither a French writer nor an English writer feels this, but a writer in the Netherlands does.

MDB: According to your views, there is no difference between a Western mode of writing and a Central European mode of writing. Rather it hinges on the size of the country.

MV: Not only. In our literature, the aesthetics of censorship had a lot to do with our general literature, so the literature of Hungary was totally different. But I always felt that my writing is not too different from the writing of someone in the Netherlands or in Belgium because my interest was always the human psyche, and this is the same.

MDB: So basically a private interest, in the sense of the soul's space rather than the space of the country.

MV: I'd like to put it in another way because, you know, everything is politics. How a woman feels after a divorce is a political statement. It's totally different in a country where after a divorce you can easily find an apartment, whereas in another country, like Hungary, your main concern would be that you almost always have to stay under the same roof with your husband, in the same prefab apartment of, I would say, ninety square feet.

MDB: Right now there is a kind of revolution taking place in Hungary, and yet I have a feeling that you will not go home and write a revolutionary novel. You will still write a novel in which the feelings and the personalities of your characters will be more important than what's going on outside.

MV: Actually I'm working on two different books right now. One is a story with the title *The United States of America*, something between fiction and nonfiction. I tried to find all the misbeliefs we were taught about the United States during my childhood and since. You probably know that in the sixties we were told that here everybody lived on drugs. The most dangerous drug was Coca-Cola, and if you tried it, you became insane. One of my friends was the son of an ambassador in a Western country, and he smuggled in a couple of cans. We tasted it at a clandestine meeting, and some of us had real hallucinations.

MDB: But, you see, the Americans have the same kind of slanted view of Russia, except it does not determine their daily lives.

MV: This will be the second part of the same book. I asked a friend of mine, an American, to collect the anticommunist beliefs on Eastern Europe in the United States, and we put the two together.

MDB: What is the second book?

MV: The second book is a novel about the hundreds of Eastern Europeans who live in this country and who all believe that they are already on the threshold of success.

MDB: This is a very rich harvest in less than a year. How will you approach Hungary anew where so many things have happened during these eight months? Maybe you will have new stimuli to write about things that are going on right now in Hungary. What do you expect of Hungarian theater?

MV: I believe that somehow these turbulent years aren't the years for the novelist. In times of disorder, first the poets begin to sing.

MDB: The joke goes that even in the worst of times you can write a bad novel. Personal courage had a lot to do with success and popularity during those years when not everything was permitted to appear. What do you think is valuable and salvageable of your oeuvre from that period?

MV: I always believed that the history of my career was the history of the very slow disappearing of censorship. When I started my career, it was rather difficult to get through, and in twenty years censorship totally disappeared.

MDB: That is an interesting point because what worked in one sense as a control also worked as support of the arts, that is, state-subsidized theaters, state-subsidized newspapers, etc. You couldn't fall: there was always somebody who held the net below you, and this is most probably disappearing. This is the price of freedom. But are you willing to pay this price? Do you think this is still the right price? Let's face it: does a free society need a writers' union? What is a writers' union in a free society? It's a joke.

MV: Personally I am ready to pay the bill. The only problem is that in a civilized society there are foundations and other sources that could help, and in Hungary we have actually one foundation only, the Soros Foundation.

MDB: There's no Fulbright or Guggenheim to support you.

MV: We would need that, and I'm totally positive that we'll have that in ten years. Now is probably the most difficult time to start a career as a writer. But if someone is ready to write junk, the market's opening up. In Hungary we didn't have horror literature, and not many detective stories were published either, but now the majority of Hungarian books are of that kind. And it's the same in the theater. My prophecy is that the Hungarian national film industry won't exist, and the films will be shot with foreign money. And, you know, whenever a foreign producer puts money into shooting a film—

MDB: Then he calls the shots.

MV: Oh, yes.

MDB: I think Hungary right now is on the map and there should be a way to exploit this beneficial moment. But don't forget that Eastern European writers also compete with one another because they address the same rather limited audience who is interested in this kind of literature. . . . How would you define yourself? Do you define yourself as a Hungarian writer? A Hungarian Jewish writer? Does the fact that you are Jewish have any effect on your work now and on your plans for the future?

MV: I have received many titles from critics, and I didn't like any of them. I think that the word "writer" is a very courageous word. It also doesn't need adjectives. I would be happy just to be a writer, but I'm afraid I won't be allowed to be a writer without adjectives. Certainly, I would be a Hungarian writer *and* a Hungarian Jewish writer, which, by the way, is a brand new term in Hungary. Previously, whenever one was labeled a Jewish writer, it was an offense, an insult. I wrote a lot about my Jewishness in newspapers and in my novels. And I will keep on doing this since more than half of my family was killed in the war, and I can neither forgive nor forget. I'm like the Bourbons. I am getting information that in Hungary there is a new wave of anti-Semitism. I don't like that, and whenever there is an anti-Semitic statement, there should be a defending statement. I think it's not enough to write your opinion once. As a Jew, my main concern would be to answer any anti-Semitic statement I came across.

MDB: But this is not a Jewish problem; it's a Gentile problem. Don't you expect your colleagues, who are non-Jews, to answer as well?

MV: Yes, I expect it, but I believe this to be one of my personal tasks.

> Gyula Gazdag (b. 1947) studied at the Hungarian Academy of Theater and Fine Arts. His first work, *Hosszú futásodra mindig szamithatunk* (The Long-Distance Runner), a documentary, was released in 1969. He directed *A válogatás* (The Selection, 1971), *A sipoló macskakő* (The Whistling Cobblestone, 1972), and *Bástyasétány hetvennégy* (Singing on a Treadmill, 1974). Since 1969 Gazdag has been working at Objektiv Filmstudio. His 1986 film *Hol volt, hol nem volt* (A Hungarian Fairy Tale) received several international festival awards.

MDB: How will the present events in Hungary affect your profession?

GG: Well, I don't know yet. I don't think anybody can predict, but I think we should look at film and how it has changed. I think that nowadays we can make films practically about anything we want or anything we can have the finances for.

MDB: So will it be primarily a question of money?

GG: Yes, I think that's the main change in the movie business. It seems that the government wants to leave culture on its own, which might be favorable on the one hand, but on the other hand it means that the government doesn't want to subsidize the Hungarian film industry.

MDB: What do you think about joint ventures and the possibility of joint ventures with Western filmmakers or bigger companies?

GG: We might be forced to make joint ventures, but until now all the joint ventures failed.

MDB: Why?

GG: Because the Western partner wants to have a marketable industrial product, and Hungarian films usually are not industrial products but art films. So what happens is that usually the films lost their character and became just baseless.

MDB: Do you believe in government subsidies without government interference?

GG: Yes. Well, if you look around the world, there is no country except the United States where a national film industry could survive without government subsidies. I think the United States is the only country where the market is large enough to keep the film industry alive.

MDB: Do you have any works in your own drawer that you can now show in public, films that you didn't have a chance to show before?

GG: I made a forty-minute documentary in 1970 called *The Selection,* which was shelved from 1970 to 1984.

MDB: What is *The Selection* about?

GG: It's about a communist youth organization that appeals to the youth by hiring a beat group and by advertising on the radio. When I heard the ad on the radio, I became interested in how they actually select the group, so I went to film all the processes of the selection.

MDB: That's very amusing, but I would think that this group now has merely historical value because the communist youth organization has dissolved itself. So this would make an interesting documentary, then.

GG: Another example is *The Whistling Cobblestone,* which was considered very controversial, and it couldn't be shown to foreigners for eight or nine years. There were some really devastating reviews about it.

MDB: You had a number of movies that were also shown in this country, and among them I'm interested in the documentary movie that you made about survivors who were visiting Auschwitz.

GG: Well, that happened in the spring of 1984, I think. It was the fortieth anniversary of the liberation of the concentration camps, and I read an ad in the newspaper about a package tour, a three-day trip to Auschwitz and Birkenau, and I found the idea very strange. I just wanted to know what it was, and I wanted to know what kind of people wanted to go on such a trip. So I started to do some research. I called this travel agency, and finally when I had the authorization to shoot the film, they gave me the names and addresses, and I spoke to all the participants separately. I called them, wrote to them, and went to visit them. It turned out that they were almost all survivors. From then on, it became a challenge for me. I never wanted to go to visit Auschwitz or Birkenau. It just was not my taste to go and see those places as a tourist. But this was a challenge, and I had to face it. There were many people who didn't want to be in the film. Those who told me in advance were not filmed, and those who told me after we finished the shooting were cut out of the film. All of them saw the film after we finished it. To my surprise, they liked it, if you can actually like such a film. I have the strangest relationship with this film because since I finished it, I just can't get myself to watch it again.

MDB: What do you say about the great success of your *Hungarian Fairy Tale?* Does it surprise you? Did you expect it?

GG: It surprises me greatly because I didn't expect it. I just don't understand it.

MDB: Weren't you planning to make movies that have a universal appeal? You are not just a Hungarian filmmaker. You are a filmmaker who happens to be Hungarian, so why does it surprise you?

GG: Well, I'll tell you why. You can plan to make universal films, but it doesn't mean that they will be universal or that they will appeal to foreign audiences as well. And even if you know a little bit about foreign cultures, it doesn't mean that you are able to think as they do. Everything that I do is so deeply rooted in Hungarian culture that it's really very difficult to think of something that would not only be interesting for a Hungarian audience but for a foreign audience as well.

MDB: But suffering, insecurity, and pain have no nationality, so obviously these problems are universal. What did you think of the American students? Is it different to teach film here?

GG: I think it's very different. Here I had eight graduate students, and I think that it's very different to teach here or to talk to students here from the way it is in Hungary. There are differences in the curriculum. Back in Hungary there are more topics required as part of the curriculum, whereas here the students can choose many things. I could see that here there were filmmaking skills in which the students excelled, but at the same time some skills were completely unknown to those same students. This is something that could not happen in a Hungarian school.

MDB: What will you do in Santa Fe?

GG: I'm working on a new system of teaching filmmaking. I think that the most important thing is to teach people how to see and not how to use filmmaking techniques. Right now I'm working on the concept of a preliminary course or something like that.

MDB: Let's make it the last, but a very important, question: what is the "dream piece" you are still hoping to make either as a filmmaker or as a director? The one thing you would like to do before you die?

GG: There are so many.

MDB: Tell us a few.

GG: Okay. I want to direct a Molière—*Tartuffe.*

MDB: On stage or as a film?

GG: On stage, but I could make it as a film too. And I desperately want to direct Mozart's *Don Giovanni.*

# Ivo Andrić, a "Yugoslav" Writer

## (1892–1975)

## THOMAS BUTLER

Ivo Andrić, the Nobel Prize laureate for literature in 1961, author of *Bridge on the Drina* and *Travnik Chronicle,* wrote in a style that is deceptively simple, in seamless sentences in which words seem to slip into place almost by accident, a style that is so "easy" we feel we are listening to the tale of a village storyteller and not to the creation of a very wise man. As Miloš Bandić notes, "Everything seems to be created without effort and strain, by some magnanimous grace. From this comes the unobtrusiveness and simplicity of Andrić's art, which really is the result of a methodological, systematic and prolonged work of filigree." [1]

Andrić showed his concern about the external form of his writing on more than one occasion. In describing the polemic between Vuk Karadžić, the nineteenth-century founder of the Serbo-Croatian literary language, and Milovan Vidaković, the first Serbian novelist, he suddenly stops his account of their acrimonious debate and wonders aloud if his own language will seem as strange to readers one hundred years thence as does Vidaković's mixture of spoken Serbo-Croatian and Church Slavonic. Andrić confesses that he is worried, yet he lightheartedly admits that he has no control over what future generations will think about his work. [2]

Given Andrić's perfectionism, the shift in his writing from his native Bosnian "ijekavian" dialect (*mlijeko* for "milk," *tijelo* for "body") to the Serbian "ekavian" variant (*mleko, telo*) cannot be considered inconsequential. As Jovan Deretić says, "Everything he did was deliberate; he left nothing to chance." [3] The question therefore arises, Was his change of dialect politically motivated (as a declaration of allegiance to Serbia and by extension to the pre–World War I "Yugoslav idea")? Was it aesthetically inspired? Or could it have resulted from a combination of factors? An examination of this problem will provide insight not only into Ivo Andrić the man but also into the times in which he developed as a writer.

It may be useful here to remind the reader that not only Bosnians and Her-cegovinians spoke and wrote ijekavian; it was also the dialect of a large Serbian minority in Coatia as well as of the inhabitants of Montenegro and southern Dalmatia.

In addition, the northern Croats in the middle of the nineteenth century had accepted the ijekavian pronunciation proposed by the Serb Vuk Karadžić and their own reformer Ljudevit Gaj as a way of promoting a single South Slavic literary language, which Gaj called "Illyrian." Ironically, the Serbs in the Principality of Serbia by and large did not accept Vuk's suggestion and continued to write in their native ekavian. In 1913 the Serbian cultural historian and critic Jovan Skerlić came up with a different proposal: he suggested that the Croats discard ijekavian and the Serbs their Cyrillic alphabet. Thus everyone would write in ekavian, and the common alphabet would be *latinica,* the modified Latin letters used by Croats.[4] In *Srpski književni glasnik* (The Serbian Literary Herald) Skerlić then conducted a poll among Croatian and Serbian writers, including those in Bosnia and Herzegovina, to find out what they considered the preferred dialect for a unified literary language.[5] The great majority of the respondents agreed with Skerlić, not because of the superiority of ekavian (as he had asserted), but for patriotic reasons. The Serbian victories at the battles of Kumanovo (1912) and Bregalnica (1913) in the Balkan Wars were mentioned by several ijekavian respondents as sufficient justification for their shift to ekavian. The fine Herzegovinian poet Aleksa Šantić, an *ijekavac* who shifted to ekavian, as did the poet Jovan Dučić, cited the need to show solidarity with the Serbs "who left their bones in Old Serbia, Macedonia, Thrace, and Albania." Meanwhile Josip Smodlaka, a Croat from Split, answered Skerlić's poll: "Croatian separatists who wish to maintain an artificial wall between the two parts of our one people are against 'Serbian' ekavian, not because they love ijekavian, but because they regard it as specifically 'Croatian,' which it is not." According to Smodlaka, "any objective person who is for our [Yugoslav] literary and cultural unity should be won over by Skerlić's reasoning." But he also reminded the Serbs that if they expected ekavian to be promoted in the Croatian lands, they should show their good faith by writing in *latinica,* "the universal European alphabet."

Not only writers but also linguists participated in the dialect discussion. The Croats Tomo Maretić and Petar Skok as well as the Serb Aleksandar Belić did not regard the difference in the pronunciation of one syllable (*vreme* vs. *vrijeme*) as significant. According to Skok, "No one would contend that there are differences in the grammar of the Serbian and Croatian literary languages. . . . Supporters of national unity should rejoice that the differences between the two literary languages are minimal." The Dalmatian Milan Rešetar, then a professor in Vienna, reluctantly decided to accept ekavian, as a token of regard for the Serbian military victories, but he reminded the Serbs that they must show goodwill by transliterating road signs into Croatian *latinica* (e.g. Šabac) and not according to German usage (Chabatz). And Vladimir Čerina, a young Croatian writer and later friend of Ivo Andrić, responded, "To adopt ekavian as the written and spoken form of speech is the duty of all those who see the cultural union of Serbs, Croats, and Slovenes as the only outlet from our battered and dismembered life, which leads nowhere."

It is against this background of accelerating momentum toward the cultural and political unification of Serbs, Croats, and Slovenes that Ivo Andrić began his writing career. As a Bosnian living in a land that had been occupied and then annexed by Austria (1908), he shared in the enthusiasm for a Yugoslavia in which Serbia would play the role that the Piedmont had played in the unification of Italy. Andrić, like other graduates of the Sarajevo gymnasium in those times, followed the lead of writer Petar Kočić in resisting the assimilationist strategy of Austria, which tried to separate Bosnia from Croatia and Serbia by fostering the notion of a Bosnian culture and language (called *bosanski*, "the land language"). A Croat Catholic for the first thirty or so years of his life, Andrić, like many Croatian writers, showed his solidarity with Serbia and "Yugoslavism" by using ekavian in his first two published poems, "In the Twilight" and "Gentle and Kind Moonlight," which appeared in 1911 in the pro-Serbian Sarajevo journal *Bosanska vila* (Bosnian Nymph). In subsequent issues Andrić published three more poems, two in ekavian and one, "Last Year's Song," in his native ijekavian. In the same journal he also published in ekavian his translations of five Slovene poems, a Walt Whitman poem from *Song of Myself* ("I am the poet of the Body and I am the poet of the Soul") and a short excerpt from Strindberg's *Red Room*.

Andrić's use of ekavian in his *Bosanska vila* phase was obviously politically inspired and quite in the spirit of the times—like waving a Serbian flag in the face of the Austrian censors. In terms of his creative development, however, far more important was his use of ijekavian in his best poem, "Last Year's Song," where Andrić found his subjective poetic voice, what Predrag Palavestra calls "the confessional character"[6] of Andrić's lyric poetry. Nearly all his subsequent published poems are in ijekavian. Thus Andrić's poems in the anthology *Young Croatian Lyric Poetry*,[7] published in Zagreb in 1914, are all in ijekavian, including "Darkness" and "Sunk," which he had previously published in ekavian in *Bosanska vila*. The change of dialect, of course, affected the rhythm, and he had to make adjustments accordingly.

Whereas Andrić's subsequent poems in *Književni jug* (Literary south), are in ijekavian as well, his review articles and other criticism in that journal are in ekavian, as, for example, his marvelous piece "Walt Whitman, 1819–1919."[8] With a few exceptions, such as his review of the Croatian novelist Tomo Kumičić's *Erna Kristen*[9] and his obituary for the Croatian writer A. G. Matoš,[10] ekavian early became for Andrić the standard medium of his nonfiction writings. Thus, whereas ijekavian was the voice of his lyrical poetry, of his heart, ekavian was the voice of analysis, of his head, bearing with it a pro-Serbian and, according to the psychology of the times, pro-Yugoslav nuance.

In Andrić's early short stories, milieu was clearly the determining factor in his choice of dialect. His "The Road of Ali Djerzelez"[11] is written in ijekavian because it is set in Bosnia, Andrić's heartland. In the love of a legendary Moslem hero, Djerzelez Ali, for a "Latin" temptress, we see a thinly disguised young Andrić. The omniscient narrator speaks ijekavian, which makes him a native of the area and thus credible. In the same vein, ijekavian is used in Andrić's masterful Bosnian stories, published in *Srpski književni glasnik* in the 1920s. But when he changes ambiance, as he does in the story about a Serbian courier in Rome during the war ("A Day in Rome"),[12] he uses ekavian.

The year 1925 was a milestone in Andrić's stylistic development. In that year he published in *Srpski književni glasnik* his brilliant short story "Bridge on the Žepa," a tale about the building of a bridge in Bosnia. Why, then, did he write it in ekavian? One should note, first, that the story is also about a grand vizier in Istanbul who had experienced a temporary fall from grace and while in prison had remembered his native Bosnia. Thus the story is about Istanbul as well as Bosnia, and it also concerns a master builder from Italy. Andrić's narrative has widened its horizons to embrace West and East, with Bosnia in between. Moreover, "Bridge on the Žepa" is rather sophisticated and cerebral, quite different from Andrić's more earthy Franciscan stories. In the closing line the narrator calls it an *istorija*, which can mean either "history" or "story." The ambiguity suits Andrić's purposes because "Bridge on the Žepa" is a chronicle of the events surrounding the building of the bridge, with only one snippet of dialogue. Clearly here Andrić has decided that for pure narrative or chronicle the less localized (as he perceived it) ekavian is more appropriate.

Andrić's second collection of short stories, published in 1931, contained four pieces in ijekavian and two in ekavian, "Bridge on the Žepa" and "Anika's Times," also a kind of chronicle. By the time Andrić published his third collection, in 1936, he had opted completely for ekavian, except where the dialogue required ijekavian. In my opinion, his now undifferentiated use of the Serbian ekavian can be attributed primarily to his gradual change in perspective and theme. His major novels, *Bridge on the Drina* (1945) and *Travnik Chronicle* (1945), concern not only Bosnia but also world events and their effects on that unhappy land. Like "Bridge on the Žepa," these works are histories (Andrić himself refers to each of them as a *hronika*), and for that genre he chooses an omniscient narrator whose language does not mark him as local. Such an approach also suits his aphoristic style.

Did Ivo Andrić consider himself a Serbian rather than Croatian writer, and could this view have contributed to his eventual decision to restrict himself to ekavian? In answering that question, one should take into account that in his student days he, like many other young intellectuals, called himself a Yugoslav, which meant that he was spiritually both a Croat and a Serb. In 1913, while at the University of Vienna, Andrić had joined both the Croatian (Zvonimir) and the Serbian (Zora) student organizations. Illustrative of the Yugoslav spirit of the times was the fact that the Croatian sculptor Ivan Meštrović, as well as many Croatian writers, drew from Serbian themes, including the battle of Kosovo (1389), the mother of the nine Jugović brothers, and the legendary hero Marko Kraljević, in an effort to create a common Yugoslav mythology and ethos. In the same endeavor Andrić offered his

Friar Marko and the Croatian Franciscan monks as historical figures of great endurance, heroes not of the mace but of the breviary, committed to their people under the ignominious conditions of the Turkish yoke. It seems significant that he published his Bosnian stories in *Srpski književni glasnik*, which was truly Yugoslav in its outlook. Clearly he did not discard his Serbian half in the late 1920s, as did many Croatian writers who were disillusioned with King Alexander and his government. In his lectures to Belgrade audiences in the 1930s he referred to Vuk Karadžić as "our Vuk" and to the Montenegrin poet Njegoš as "our poet." Apparently he never lost his youthful vision of a united Yugoslav people, and for that reason the Nobel Prize committee was quite correct in referring to him in their award as a Yugoslav writer.

## Notes

1. Miloš Bandić, "Ivo Andrić—neki momenti duhovnog razvoja i stvaralaštva," in *Zbornik radova o Ivi Andriću*, Srpska akademija nauka i umetnosti, Posebna izdanja, 505 (Belgrad: SANU, 1979).

2. Ivo Andrić, "Beleške za pisca," in *Sabrana djela*, vol. 12 (Sarajevo, 1976).

3. Letter to Thomas Butler, November 6, 1989.

4. Jovan Skerlić, "Istočno ili južno narečje?" *Srpski književni glasnik* 31, no. 10 (1913): 756–770; 32, nos. 11–12 (1914): 862–873.

5. "Anketa o južnom ili istočnom narečju u srpsko-hrvatskoj književnosti," *Srpski književni glasnik* 32, nos. 2–5 (1914).

6. Predrag Palavestra, "Andrićeva lirika," in *Zbornik radova o Ivi Andriću*.

7. *Mlada hrvatska lirika*, ed. Ljubo Wiesner (Zagreb, 1914).

8. "Walt Whitman: 1819–1919," *Književni jug* (August 1919).

9. "Erna Kristen," *Književni jug* (January 1918).

10. "A. G. Matoš," *Vihor* 5 (1914).

11. "Put Alije Djerzelez," *Književni jug* (July 1918 and June 1919).

12. "Dan u Rimu," *Srpski književni glasnik* 1, n.s. (1920).

# Women's Voices from Yugoslavia

## NEDA MIRANDA BLAŽEVIĆ, TATJANA LUKIĆ, DESANKA MAKSIMOVIĆ, VESNA PARUN, DRAGINJA UROŠEVIĆ, AND IRENA VRKLJAN

Translated and Introduced by Dasha Čulić Nisula

This selection features the work of six women poets spanning three generations. The pieces reflect some of the concerns shared by poets from Yugoslavia. Among these are human relationships (Lukić, Parun, Vrkljan), the relationship between people and nature (Maksimović, Parun, Ugrešić), and the relationship of a poet to her craft (Blažević, Lukić, Maksimović, Parun, Vrkljan). Most of the poems were first published in the 1980s, except for Parun's, which appeared in print in the 1950s, and Maksimović's, in the 1970s.

> *Desanka Maksimović*, born in 1898 in the village of Rabrovici, near Valjevo, completed her studies in philosophy in Belgrade and worked as a teacher in Obrenovac. She has published numerous collections of poetry, writes prose, and translates from Bulgarian, Russian, Slovene, and French. She lives and writes in Belgrade.

## Work Is Done

I have nothing more to do here.
I accompanied the moon home
to the last turn
and watched after it for a long time
as if after a loved guest.
I took the stars as a herd
from the heavenly meadows,

as a shepherd left last in the field.
Silently as if in a temple
I kept distance at an owl's funeral,
and before dawn I shook
from the branches horror and darkness,
freed from the fog rivers and rocks.
I waited until runaway meteors
hid in the abyss.

I waited until the birds' belfries
rang the morning service,
until the morning moments burst into flames
like twigs
and took them dry across the water.

And now,
I have nothing more to do here.


## The Last Testament

I will leave you only words
dug up from the depths of hearing
as a treasure from a well,
inherited from the wind's flute,
forged where the sickle is wrought,
words stolen from the bird's beak
that flies above the clouds,
words spun at the hearth
which know the secret of the fire and ashes,
a word read in animal language out of a gaze,
wrested from a man crying,
words which children and underground streams
utter first when they notice the sun.

I will leave you nothing
except words studded in verse
as an ancient insect in amber.
After me will remain
neither a drop of blood in anyone,
nor a bone
nor a heart even as small as a bird's.

*Vesna Parun* was born in 1922 on the island of Zlarin. She studied in Zagreb, where she still resides. Since her first collection of poetry in 1947 she has published numerous collections which include love lyrics, war poems, children's verse, and dramatic works for radio and television.

## A Return to the Tree of Time

You who ask whence my daring
that here again I sing of love
after I locked it away from a black song in a chest
and placed it in the laps of birds.

Listen: I always return to myself
and in the bark of each tree into which I cut
with a knife of remembrance, a surprise awaits me.

But if the tree has died
and already turned into coal,
I'll dig deeply with my hands into the earth
and dig it up as coal.

If I return after ten years,
I'll dig it up as stone.
And if I return in a hundred years or more,
I'll dig even deeper, and I'll find nothing.

For even a stone doesn't remain a stone.
For even a stone goes somewhere
and don't ask about its whereabouts
but let me sing and return
to the roots of my song, deep inside myself.

## Sleeping Youth

Spread out on the beach of a shaded bay
he lies as a fenced in vineyard,
solitary and turned toward the waves.
His face is sweet and serious.
Noon wind plays around him.
I don't know whether a pomegranate branch,
full of chirping birds, is prettier than
his bent waist, as nimble as a lizard's.

I listen to the roar of low thunder,
which twists from the sea closer and closer.
And hidden in the leaves of an old agave
I watch as the youth's throat becomes a seagull
and flies off toward the sun, shrieking sadly
in the yellow clouds. And from his
magnificent bronze belly rises gloomily
a flower cliff on which beautiful
nymphs and fairy tale queens rest.

The shore rustles and the sea grows grey.
Golden shadows screen the vineyard.
Pillars of clouds rise in the distance,
and lightening touches the wooden cove.

I inhale the smell of summer in the trees,
and I let the nakedness of plants intoxicate me.
Then I look at my shining hands
and thighs, gilded by the foam of the sea,
from which oil flows in the olive grove.
And returning peaceful eyes toward him
who sleeps, immersed in the roar of
a slow storm, ancient as agave,
I think, full of scattered yearning,
how many white open-winged birds
tremble in the cloudy blue ravines
of this body, which in its silence confuses
the roar of the sea and the solitude of grass.

*Irena Vrkljan,* born in 1930 in Belgrade, studied philosophy at the University of
Zagreb. In Berlin she studied film and television and has worked for radio and
television in Zagreb. She writes poetry, drama, and prose and translates from
German, dividing her time between Berlin and Zagreb.

## A Romantic Poem

Sand color of honey,
hair color of sand
and a gentle touch of darkness,
which shields you, which takes you away,
to some other planet

to which you travel so indifferently
each day,
together with your shadow,
together with your face of sand
that dissipates between my hands
and I cannot save you,
smooth are the walls of night
and I cannot capture you,
the wind scatters you across the whole room,
on all things which I touch,
and I cannot catch you,
you are a sand clock
that broke
suddenly,
as if tired,
you pass through my fingers,
fall softly and easily
on the lips,
on the hair,
you turn into a distant dune
in the lost parts of the sun,
you are only a man of sand,
and I a wind
that scatters you


## For Elsa Morante

An unspent smile travels on a postcard from Rome
which you show me in front of windows of your home,
and it turns into an unknown street,
approaches me between facades
which I have never seen, waves to me from the bell tower
and falls into the abyss, I cannot stop it,
it doesn't know me and it's from another part
of the world, that which we do not know yet.

A patient hand lies on the tablecloth and sleeps,
a frozen bird in a tree top of nothing,
in weakness to be an arrow which I could throw
into the region of friendship that's already ending,
while an agitated glance travels about the dress design,

entangles in the folds, it's afraid of anger
because of an inaccurate world of words
I didn't utter.

The ensuing silence entangles with silk lips
and remains lying as a veil, I cannot lift it,
forgetfulness already drips through cracks of time
and around emptiness flows a brook,
a conversation we never began is ending.

Unuttered prayer, return some possibility
that we begin it, wherever or whenever,
return the voice which wasn't unfriendly, but kind,
or at least a night in which you stay,
in which you are silent and suddenly sing
in the midst of far and sunny Rome.

*Draginja Urošević* was born in 1949 in Kraljevo and studied literature at the University of Belgrade. In addition to poetry, she writes literary criticism. She lives in Belgrade.

## The Deer and Death

Death supervenes as a flood
purple waves circle
around the Deer who just lifted his head
while drinking light green drops
so as not to look at his reflection in the lake
because then his spirit always senses a duality
the reality of matter—the reality of shadow

and fear overtakes him

Death wandered off all in purple
among his hills
now all the foresters are poisoned
and with their garb they infect
equally does, dogs, and people,
silvery butterflies and reddish-brown wolves

Death wandered off all in purple
the Deer stopped for an instant by the shore of the lake

mesmerized by Death's gait
by its fragile gait
which intoxicates and murmurs from all sides

## My Organism Corresponds with Nature

Three days it pours from the sky and out of earth
it pours from the north and the south, from the east and the west
Three days lightning steps into the room
and here it quiets down and takes a nap
but the thunder, supreme god, roars in the midst of the flat
in the whirlpool of a powerful natural symphony
at lunch, at dinner
tinkling the porcelain on the birthday of the storms

Three days it celebrates the child of lightning and thunder

Three days my organism corresponds with nature
with the sun through rain
with rain through the sun, a perfect postal carrier
letters fly
one moment I am elated, one I am foundering
my ship stops before a wall
the voyage is invariably uncertain
and the captain, my head, writes out lines
points, and coordinates of time
giving hour after hour the state of the organism

> *Neda Miranda Blažević* was born in 1951 in Gračac and studied comparative literature at the University of Zagreb. The author of four collections of poetry and two collections of prose, she has taught in creative writing programs at the University of Minnesota in 1984 and the University of Iowa in 1990.

## Shortages

A question does not help.
An answer even less.
But even in their chains they show strength
as does a slave whom the owner
drags from market to market, from sentence to sentence.

A girl at the train station
holds an arm akimbo
swinging slowly one foot forward.
An old man is stealing a can of sardines in a shop.
While he is hiding it, in a mirror above a shelf
swim swarms of fish, water ripples,
someone is slamming the door.

A letter arrives from America.
Trish got married, Saint Michael's summer
returns the land to the Indians
Joseph Brodsky's new book is out
Raymond Carver is terminally ill
Martha Roth will visit Lublin with her husband.

All right, I will go with you, the room is around the corner,
later we will eat the sardines, I am hungry
there are so many shortages this fall
like books with only one ending.


## Croatian/English

As if I twice
open the door,
twice I check
is it right
that the sound has deeper meaning
than action which
in two languages,
of which one is more mine,
verifies
how much the other
less mine
becomes equally mine.

It's like when I gauge
the space between
the musical instrument
and the movement necessary
to play it.

*Tatjana Lukić* was born in 1950 and studied philosophy and sociology at the University of Sarajevo. She has published several collections of poetry and lives and works in Osijek.

## Measured Units

you were pregnant with a son
I was pondering comparisons

time is one
but the hours are different

your clock—a wall decorated
with a barometer, a spoon
a red box for pepper
cinnamon and salt

as a second hand
you tiptoe quickly after a man

while you quiet a child with a pacifier
I erase a title
before dawn I question: should I put a period?

you change diapers

you have your own noon
—a line full of clothes
your own midnight next to your husband's breath

you made all repairs this summer
in my home
a drinking fountain
which no hand
closed

day and night
from it drips
bitter honey

—my clock

## Third Person Singular

she
writes poems
makes a great fish stew
and each afternoon teaches children

how to take a fly out of the eye
the quickest way to clean glasses

from knowledge herself acknowledges
only inquiry and amazement

into her box
the mailcarrier drops greetings
from a lonely tollgate guard
seed seller
and village teacher

not in one drawer does she have
gold lettered invitations

she doesnt change people
only bed arrangement
night lamps and chairs

she keeps a broom by the door
just in case
for a flier or a cigarette butt

on rainy days
when tents are being prepared
parades and plays

behind a window
she pulls a needle through
green flax bought on sale
she sews a pillow

she makes up a new recipe
and like a fragrant bonbon
feeds on metaphor.

# Twelve East German Artists

VICTOR H. MIESEL

The first of its kind in the United States, the exhibition "Twelve Artists from the German Democratic Republic" opened at Harvard University, where it had been organized by the Busch-Reisinger Museum, in September 1989. Subsequently, this showing of sixty-four paintings, drawings, and prints—none a minor effort—by twelve notable and mature artists, the youngest thirty-seven years of age and the oldest eighty-eight, traveled to two more academic venues, the University of California at Los Angeles and the University of Michigan, as well as to the Albuquerque Museum of Art, Science, and History.

No megamuseum joined in this enterprise, and that was unfortunate, for obvious reasons. Events in East Germany provided such a dramatic, albeit coincidental, context for the exhibition that protestations of the if-only-I-had-known variety were soon forthcoming from all quarters. I suspect that the organizers had no easy job finding any small museums for the exhibit either. As far as the University of Michigan was concerned, I must confess that though my special field of study is German Expressionism, I was not very interested. Fortunately, the acting director of our museum, Professor Graham Smith (a scholar of Renaissance art), was. For me, it was especially ironic that a fellow Detroiter and someone I have known for forty years, art patron Stanley Winckelman, played an important role in the development of the show.

But no matter: once the exhibition was mounted, it became clear that here were powerful works well able to make for themselves a space that in the best sense was a *museum* space, that is to say a space where one experienced significance beyond the merely sensational or fashionable or informative. For Americans, the works on display demonstrated that, as far as cultural politics in East Germany were concerned, we were in a new era. This new era, however if one dares to judge from such slim evidence, declares itself to be one where traditions persist to be confronted but also cultivated, to be acknowledged but also sublimated. I have different traditions in mind, art traditions as well as traditions having to do with general attitudes toward one's self and one's culture. It is also worth noting that the word "tradition" need not

Sighard Gille, *Gigi and Dietmar* (1966), oil on canvas, 200 × 100 cm.

connote anything authoritarian and can be understood as both a handing down, a passing along, and a delivering up, even a surrendering, to others.

Clearly, the works bore witness, and the artists' statements about their art confirmed, that a tradition having to do with the self-reward of art was a vital component to be celebrated. I am reminded of what Diderot observed more than two hundred years ago: "My friend, one must work for oneself. Anyone who does not pay himself with his own hands by getting most of his reward in his own room through the intoxication, through the exaltation, of his craft would be well advised to remain idle." He prefaced this good advice, admittedly, by gently ridiculing the faith of artists in "an invisible church of the elect . . . underground apostles converting the unenlightened." And yet that is what has happened in the past and, I think, will continue happening, notwithstanding the missionary activity of the highly visible, aboveground apostles of contextualism, race and gender politics, and "creative criticism," who experience art primarily as ideology and propaganda.

Personally, I was disappointed that the only excitement during the exhibition's University of Michigan symposium was generated by feminist concerns about the absence of women artists in the show. After all, one of the three selectors for this project was the noted art critic Doré Ashton, a woman. That there were neither sculptures nor photographs to be seen and not the slightest trace of "antifascism" bothered nobody, apparently. Incidentally, when I first heard about the role of the Busch-Reisinger Museum in launching an East German art exhibition, I recalled my father's alarming jokes about the opening of that museum (1903), funded by a brewer, inspired by the gifts and cultural vainglory of Kaiser Wilhelm, and characterized by plaster reproductions of medieval church facades. For my father (fifteen years old at the time), but especially for his father, a wine enthusiast, anarchist, and freethinker, the museum was a "palace for beer hall politics and plaster saints," a symbol for *Kaiser, Kitsch und Kirche.* Frankly, such ancient history was wiped away by a quick glance at what the exhibition revealed. To be sure, oppressive memories of Germany's more recent history remained. Or as one reviewer put it (foolishly and inaccurately), "And what of Bismarck, Hitler, the Holocaust and Erich Hönecker's hunting lodge? The German *Angst* is certainly omnipresent. But remorse, repentance—they are more difficult to find" (*Detroit Free Press*). I disagree. I found it: it was evident enough even though devoid of blatant *j'accuse* finger-pointing or *mea culpa* breast beating.

Admittedly, the works initially, and sometimes with misleading ease, evoke a comfortable, almost nostalgic sense of art history. Reminiscences of an earlier generation of German expressionists—Max Beckmann, Oskar Kokoschka, Lovis Corinth, Paul Klee—abound. Nevertheless, this experience of déjà vu is a fleeting one. What one comes to see is a re-vision at the service of a *müssen,* not a *können,* a profession of a compelling need instead of a cleverly updated appropriation. I suspect that it was the raw energy as well as the confidently crafted and controlled force that won me

Gerhard Altenbourg, *Unscattered* (1974), mixed media, 103 × 72 cm.
Private collection of Dieter Brusberg.

Bernhard Heisig, *Volunteer Soldier* (1983), oil on canvas, 101 × 90 cm. Galerie Brusberg, Berlin.

over so quickly. It is possible that some "postmodern permissiveness" and a diminished capacity to care about art progress also played a role in muting, if not entirely suppressing, my curiosity and the curiosity of others about the vanguard significance of the show. Anyhow, I am convinced that among recent exhibitions of contemporary art, nothing better has appeared in the midwest than this show of East German art, with the exception of the 1988 presentation of Central European art called "Anxiety."

Having mentioned "Anxiety," and with that show's use of media besides paint-

Sighard Gille, *Fasching* (1988), mixed media on canvas, 175 × 125 cm.
Collection of Reinhard Botcher.

ing, prints, and drawing in mind, I should acknowledge that I do regret the absence in the East German exhibit of any sculpture, photography, or documentation of performance art. *Aktionskunst*, sometimes called *Autoperforationskunst*, seems to be becoming increasingly important in East Germany. Also, I could not help wondering if sculptors like Peter Lewandowski and Susanne Rast and photographers like Ute Mahler and Helfried Strauss were considered. Or were they thought too young? It occurs to me that the next time round, one might try the approach used for the interesting "Der Eigene Blick" exhibition (1988), for which ten East Berlin critics of obviously different tastes and concerns each chose several artists without the slightest worry about a consensus.

Of course, what has just been rehearsed is simply the trite, old routine of proposing a different exhibition from the one actually mounted. The main reason for this exercise, however, is to make the point that the East German exhibit is only a first step in a direction that is filled with promise. The show convinces me that there is a lot more where that came from. There is also, it should be emphasized, a lot more to the East German exhibit than what literally first meets the visitor's eye. Not unlike many of the best exhibitions these days, a catalog is featured that complements what is looked at so effectively that one runs the risk of having one's attention diverted from looking at original works of art to thinking about them as examples of larger issues or, even more reductively, as additional items of information in an extended context of issues. It is a risk worth taking because it is necessary—necessary because the originals, to their credit, provoke so many questions to which one needs answers and necessary also because, like it or not, history, present politics, and fashionable discourse cannot be ignored.

The catalog is indispensable.[1] First of all, it indicates that the organizers of the exhibit are well aware of the contextual issues that many people find more interesting than the art itself. Thus, it features an annotated chronology, "Developments in the Fine Arts in East Germany from 1945 to 1988," accompanied by an excellent bibliography. The chronology includes a number of illustrations, and these function as a valuable supplement to the color plates, which in the catalog proper reproduce all the works in the exhibition. Ironically, it is this supplement, with its plentiful and wonderfully revealing quotations from such official sources as the Ideological Commission of the Politburo of the Sozialistische Einheitspartei Deutschland (Communist party) that while speaking to one set of concerns—"Erich Hönecker hunting-lodge concerns—unaccountably and woefully neglects a far more serious one—the Holocaust. Surely some space should have been given over to illustrations and documentation of those works, occasionally monumental works, that bear witness in the GDR to Nazi crimes. The organizers' single-minded attention to painting, prints, and drawings may have had something to do with this omission. In any case, references in the chronology to political and moral issues may alert us to what has been left unsaid.

Thomas Ziegler, *Soviet Soldier,* 1987, mixed media on canvas, detail, first of four parts, each 158 × 127 cm. Gesellschaft für Deutsch-Sowjetische Freundschaft.

The catalog introduces one to other contexts as well. For example, in the nicely titled "Revival and Survival of Expressionist Trends in the Art of the GDR," an organizer of the exhibition, the distinguished scholar of German Expressionism Peter Selz, emphasizes that what one sees is not an exploitation of the past in the "postmodernist sense of replication, appropriation or simulation (the simulacra of Baudrillard)" but rather an example of "elective affinities in Goethe's sense." This is not to say that the art cannot be placed in an ambiguous light. An interview a few months ago with the East Berlin art historian Christoph Tannert used the following headline: "Gestern—Avantgarde von drüben, Jetzt—Weltkunst für hüben?" It seems to me that one must concede that this headline—with its contrasts of a "yesterday" and a "now," an "over there" and a "here," a vanguard elect, doubtlessly encouraged by underground apostles, and international renown—lends itself to a number of interpretations, none without irony. The headline sets one thinking about success in the art market but also about issues of late-arrival or retarded modernism or, better yet, "timely" and "untimely" achievement. As far as I am concerned, the inclusion in the exhibition of paintings by Rosenhauer, born in 1901, who works in a style that makes one think of artists born a generation earlier than that, was a splendid *idea* even though it was not intended as such, that is, as a calculated snub vis-à-vis obligations to be "on time," if not "ahead of time," in art. Rosenhauer's slowly and densely painted little pictures are impressively timeless, like Giorgio Morandi's (born 1890), and like Morandi's, they are that way without becoming a "flight out of time," to use the words Dadaist Hugo Ball chose for the title of his 1910–1921 diaries.

Besides Selz's essay, the catalog offers another context for the East German show in "*Concordia Discors:* Common Elements among Incomparable Temperaments," by the East German scholar Hermann Raum. Like Tannert's headline, the title of Raum's essay lends itself to uncertain, multiple readings and tones. The scholastic-sounding "Agreement and Disagreement" strikes a note of lofty but not unkind dissent. "Common Elements" but "Incomparable Temperaments" might conceivably refer to the judges and their judgments of East German art as well as to the artists and their art. It sounds conciliatory but nonetheless leaves the impression of an implacable unlikeness. If the exhibition itself was premised on a "mystique of quality" that "all" could respond to, Raum presents a "mystique of context," which, in the final analysis, insists that a correct response is limited to those persons within that context. His essay begins by conveying, gently but firmly, that notion:

We in the GDR are well accustomed to viewing the art—particularly the newer and the newest works—in contexts that do not exist in the U.S., contexts that are provided neither by the images nor by the accompanying texts. I speak here of the social, cultural, and psychic environment that determines how the works take shape. . . . I also refer to the impact of these works—their reception and

Michael Morgner, *Crucifixion*, drawing, embossing, tar, ink wash on paper, 70 × 53 cm.
Collection of the artist.

evaluation in a surprisingly wide and well-informed audience. . . . It is difficult, however, for me to imagine the distance from which viewers in the U.S. look at these pictures now displayed away from the environment in which they took shape. . . . The show's organizers have, understandably, not made their selection with the intention of shedding light on the characteristics of internal social and cultural processes of GDR society. The fruit of their labors reveals, rather, that they have attempted to adapt to the need and customs of a viewer, in whose world art is produced and functions differently. . . . They are firmly rooted in the same art world as their audience. . . . they purposely steered well clear of being influenced by our public's predilections for works that treat problems in their own lives.

Unfortunately, Raum does not make much effort to illustrate these cautionary observations with specific examples. I recall my mother prefacing remarks that would be blunt and critical by saying in German, "Now I'm going to talk Latin!" Raum begins literally in Latin, but the issues that so richly merit frankness in his essay are mostly skirted.

The works themselves, however, through the sheer authority of their presence, make details about their modes of production and reception seem, if not irrelevant, certainly of secondary importance. This is not to assert that one is invited merely to savor what Raum calls the "pure state of form alone"—an experience he grants is necessary from time to time. I submit that here is indeed, as the *Detroit Free Press* reviewer put it, an omnipresent German *Angst*. Or rather, there is *Angst*, but to be precise, it is an *Angst* that is not so much a panic stricken apprehension as a solemnly alert and sorrowful concern. There is little that is festive about any of the works. If one felt at times a little bravado (Gille's *Party in Leipzig*) or something aggressive (Sitte's *Male Nude Putting on Trousers*) or frivolous (Claus's *Emotional Movements in the Process of Formulation*), a little more attention indicated that one was looking at something quite different—no melodrama, no histrionic rage, and no Dadaist tricks. Nietzsche's *Geist der Schwere* reigns. As another Detroit critic put it, "The show is a downer." Nietzsche of course proclaimed an overcoming of this Spirit of Gravity by a liberated "personal taste" that would "run, jump, climb, dance" and ultimately "fly" (*Also sprach Zarathustra*). It would be a simple matter to agree with the philosopher if one simplemindedly associated the Spirit of Gravity with a political system or some set of social conventions and customs. But suppose the Spirit of Gravity involves that weight imposed by the last fifty years of German history? Is this why nothing in the exhibition runs, jumps, climbs, dances, and flies? I believe no artist in the East German exhibit showed much inclination even to slip to one side of that weight, let alone overcome it. In praiseworthy ways they carry it.

Artists as utterly different stylistically as Carlfriedrich Claus and Thomas Ziegler submit to it. Claus's *Sprachblätter*, for example, uses scribbled words on one side of a sheet and delicately drawn landscape shapes on the other, so that when held

Max Uhlig, *Portrait of A.S., January/February 1988*, oil on canvas, 140 × 100 cm.
Photograph by Robert Chase.

up to the light, they fuse into a verbivisual labyrinth of indeterminate sense. The effect is that of an elegant but mournful counterpoint to the directness and pedantry of lengthy titles, such as *Conjunctions, Unity and Struggle of Oppositions in Landscape Related to the Communist Problem of the Future, Naturalization of the Human Being, Humanization of Nature*. In stunning contrast to Claus, Ziegler paints stiffly precise portraits of Russian soldiers placed against bright red backgrounds like ducks in a shooting gallery. These pictures do not tease us into painfully conscientious attempts to unsnarl and read *Gedankengänge* as Claus's do. They command us to stare. If we obey, then we experience a confrontation that is in a sense fiery: the green uniforms of the soldiers against red backgrounds produce flickering afterimages that turn a rather cold brightness into a burning. The effect is felt as neither clever nor angry but rather mysteriously heavy-hearted.

Likewise, the dissimilar works of Max Uhlig, Wolfgang Smy, and Michael Morgner seem companions in sorrow: those of the first are impulsively gestural; the second, awkwardly schematic; and the last, darkly explosive. Their ostensible subjects were easy to identify: Uhlig's were portraits and landscapes, Smy's were bathers, and Morgner's were unambiguously named—*Death and Child, German Requiem*, and so on. They all, however, seem to go beyond unspecific heavy-heartedness or, for that matter, self-pity, to engage the imagination in ways that conform to Raum's observation about Smy's bathers. He thinks they look "happy" but then adds that they "conjure up atrocities from our historical memories." Uhlig's people and places, which, to be sure, are "Jackson Pollock-inspired" (Raum), also conjure up similar historical memories—memories of killing and being killed, memories to which one falls heir, whether one was an eyewitness or not. In this respect Morgner's tar-and-ink series of drawings entitled *Ecce Homo*, with its concluding crucifixion scene, is conspicuous and exemplary. It is both a Lamentations and a Miserere.

"Lugubrious" might be the cynic's word for this art. Walter Libuda's darkly glowing *Listeners*, Heinrich Tessmer's *Rat's Game*, Willi Sitte's *Self-Portrait in a Swamp*, and Bernhard Heisig's *Prussian Still Life*, its military paraphernalia surmounted by a skull, are all heavy-hearted. And yet the heavy-heartedness is not despair. Though I must concede that this judgment is based on the slender evidence of artists' statements used in the catalog, the artists themselves are men of courage who, as has already been noted, seem sustained by the self-reward of art:

In my painting white is the earth, in order to conjoin different layers of color. White can become visible when uncovered and lie exposed like a wound. It shapes itself into crusty roads of color thrown to the surface, into islands on which points, crosses and spots emerge, awaken memories of concrete things.

Lines drown in masses of planes, resurface and grow on, strengthened and intensified. They form veins in the plains, traverse areas, or cling to them. Planes are often overlaid three or four times (sometimes more); the ones below shine through and reach into the upper ones, joining themselves to them.

Wolfgang Smy, *Small Sulphur Bath* (1985), latex, acrylic, wax crayon on paper, 73 × 102 cm.
Collection of the artist.

The first passage is taken from Libuda's poem "For the Lovers of Grottoes, Gorges, and Narrow Islands"; the second is from an essay by Gerhard Altenbourg, whose ironic and elegiac drawings in the exhibition evoke, as Raum puts it, "Ensor, Klee and Kubin demonstrating a clear affinity for Dubuffet and Wols." Both passages convey what all the works in the show convey—if not an exaltation then certainly a devotion to métier, a devotion that reminds me of something that the American painter (and teacher of such major artists as Edward Hopper and Stuart Davis) Robert Henri emphasized: "Art is the giving by each man of his evidence to the world. Those who wish to give, love to give, discover the pleasure of giving. Those who give are tremendously strong."[2]

These twelve East German artists impress me as givers. Sorrowful, anxious, and at times perplexed, their giving does nevertheless convey love, pleasure, and strength. It is of the utmost relevance, I think, to take note of the following remark by Tessmer, not for art historical but for human reasons: "I love greatly the gentle, tolerant transition from gray to pink in Mark Rothko and the soft, democratic light in Rembrandt's pictures." Emphatically, consciousness of history is not evaded by these artists. Heisig speaks about the "calming feeling" that artists have when they realize that they are "part of a long process that began before us and will continue after us." He goes on to acknowledge that this historical feeling is a "feeling for larger connections" that "must be a disturbed one." He adds, "Without a past, no people can live; there can be no nation and of course no visual arts, architecture or cities. A people is unable to produce art without its own history." One need only glance at his paintings, which overflow with a pathos that reminds one of Beckmann, Kokoschka, and especially the late Corinth (not to mention, as Doré Ashton has pointed out, Ludwig Meidner), to recognize that that "calming feeling" of Heisig's has nothing to do with the placid satisfaction of an heir to some grand tradition. What I see is evidence of brave acceptance of duty, an acceptance of a Spirit of Gravity that does not in the slightest try to veil the fear and trembling produced by the "larger connections" of German history. It is evidence of working with tradition understood indeed as a delivering up and a surrendering to others. It is not a despairing, self-indulgent *Angst*.

A concluding thought, or to be more precise, a hope, occurs to me in relation to what one might discover in the work of all twelve of these artists from East Germany. This hope has to do with how individual conscience and artistic probity might combine to intersect politics, combine to become a "living in truth," exemplary of what Václav Havel envisioned when he wrote, "Living within the truth covers a vast territory whose outer limits are vague and difficult to map, a territory full of modest expressions." [3]

## Notes

1. *Twelve Artists from the German Democratic Republic*, ed. and intro. Peter Nisbet, with essays by Doré Ashton, Peter Setz, and Hermann Raum (Cambridge, Mass.: Busch-Reisinger Museum, Harvard University, 1989), available from the Harvard University Art Museum, 32 Quincy St., Cambridge, Mass. 02138.
2. Robert Henri, *The Art Spirit* (New York: Lippincott, 1951).
3. Václav Havel, *Living in Truth* (Amsterdam: Meulenhoff, 1980).

Prague punks in front of the Jan Hus statue. Photograph by Thomas G. Winner.

# Skinheads and Faschos in East Germany

## The New-Old Danger of Fascism

KONRAD WEISS

Translated and Introduced by Luise von Flotow

Independent samizdat periodicals, sponsored by the Lutheran church, have been appearing in East Germany for years. They differed from the official publications of the church in several ways. Most important, they were able—at least to some extent—to avoid state censorship. Although the samizdat papers were published by the Lutheran church, their tendency was pluralistic and usually characterized by liberal humanism. Produced privately in church halls or the homes of those who dared, these magazines were issued in tiny editions, passed from hand to hand, and read carefully. Church groups, peace seminars, human rights activists, and ecologists met regularly to discuss such publications and then devise responses and commentaries.

One of the samizdat magazines, *Kontext: Beiträge aus Kirche und Gesellschaft,* was published by the Evangelische Bekenntnisgemeinde in Berlin-Treptow. The issue from which the following essay is taken contains texts on the greenhouse effect, pollution, and ecological disasters. The entire issue is characterized by a pastoral and moralistic tone, although the authors are not necessarily churchmen. This essay, "Die neue alte Gefahr: Junge Faschisten in der DDR," addresses the moral bankruptcy of a society trying to solve its problems through violence. Since the first-person narrative and the emotional rhetoric are evidently intended to provoke the reader, I have tried to preserve in the translation these characteristics of the texts with only minor abridgments.

Although the piece was published in the spring of 1989, it has not lost its relevance. Its author, Konrad Weiss, is a filmmaker who worked in the section for documentary film at the East German film studios. In 1964, at the age of twenty-three, Weiss joined a group of young Germans whose purpose was to find ways to understand and take personal responsibility for German history. He became one of its first members to visit Auschwitz after World War II. This experience had an important influence on his moral and professional development, and its effect is evident in the work he subsequently produced. *Flamen* (Flames), a film made in 1968, deals with the Herbert-Baum-Gruppe, a Jewish resistance movement of the 1930s. *Davids Tagebuch* (David's Diary) is based on a young Jewish boy's diary of events in Poland after 1939. His 1988 documentary *Ich bin klein aber wichtig* (I Am Small but Important) traces the thought and work of Janosz Korczak, a Polish doctor, educator, and writer, whose commitment to the Jewish children in the orphanage of the Warsaw ghetto led him to accompany them to Treblinka. But Weiss's career has not been smooth. Films were made but never shown. The emphasis on Jewish questions challenged the censors and government administrators in East Germany. It took Weiss half a year of struggle to get *Davids Tagebuch* released. The publication of this essay in the Lutheran samizdat cost him his job at the state film studios, and as further punishment, his youngest daughter was not accepted to the university. After the political upheaval at the end of 1989, Konrad Weiss ran for a seat in the Volkskammer on the ticket of the small liberal party called Democracy Now.

In the early 1980s there were only a few skinheads in East Germany. They served to indicate a certain right-wing potential that was still unorganized. At that time such an ideology was not visible, and acts of violence appeared to be spontaneous. The assumption was that the skinheads were just one among many other youth groups and that they would disappear of their own accord. It was unthinkable that young people raised in East Germany could become the carriers of a new fascist thinking.

Around 1983 the new fascists began to organize. At first right-wing groups made appearances in the football stadiums, a development similar to that of other countries, and instigated nonpolitical fights and rampages, usually under the influence of alcohol. Acts of violence together with racist and anti-Semitic insults became the norm at football games in East Germany. The irrational hatred between Saxons and Berliners, formerly taken lightly, has became part of fascist ideology. The game between LOK Leipzig and Union Berlin on April 23, 1988, was a sad climax, as police had to use rubber bullets against the warring "fans."

Besides the skinheads, who are identifiable by their martial appearance, there is a second, in my opinion more dangerous, group—the faschos, who clearly adhere to a fascist ideology. At first glance they are unobtrusive conformists and good workers. Yet in their own closed circles they are engaged in the secret elaboration of their new-old *Weltanschauung*.

These developments have probably overwhelmed those responsible in the state and the Communist party. Perhaps they were too occupied in the early 1980s with struggles against the advocates of environmental reforms and the peace and human rights activists. Was the socialist German state blind in the right eye, or at least myopic? The official response to fascist incidents was simply to blame them on influences from the capitalist West.

In his book *Die Rebellion der Betrogenen* (The Rebellion of the Betrayed) Thomas Haubner takes the same position. Even in the most recent edition of the book he lays the blame exclusively on the West: "In their thinking and their actions, the skinheads are a mirror image of capitalist society." But I do not think things can be that simple.

In the early 1980s the number of young people belonging to fascist groups in East Germany was estimated at about one thousand. But by 1986 skinheads had already begun terrorizing punks, who were considered left-wing and proletarian, and attacking other marginal youth groups, members of visible minorities, and members of grass-roots alternative groups. Acts of violence increased fivefold between 1983 and 1987, and most of the perpetrators were not identified or brought to justice. Now the potential for politically motivated criminality has increased enormously. Fascists are on the move. Vocational schools count on two or three right-wing extremists per class, and there is no great territorial differentiation. At least three-quarters of the young fascists are more than twenty-six years old. Furthermore, fourteen and fifteen year olds are strongly attracted by the right-wing scene.

Among the new fascists we find children of working-class as well as intellectual and middle-class families. Skinheads often have proletarian backgrounds or are young workers. The fascist groups are heavily dominated by men, in contrast to other independent groups, in which females participate. Less than one-fifth of the members of the right-wing groups, however, are women. Most of the members are single, and as far as I have been able to ascertain they marry relatively late. But it is not clear whether these sociotypical indications are a significant or a chance development.

If we consider skinheads and faschos as a fighting, rampaging mob, as a horde of uncontrolled criminals misled by Western idols, then we can avoid the issue of their political program. But that is exactly the attitude that caused the most far-reaching error ever made by the left and the middle class in German history. It seems to me that today, many first- and second-generation antifascists have literally taken as their credo the assumption that the new social order and forty years of antifascist education cannot have been in vain. For them it is unthinkable that young Germans who know about the horrifying national socialist terror and the fascist mass murders could again succumb to the madness of right-wing ideology.

And what exactly do we know about the way the new fascists—the skinheads and the faschos—think? Both groups embrace the principle of violence. Their social values are not those of democracy, the French Revolution, socialism, or Christianity. Instead, they are founded on strength and violence—in the *Herrenmensch*. In political terms this attitude is not limited to a group or small clique whose members think along similar lines. The faschos, more clearly than the skinheads, draw inspiration from national socialism. Hitler's *Mein Kampf* circulates readily among the new right in East Germany. But antifascist writings also serve as material for an education in ideology!

Both skinheads and faschos have reservations with regard to West German democracy: "We stand for a unified Germany, but we aren't yes-men, and we stand up for what we think." The faschos want a return to the German Reich and the boundaries of 1938. They see their task as the reunification of *Grossdeutschland*.

Occasionally, the new fascists also engage in activities related to external affairs. Their hatred is directed, logically, against the allied countries, victors in the Second World War, who destroyed the fascist state. Apparently the new fascists have contacts with the neighboring socialist states, and especially with the right-wing groups in Hungary, Czechoslovakia, the Baltic states, and the Ukraine. There is some indication, too, that common ideological bases and logistical processes make it easier for them to acquire propaganda material, martial-arts equipment, and weapons, although relations with the new political fascists in West Germany have probably been exaggerated. In any case, I am convinced that the thinkers and leaders of the new fascist movement in East Germany are not located in the west but rather that they "hibernated" or grew up in East Germany.

Most recently a real anti-Americanism has developed among the faschos; the right needs a new enemy. Anti-Semitism and racism already exist in latent form, and we can expect a series of anti-Semitic actions and graffiti in the near future. Anti-Semitic jokes and comments are already a commonplace on the football fields and in the bars frequented by the new right. In fact, any belief that the roots of anti-Semitism have been totally eradicated in East Germany is nothing but wishful thinking.

Right-wing radicalism is already finding increasing support among workers and educators. According to one insider, the antifascist resistance in the population is wearing thin. This is most certainly a result of the values propagated and systematically lived by the faschos. The apolitical observer, the *Kleinbürger,* perceives them as industrious, orderly, and disciplined young citizens who are active and seem to know their purpose in life.

The new right rejects any type of anarchy and exercises self-discipline. Physical training and healthy life-styles are part of their political program; generally they are extremely fit. "We are the elite of the German youth." The current rejection of alcohol by one part of the new right supports this view. Other important values are a personality cult and a pronounced sense of comradeship—and here again the historic role models are undeniable. Weekly meetings serve as forums where members educate one another in absolute adherence to the idea and the idols. The new right deliberately promotes elitism and confidence in right-wing beliefs. Each member has to submit to certain test rituals, in which he proves his willingness to use force; inhibitions to do so are gradually dismantled. Cowardly ambushes on passersby are usual as a test of courage. Some groups spend weekends in camps where battle strategies or paramilitary exercises are practiced. It is no accident that military values are culti-vated—discipline, obedience, perseverance, trustworthiness, and especially the sense of *Wehrmacht* comradeship. An integral aspect of the personality cult of the right is the view that those convicted of violent crimes are heroes. There is a definite danger that without some kind of sociotherapeutic program, prison will truly turn into an academy for many of these young men, a place where their opinions will harden and their self-confidence develop. For the faschos and the skinheads, those who have been convicted are real martyrs of the movement.

It is relatively simple to identify determining characteristics and common values for the various independent groups, but it is almost impossible to verify the existence of organizational structures and mechanisms. Since all the new fascist groups operate under strictly conspiratorial rules, there are no clear indicators of a central organization. Yet the logistics of the faschos and the skinheads do point toward a central and ideologically based leadership.

The right-wing groups are generally small, with no more than ten to fourteen members—according to sociologists an ideal size, enabling such groups to insulate themselves against the outside and thus control any leaks of information. The lead-ers' hold on power is based not on democratic principles but on strong personalities. Once their authority has been accepted, unquestioning allegiance is required. Group leaders are typically of above-average intelligence. They have access to *Elitewissen* (privileged knowledge), suggesting the participation of higher authorities. Instances of well-timed and simultaneous actions and activities of the new right also indicate an ideological structure and a central authority.

It is evident that there are countless threads that connect the new right to German national socialism. How is it possible that this dreadful seed could fall on such fertile ground in East Germany in the mid-1980s? Antifascism has been an integral part of the East German constitution and of East German state poli-cies. Nazi criminals and their collaborators were more rigorously punished in East Germany than in West Germany. By the mid-1970s, 12,876 Nazis had been sen-tenced, and every year since then there have been further trials.

Yet all of that tells us nothing about the psychological or moral condition of the Germans in East Germany. Many of those who welcomed Hitler in 1933 or were part of the silent majority that experienced the fascist crimes and the war never really turned over a new leaf. Some—and they were probably the ones who shouted "mea culpa" the loudest, may have changed flags, uniforms, and party cards, but basically they stayed the same. For most of the silent conformists, though, the knowledge that they were criminally misused and led astray for twelve years is so terrible that it has simply been repressed. Excessive guilt and shame have rendered a real confrontation with the past exceedingly difficult.

Neither the church nor society in East Germany has ever recognized the problem: none of those involved in the Third Reich was able to confess publicly or to discuss their actions publicly. The criminals were punished. Millions of conformists, however, and all those who are guilty by silent acquiescence, were reduced to silence. The relief of repentance was denied to them. The Germans in East Germany moved too quickly into the new order of things.

Shame and sorrow were further hindered by the claims of superhuman purity and humanity made by many antifascists and especially by the communists. But this noisily proclaimed humanism soon met the obstacle of the postwar Stalinist terror. The result was the total discrediting of the purveyors of the antifascist state and of the antifascist idea, and a reversion to a latent fascism. Every error, every problem that developed in East Germany and in East German society, became an argument in support of a renewed interest in fascism. A new, yet deeply concealed fanaticism developed. These reconverted fascists spent forty years in apparent conformity, behaving like politicaly indifferent citizens or playing the role of socialists. Yet they are the ones who have been patiently awaiting their turns and who have now passed the brown baton on to their grandchildren. They are the ones—unobtrusive, apparently harmless, and hard to pin down—who hold the reins of control in their hands, and not the handful of former SS-men or party bosses who may have been able to hide somewhere under false names and papers. This is of course all hypothesis. Maybe it is all much simpler. Maybe there really are families who have lived the fascist idea openly and without interruption and who display a fascist elitist consciousness. Maybe the widows of those who were executed passed their husbands' heritage on to sons and grandsons.

There is no full explanation, however, for the popularity that the right is presently enjoying, a popularity that can only be based in the present. Even in those cases where an honest reversal of values occurred, traces of the Third Reich remain in the subconscious and the unconscious, in our everyday language. Our everyday culture was never completely denazified: it is still not the individual, the unique element, that is placed at the top of our scale of values, but rather the mass. Similarly, originality and innovation are not highly valued; submission and conventionality are. Criticism and argument are not welcome; conformism and moral cowardice are.

The East German state has never had the opportunity to take up or carry on the democratic traditions of the 1848 revolution or of the Weimar Republic; a proletarian dictatorship with a Stalinist core was forced upon it. The antifascist-democratic societal structuring has not touched all aspects of life; often it has remained nothing more than a scheme. The communist Kaderpartei (party of specialists) has not supported the development of democratic values but has created a system of new privileges designed to reward loudmouthing, servile behavior, and party discipline. The *Fürher* principle, which proved so disastrous for Germans, experienced a renais-

Skinheads in Halle, (East) Germany. Photograph by Luise von Flotow.

sance in different constellations: first the Stalin cult, then the unconditional claim by the Communist party that it functions as a vanguard. Grass-roots control of those in power and of their structures has never existed in the East German state.

The socialist society accepts the principle of violence, recognizes it, and practices it. Time and again conflicts are resolved through violence. All of this does not constitute fascism. But the basic approval of violence and the lack of a democratic culture have provided the propagandists of the fascist movement with a ready public. People growing up in East Germany and educated in the East German schools have not been sufficiently immunized against the bacteria of radical thought.

An additional factor is that the national pride of Germans has been severely disturbed for more than half a century. After the pathological nationalism of the first decades of this century all nationalist thoughts and sentiments were suppressed by the division of Germany. For many years it was a disgrace to be German. Patriotism was supposed to be replaced with internationalism—but how can you be an internationalist if you have no national identity? The synthetic construct of the East German "socialist nation" has never really been accepted by the Germans of East Germany. Is it this suppressed and repressed nationalist feeling that is turning into extreme nationalism? History offers more than one analogy.

Moreover, the return of much of the East German population to petty bourgeois values and life forms, its evident retreat into private niches, its flight from the public into the private sphere, all these phenomena have caused susceptibility to fascist thought.

Painful as it may be to recognize, the young fascists in East Germany are a product of East German society. They are our children. We must not give up a single one of them. And we must avoid prejudices, for how often have prejudgments become judgments? Of course, after all the damage done to Germany and the world by the National Socialists there can be no tolerance for fascist opinions and deeds. But we owe even the worst culprits compassion, warmth, and discussion.

Many of the skinheads who have been sentenced grew up in "proper conditions," in "good families": they were good students and workers. One begins to wonder whether there wasn't a certain lack of warmth and understanding in the homes of these children who got involved in right-wing activities; whether they were raised according to authoritarian principles or in homes where parents did not practice what they preached, or whether perhaps the parents forced their values and philosophies on the children instead of providing examples. The legitimate, inevitable, and healthy opposition toward all authority that young people need to experience for balanced development may very often have been broken through methods of "black pedagogy"—psychological and physical violence. Hence the fertile ground for hatred of all authorities: the children knew only too well that their embrace of fascism would cause their parents and the social and state authorities great pain. How long a period of mourning must we all experience now, in order to recuperate from this flood of hatred and pain!

The danger of a new fascist movement, carried forward by young people in East Germany, has become a reality. It constitutes a challenge for the whole population. Bitter questions will have to be asked about personal failings and failures.

I am afraid that for some time a certain right-wing "potential for politically motivated criminality" will continue to exist. Violent countermeasures by the state are not an appropriate therapy. Rather, the powers of seduction held by right-wing extremism must be stripped off and replaced by humanist alternatives. And that is only possible through a systematic and democratic reform of our society and the rejection of violence as a social option. Community service should replace military service. Violent attitudes toward unborn life and the environment must also be countered.

A new culture of public dialogue must be initiated and practiced. Young people must be guaranteed legal and social protection in experiments in alternative and democratic life-styles, based for instance on the Israeli kibbutz. Only true democracy can permanently immunize our youth against fascist thought.

# A Gambler in Life and Art

Franz Werfel (1890–1945)

EMERY GEORGE

Even Franz Werfel's family name suggests dice (one great-great-grandfather spelled it Würfel); his middle name was Viktor.[1] When the woman he worshiped and married first met him, she recorded in her diary that his forehead reminded her of Goethe's.[2] With Werfel's gifts as poet, singer, and speaker, and with no less a casino mistress than Alma Maria Mahler Gropius to keep a watchful eye on her player, how could he emerge a loser? Yet Werfel gambled hard, staking work, financial security, and mental health on all of a complex personality. Eager to embrace the world, he was also a tormented man, full of contradictions. Jewish by birth and deeply Christian in his sympathies, he was at various times also a Bolshevik revolutionary and an opportunist just short of being a Nazi collaborator. He was a child who never grew up and who even cherished the deep divisions within his nature. As an artist, he was uneven. A leading expressionist poet before World War I, a playwright whose works were staged by Max Reinhardt and performed before sell-out audiences, in the United States a best-selling novelist whose works were made into films, today he is remembered for parts of his oeuvre, depending on who does the remembering. Mention Franz Werfel, and some member of the Book-of-the-Month Club will mention Jakob Wassermann or Stefan Zweig. Critics have sworn by the early poetry. To us, Werfel looms large as a period phenomenon and as a man of fabulous luck, some say undeserved. And yet now that his centenary is here, his star is on the rise once again.

The Prague where Franz Viktor Werfel was born, on September 10, 1890, one of the major capitals of an ancient and overripe *Donaumonarchie,* was ethnically and linguistically a divided city. It was also a place of nature and of magically evocative civic beauty. Werfel's family, members of the German-speaking Jewish haute bourgeoisie—his father was a wealthy glove manufacturer—lived in a spacious and aseptically clean apartment at Mariengasse 41, in one of the city's most prestigious districts, near the City Park and the Neue Deutsche Theater (today the Smetana Theater). Barbara Šimůnková, the family cook and Franz's nursemaid, would often take the boy on walks of natural or architectural exploration. Franz regularly accompanied Barbara to morning mass, whereas his father would take him to synagogue on the Sabbath. Young Werfel thus had ample early opportunity to feel a religious split within him yet also to learn to know the essential oneness of the Judeo-Christian tradition. His sense of that oneness was nurtured by his developing affection for European culture—for books, classical theater, music, and opera. Angelo Neumann's May Festivals attracted the entire family, and Enrico Caruso's visit to Prague in 1904 was most assuredly the one event that kindled Werfel's lifelong love for the work of Guiseppe Verdi.[3]

Young Werfel was a disappointing student—his third year in the Piaristengymnasium had to be repeated—and very good all along at shirking unpleasant duty or responsibility.[4] As if to make up for this, he was a dreamer and talker like no one else around him. With Ernst Deutsch, Willy Haas, Franz Kafka, and other friends, Werfel caroused and discussed philosophy and literature deep into the night, at the same time writing and reading aloud an abundance of poetry. His earliest efforts are little more than sketches, notes, and some juvenile love lyrics (to a pretty but unresponsive adolescent flame named Maria Glaser). Willy Haas encouraged Werfel to revise, submit, and think of assembling a first collection. A debut of sorts came with the printing, in a February 1908 Sunday supplement of the Vienna daily *Die Zeit*, of Werfel's poem "Die Gärten der Stadt" (The gardens of the city). His first poetry collection, *Der Weltfreund* (The World's Friend), published by Axel Juncker in Berlin in December 1911, was reprinted several times and established Werfel as a leader of the expressionists. With Karl Kraus, who as a preview printed five of the poems in his magazine *Die Fackel* (The Torch), Werfel soon had a falling out, but by then the eyes of the literary world were on him. At Hellerau, near Dresden, in the summer of 1913, he met Rilke, who had written Werfel to express his admiration, suggesting they get together.[5]

Literary aspirations did not impress the young poet's father, and Franz soon had to yield to parental demands that he prepare for a livelihood. After ruining his "journeyman piece" (a glove he was assigned to make on his own), he was sent to a shipping firm in Hamburg, where he was soon fired, then up to Hradčany Castle for a year of military service. Werfel found his year with the artillery, from the fall of 1911 to the fall of 1912, burdensome but in some ways also interesting. He began to think about power and to feel sympathy with Czech nationalists, whose thinking seemed to him "close to Bakunin's anarchism."[6] Happier times came in the fall of 1912, when Werfel obtained a position as editor with the publishing firm of Kurt Wolff in Leipzig. Once there, he began a successful series of inexpensive paperbound volumes, named Der jüngste Tag (Doomsday); its aim was to publish the work of little-known writers, among them Walter Hasenclever, Kafka, and—a poet superior to Werfel—Georg Trakl. At Leipzig Werfel also met such writers as Martin Buber,

Franz Werfel. Line drawing by Adolf Hofmeister.

Else Lasker-Schüler, Carl Sternheim, and Franz Wedekind, and because of the associations of place, he felt close to Lessing and Goethe.[7]

War broke out in July 1914, putting an end to Werfel's work with Kurt Wolff; for many, it was also the end of an era. Werfel was called up, and here too he was a gambler and a child of luck; he was excellent at convincing the authorities that they should be lenient with him either for health reasons or because he was a well-known poet. To his surprise, he was treated with respect, and it is absolutely accurate to say that Werfel never spent a day in the trenches. Even on the Russian front, at Hodóv, in Galicia, he was given the coveted assignment of telephone operator and thus left with plenty of solitude and time to write. It was a time of essays and plays, significantly, of the early unfolding of the talents of the playwright. Already back in the May 1912 issue of the short-lived *Herder-Blätter* Werfel had published a one-act play entitled *Der Besuch aus dem Elysium* (The Visit from Elysium);[8] now his most important achievement was to be a translation-adaptation of Euripides' *Trojan Women*. First published by Kurt Wolff in 1915 and performed to great acclaim in Berlin in 1916, it was a very timely piece. Its themes of war, suffering, and pacifism made it an allegory of wartime Europe, and in Euripides himself Werfel saw an early forerunner of Christianity. These were also days of reading and study; Werfel read the works of early Christian writers—church fathers, Scholastics, and above all Dante. After these encounters Werfel decided that his real home was nowhere on earth but rather between worlds and, most important, in a realm secured for him by his work.[9]

Let us not gather the wrong impression: earth-man Werfel was very much around during these solitary war assignments, wherever in Europe they may have taken him, often in mufti. The question emerges, Was there to be a woman in his life at this time? and the answer is yes. One day in the spring of 1915, near Bozen (present-day Bolzano), on a funicular ride, he sustained severe leg and foot injuries when he jumped off the cable car too soon as it was approaching the platform. He had to walk on crutches and as late as November underwent tests and observation at the Prague garrison hospital. There he fell in love with one of his nurses, an unmarried young woman of thirty named Gertrud Spirk. They had actually met once before, and she had to remind him of it. She was from Prague, of a family of German-speaking Evangelical Lutherans. Spirk was the first woman whom Werfel thought seriously of marrying. The two kept up a long correspondence, but nothing became of it. Their relationship was broken off in Prague, in the summer of 1918, at a time when Werfel already knew that he was looking for a much stronger guiding light than Gertrud Spirk could ever be to him.[10]

Luck was with Werfel once again—uncanny, metaphysically directed luck, and he would have agreed. In February 1917 Count Harry Kessler, Kurt Wolff, René Schickele, and other intellectuals intervened to have Werfel recalled from frontline duty. His release from Hodóv came at the end of June. Just after the long-awaited and "feared Russian offensive [had begun], with considerable ferocity,"[11] a communication reached Corporal Werfel that by order of the Imperial and Royal Military Press Bureau (K. u. k. Kriegspressequartier) in Vienna, he was to leave the front immediately, proceed home to Prague, and there await his assignment to go on a propaganda lecture tour in Switzerland. That is how Werfel came to Vienna, in midsummer of 1917, to work long hours at the Press Bureau and once again to seek the company of kindred souls at such haunts as the Café Central, on the Herrengasse. It was like old times; here, in the company of his old friend from Prague, Egon Erwin Kisch, Werfel met writers of the stature of Robert Musil and Alfred Polgar, not to mention many other interesting people. But even that was a mere prelude to an impending brilliant future; much bigger action than haunting cafés lay in store for Franz Werfel. For late that fall, by courtesy of another friend and café acquaintance, the gregarious Franz Blei, Werfel met the woman who was to become his wife and companion of almost three decades, Alma Mahler.[12]

Alma Maria Mahler Gropius, née Schindler (1879–1964), was, at the time she and Werfel met, reputed to be the most beautiful and most interesting woman in Viennese high society. The daughter of Jakob Emil Schindler, a distinguished Austrian landscape painter, and the widow (since 1911) of the composer Gustav Mahler, she possessed a gift for drawing into her magic circle men of genius. Married at the time to the architect Walter Gropius, founder of the Bauhaus, and still in the throes of a hectic and visually rather obvious love affair with the painter Oskar Kokoschka,[13] Alma Mahler was drawn to Werfel at once. Two years before they met, she had already set to music one of his poems, "Der Erkennende" (The cognizant one); now that they were face to face, she was deeply impressed with Werfel's ability to speak and to sing and with his beautiful reciting voice. Werfel himself was glad to be introduced to Alma in part because he loved Gustav Mahler's music. He may have recalled how in Munich in September 1910 he and his family had heard the world premiere of Mahler's Eighth Symphony (the *Symphony of a Thousand*).[14] A personal meeting made it very clear how much Werfel needed and was drawn to a woman like Mahler's widow.

Their attraction proved mutual. Werfel visited Alma's salon frequently, sang Verdi arias to her piano accompaniment, recited poetry, and talked into the night. While Alma was still married to Gropius, she and Franzl came to live together (at Haus Mahler, in Breitenstein, where Werfel would write many of his works), and in early August 1918 they had a son, baptized Martin Carl Johannes. Born hydrocephalic, the child died a year later. Werfel wrote two plays in his memory, *Die Mittagsgöttin* (The Noon Goddess, 1919; included in *Der Gerichtstag* [The Day of Judgment]) and *Bocksgesang* (Goat Song, 1921). It is a tribute to three remarkable people that they remained friends through years of a triangular arrangement, when Gropius saw action on the western front and, once the war was over, returned to Berlin to rebuild his architectural consulting firm. Having read Werfel's work, Gropius came to love him. Alma and Walter Gropius were divorced in Weimar in October 1920, but they remained friends, and their daughter Manon did often visit her father in Weimar and Berlin. Owing in part to Alma's hesitation concerning her poet-lover's Jewishness, she and Franz did not get married until early July 1929.[15]

What quirk of fate brings together two people as utterly different as Alma Mahler and Franz Werfel? She was tall and amply built, he short and heavyset; she was drawn to the feeling of greatness within a small physical frame; to him she became an earth goddess, whom he came to worship, while to the end of his life he was her "man-child."[16] She longed for articulateness, and unlike Walter Gropius, Werfel was able to deliver it. She in turn became his polestar and solidest guiding light. She supplied him with encouragement in his work, with sage advice concerning the choice of subjects and a house where he could work comfortably, living "the life of a hermit."[17] There is an important sense, then, in which the mutual attraction between Werfel and Alma Mahler was perfectly natural, in which they enriched—in fact complemented—each other's natures. It is important to stress that Alma was much too mature and complex a person to allow a desire for condescension—in this case toward a man of short stature—to dictate her choice of a lover. It is clear that she had deep respect for Werfel as a creative artist; toward the end of his life she especially revered him for having written *Das Lied von Bernadette* (The song of Bernadette, 1941).[18]

Yet if there were natural forces that brought these two interesting people together, there were also serious differences between them, some of them never resolved. That he was Jewish and she Catholic was simply the groundwork on which rested a mansion of many rooms. She was anti-Semitic, but he was *not* anti-Catholic; he idolized Verdi, whereas her ideal in opera was Wagner; she was solidly conservative and royalist, whereas he time and again displayed sympathy with workers' movements and with progressive ideas such as socialism and mystical Christianity on a Dostoyevskian or Tolstoyan model. Their political differences came to a head on the night of November 12, 1918. Earlier that day, great crowds in front of the Parliament building on the Ringstrasse heard the proclamation of the Austrian Republic. After having addressed the assembled workers with inflammatory words, encouraging them to attack the Bankverein building, Werfel came to Alma's apartment, grimy and in work clothes, and she would not let him in. We are talking about little more than the merry political pranks of an impressionable soul; as was the Red Guard, Werfel the communist agitator too was largely the creation of his friend Egon Erwin Kisch.[19] Perhaps Alma should have seen through her companion's attempt at originality.

Be that as it may, from then on Werfel knew that he was on notice. If he was to retain his mother goddess's affections, he would have to conform in his social and political views as well as in his general religious outlook. With religion Werfel never had any trouble. He felt distinctly attracted to Roman Catholicism generally speaking, to a simple and childlike faith in Christian values. Just before their wedding he even offered verbal renunciation of his Judaism, although he never formally converted. (Yet to Max Brod and Martin Buber he wrote that he remained very much a Jew.) With politics Werfel had a slightly more turbulent time, but he eventually reached an ambivalent accommodation, one that makes us see Werfel the man in a very different light from Werfel the writer. The man, for example, could publicly endorse such a political leader as Kurt von Schuschnigg, against his better knowledge of the means by which the clericofascist government in question was maintained. Werfel also signed the declaration of loyalty to the Nazis, in a misguided attempt to save from the pyres his novel *The Forty Days of Musa Dagh*, which is a warning against nazism.[20] The writer has much more elbow room, and the low point of Werfel's politics we can probably see in such a book as *Barbara oder Die Frömmigkeit* (Barbara, or Piety, 1929; translated as *The Pure in Heart*). The high point we see in work in which the religious vision triumphs—the writer's abiding faith, in the face of the hostility and indifference shown by the age, as he puts it in the preface to *Das Lied von Bernadette,* "in these ultimate values of our lives."[21]

It is worthwhile stressing that two such memorable people as Franz Werfel and Alma Mahler, very much children of their times and cultural settings and successful to the point of being morally suspect, exist first of all not in realms purely moral or aesthetic but in the realm of the practical. Both sought and found a way to live with their times, the rich but also turbulent interbellum era in Central Europe. Their concern was in part economic; they liked to live well, and Alma expected Franz to support her on at least a moderate level of luxury. In this too they were fortunate; the box-office successes of Werfel the prolific playwright almost always significantly surpassed the success of his plays with the critics. Alma had a decided weakness for fine houses. Besides Haus Mahler she owned a remodeled palazzo in Venice; purchased in 1923, it was sold in 1935, shortly after Manon's tragic death.[22] Her most spectacular purchase of real estate, however, was the villa on Hohe Warte (with a prestigious address: Wien XIX., Steinfeldgasse 2), acquired in part with monies contributed by Alma's stepfather, Carl Moll, now to be a neighbor, and by Franz's father, who generously came up with the sum of forty-thousand schillings.[23]

Hohe Warte became the site of Alma's greatest successes as a society hostess. The luxuriously appointed building of twenty-eight rooms was filled with art works, and her parties, attended by a who's who of Austrian society, often lasted into the morning hours. In time the list of invited guests came to include persons from both worlds, art and politics. Although such gracious living aroused envy, Werfel never felt comfortable there and much preferred to continue working at Breitenstein. Hohe Warte was sold in 1937; Alma seems to have been skilled at selling just in the nick of time. It is also interesting that on the Werfels' second trip to the Middle East, in the early months of 1930, Alma, with all her anti-Semitism, "liked Jerusalem so much that she toyed with the idea of acquiring a house there."[24] This is not to say that Werfel himself did not enjoy affluence, leisure to work, and the freedom to travel. The price he paid in moral guilt was acknowledged to be high. Werfel did on occasion express the social concern he bore to the end of his life. From Italy, for example, he wrote to Alma, analyzing the four-day civil war of February 1934, which resulted in the fascist dictatorship under Engelbert Dollfuss. But that does not change the fact that the Werfels' "style of life depended on the maintenance of a specific social and economic order"[25] and that for the sake of living under such an order Alma and Franz found their accommodation with all rightist systems short of national socialism in *Anschluss* Austria.

The couple always enjoyed traveling, and it is fair to say that it was their willingness to explore possibilities for making their home abroad that saved them in the end. Above all, for the playwright and novelist, travel was a sine qua non for fresh subject matter. It was the Werfels' first trip to the Middle East—to Egypt and to Palestine—in 1925 that helped him write the historical drama *Paulus unter den Ju-*

*den* (Paul among the Jews, 1926), and an encounter at Santa Margherita in 1931 triggered the novel *Die Geschwister von Neapel* (The Pascarella Family, 1931). The travel experience that most impelled Werfel to write was the one that formed the background of *Die vierzig Tage des Musa Dagh* (The Forty Days of Musa Dagh, 1933), the epic novel treating the genocide of the Armenians by the Turks in 1915–1917. In a carpet-weaving shop in Damascus he met neglected and starving children and young people, "orphans, children of Armenian Christians."[26] The resulting novel, which not only established Werfel's international fame but also made him into the de facto epic poet of the Armenian people, is meticulously researched and is written with a great deal of empathy. If any one work victoriously redeems Werfel the social opportunist, the political compromiser, it is *The Forty Days of Musa Dagh*. Its publication date, 1933, is deeply symbolic. Deservedly, the Armenian communities in New York and Paris feted the Werfels to the point of exhaustion. Turkish interest groups in the United States prevented the filming of the novel by Metro-Goldwyn-Mayer, however.[27]

Travel was a means for Werfel to bring his work abroad. One play, the biblical extravaganza *Der Weg der Verheissung* (The Eternal Road, 1935), was staged by Max Reinhardt in New York. It was to take the form of a kind of oratorio, with music by Kurt Weill. The production ran into prohibitive expense and was a resoundingly successful failure. The Werfels, who had come to these shores partly to distract themselves from their grief following Manon's death, found New York filled with admiring friends; shortly before their arrival, in 1934, Ben W. Huebsch had already brought out the first American edition of *The Forty Days of Musa Dagh*. There were to be other trips; Gerhart Hauptmann was an acquaintance from Italy, and in June 1937, when Werfel attended the International P.E.N. Congress in Paris, he met James Joyce. The two, made into a trio by Joyce's son, Giorgio, spent much time in a café on the Champs-Elysées, singing arias from Italian opera, primarily from Verdi.[28]

In the meantime, back in Europe the political situation was growing steadily worse. The event that elevated Schuschnigg to power was an unsuccessful Nazi coup d'état in the summer of 1934 that saw the assassination of Chancellor Engelbert Dollfuss. Schuschnigg himself was arrested as soon as the Germans entered Vienna in mid-March 1938. When it happened, Franz was in Capri, working on a new play; Alma, accompanied by her daughter Anna Mahler, fled within hours, saving what possessions she could in a couple of suitcases. The two women went first to Prague, then to Milan, where they joined Werfel; then the three of them went on to Zurich, where they were guests of Werfel's sister, Marianne Rieser. The Werfels got no rest until, following a brief visit to London, they were in Paris and could find something resembling a permanent home in Sanary-sur-Mer, on the French Riviera. There they rented a small house, in the shape partly of a tower, overlooking the sea, and they moved into it in early August 1938. On July 1 Werfel had suffered his first heart attack, but he recovered more quickly than expected.

After this, events came in rapid succession. November 9, 1938, is the date of Kristallnacht; on September 1, 1939, the Germans invaded Poland; on June 14, 1940, they marched into Paris. Now the Werfels knew they would have to attempt to leave for the United States. Their rather complex escape route, partly in the company of Heinrich and Golo Mann, took them through Lourdes, where in early August Werfel made a solemn vow. If he and Alma succeeded in reaching America safely, the first book he would write in his adopted land would be the story of Saint Bernadette of Lourdes. Once again, the Werfels—he, not long after his heart attack; she, now over sixty—took their chances and, in order to cross into Spain, walked over a steep hill in the Pyrenees. They made it. After additional difficulties securing proper visas and travel to Lisbon, the Werfels and their small party of fellow refugee writers sailed on the Greek ship *Nea Hellas*. They reached New York, and safety, on October 13, 1940.

Once settled in Beverly Hills, Werfel did write *Das Lied von Bernadette*. In English it sold a million copies, and it was made into an award-winning film. Werfel also wrote one last play, *Jakobowsky und der Oberst* (Jakobowsky and the Colonel, 1945), which became a Broadway hit and was first published as a college textbook. One more major novel followed, a quasi–science-fiction work entitled *Stern der Ungeborenen* (Star of the Unborn), which Werfel completed on August 17, 1945, nine days before his death. At his funeral such musicians as Bruno Walter and Lotte Lehmann performed works by Bach and Schubert.[29] As to Alma, who did not attend the funeral, she had lost her "man-child," and that would not sink in for some time.

What kind of writer did Alma make of her husband? That, I submit, is one of the few truly urgent questions concerning Franz Werfel's development. His talent was precocious in but a limited sense. *Pace* the critics who have called *Der Weltfreund* great poetry,[30] I would like to say that it is not, although there are without question good moments in it. Werfel's early poetry is for the most part appealing *Gedankenlyrik*. The work that spoke so successfully to a generation did so for one reason, and for one alone—its offer of friendship, its resounding joy and optimism, its irrepressible "Seid umschlungen, Millionen" mentality, which made Werfel the sounding board of the longings of his contemporaries. It is no wonder that Karl Kraus, in one of his most amusing polemical thrusts, called Werfel "the other Schiller."[31] Metaphysically, then, Werfel was a leading intellectual from the very beginning. But poetry also has a physics; its depth lies to a great extent on the surface, and it is this dimension that Werfel was not able to master. Reading diligently through the well over six hundred pages of *Das lyrische Werk*, one has the impression of overwhelming doggerel. Werfel's verse has been praised for its musicality, and it is true that Werfel had formidable knowledge of music and used this knowledge in his work. But the music of poetry is not the same as the music of music; in fact, they have very little to do with each other. It is a disturbing but illuminating thought that Werfel's talent as a lyric poet is primarily that of the librettist. This talent continues into the (early) verse plays, *The Noon Goddess* and some of *Spiegelmensch* (Mirror Man, 1920). The propensity in poetry and in the early plays to do opera is yet one more sense in which Werfel may be said to have an Austrian baroque gift.[32] This too is one reason why it is not fair to try to compare his poetry with that of Trakl or even with the Rilke of *Das Stundenbuch* (1905). It is highly significant that Werfel's last activity, just before his death, was the editing of a retrospective selection of his poems; he was weeding and revising for all he was worth.

Werfel was an excellent weeder of his own work. In the prefatory remarks to volume 1 of the plays in the *Gesammelte Werke,* the editor, Adolf D. Klarmann, is puzzled as to why Werfel was so highly selective in the first collected edition of his plays, brought out by Paul Zsolnay Verlag in 1929. "Why, one asks, did the poet exclude works that had helped carry his name through the world? *Mirror Man,* or *Goat Song,* or *Schweiger?*"[33] Klarmann's answer, namely, that to Werfel these early plays seemed too drab and expressionistic, has some truth in it, but it is only a partial answer. Certainly by 1929 Werfel had long since made his break with expressionism, and he had already profited richly from what the *neue Sachlichkeit* (new objectivity) had taught him. But behind this reply there is a far simpler and more forceful one— he simply no longer considered these early efforts good enough. And he was right. By then he had written such solid and lasting works as the historical prose plays *Juarez und Maximilian* (1924) and *Paulus unter den Juden;* the following year, 1930, was to see the publication of a third historical play, *Das Reich Gottes in Böhmen* (The Kingdom of God in Bohemia), not to mention the fact that by 1929 he had also made his major foray into the novel, with *Barbara oder die Frömmigkeit.* There is a great deal of truth in the suggestion that Werfel the dramatist relieves Werfel the lyric poet, as toward the end the novelist relieves the dramatist.

The year 1924 is critical in Werfel's career. His new publisher, Paul Zsolnay, to whom he went over from Kurt Wolff, brought out both *Juarez und Maximilian,* the first of the historical plays, and *Verdi: Roman der Oper* (Verdi: A Novel of the Opera). In the former, the noisy playfulness and lyrical bathos give way to the se-riousness and silence of prose; in the second, the frustrated musician in the writer points the way to the fulfilled narrative artist. Not that *Verdi* is Werfel's greatest novel; but it is a milestone, all the more so since it calls attention to all else that Werfel did to further, in fact establish, Verdi's stature among opera audiences in German-speaking countries.[34] *Verdi* also tells a gripping story, that of the composer concerned with communication and melody, caught between the monumental ego of Wagner and the coming twelve-tone aesthetic.[35] One step higher, *Juarez und Maxi-milian* is a masterpiece, one of the few works on which Werfel's claim as a major artist rests. An extraordinary probing study of the character of Maximilian, a sensitive and idealistic soul whom the French set up as emperor of Mexico against his will, the play is also a tour de force of stage effects. Many of its thirteen scenes are set in different locales, and the peculiar combination of the European and the exotic, the Hispanic and the Germanic, the old order and the new, not infrequently reminds us of moments in Schiller's *Don Carlos,* Goethe's *Egmont,* or Grillparzer's *König Ottokar.* Yet Werfel's contribution—strict economy of dramatic means, spareness of language, probing characterization, depiction of female heroism (in the person of Princess Agnes Salm)—remains his own. *Paul among the Jews* is of comparable quality, although it is but part of a planned trilogy never completed.

Surely the last of Werfel is also some of his best, and this holds for the last play, *Jakobowsky and the Colonel,* as it does for the novels. Werfel the artist is in good measure Werfel the mature novelist, author of *The Pascarella Family, The Forty Days of Musa Dagh,* and *The Song of Bernadette.* John Simon can call these works "prolix blockbusters" if he wants to;[36] I maintain that here, if anywhere, the religious philosopher and the verbal artist meet. Thomas Mann's condescension in particular toward *Bernadette* is well known. We are invited to immerse ourselves in the ways in which the world of Bernadette comes close to us. François Soubirous's silver watch, in the first paragraph, glows in the dark. He no longer has it—it belongs to the pawnbroker—and yet it is there. That is miracle number one. Later, in chapter 2, the artist lets the village postmaster express an idea that summarizes Werfel's entire metaphysical position: "Our good fortune comes from God. . . . Our ill fortune comes from ourselves, my friend."[37] An understated sentence or two, and we are inside this world. We are taken beyond Coleridgean suspension of disbelief. The faith that is the theme of this novel becomes an overriding metaphor of the method of the artist.

Those who judge Franz Werfel to be a good writer and also a bad one, who say that his work is very uneven and that next to the best-sellers the nuggets are buried under much dross, are of course right. There were many talented writers around Werfel, and it is not difficult to find achievement superior to his in almost every genre, even if for our comparisons we do not go to such stars as Rilke, Brecht, and Mann. But in Werfel's case the issue of literary stature tells only half the story. Werfel remains of interest to us because he was himself a fascinating personality—outgoing, verbal, improvisatory, eager for new faces and ideas—and because he had the capacity to react to all the important happenings of his time, artistic, intellectual, religious, political. It is no accident that his life reads like a chapter in a cultural history of the golden epoch in Central Europe between the two world wars, of which in fact he is a key figure. One additional salient feature of Werfel as a writer and intellectual is that his subjects came to him. To a degree a magpie of glittering themes, Werfel was at all times also the lucky player, one for whom the cards arranged themselves with compelling logic.

One closing thought on his interesting surname: it conjures not only *Würfel,*

Bust of Franz Werfel, placed in 1990 to commemorate the centenary of his birth. The marker reads, "In this house was born, on September 10, 1890, the poet and writer Franz Werfel, friend of the world."

"dice," but also *Entwurf*, "plan, sketch, draft"; the noun comes from *werfen*, "to throw." As the potter throws his form in clay, so the artist sketches his design. It may just be possible that the Great Artificer only designed this man-child; he sketched but never came to be finished with him. We will never be finished with Franz Werfel either.

## Notes

1. See Peter Stephan Jungk, *Franz Werfel: A Life in Prague, Vienna, and Hollywood*, trans. from the German by Anselm Hollo (New York: Grove Weidenfeld, 1990), 3. For encouragement and valuable assistance with this essay I would here like to express my thanks to Professor Ladislav Matejka, editor of *Cross Currents;* Professor Harry Zohn, of Brandeis University; and Mr. Gregor Hall, associate editor at Grove Weidenfeld. Mr. Hall had the kindness to send me a copy of Mr. Jungk's book before it was available for purchase.

2. Alma Mahler-Werfel, *Mein Leben*, with a foreword by Willy Haas (Frankfurt-am-Main: Fischer Taschenbuch Verlag, 1963), 74.

3. See Jungk, *Werfel*, 3–4 (family's circumstances, Barbara), 4 (church and synagogue), 8, 27 (Angelo Neumann), 13 (Caruso).

4. Ibid., 9 (illness, truancy), 9–10, 14 (repeats third form of gymnasium).

5. Ibid., 34–35 (meeting with Rilke), 16–17 (Maria Glaser, friends), 17–18 (Willy Haas's encouragement), 18 (debut in *Die Zeit*), 27 (first appearance of *Der Weltfreund*), 35–36, 41–42 (falling out with Karl Kraus).

6. Ibid., 27; 24 (ruins glove), 24–25 (fired from Hamburg shipping firm), 26–28 (year with artillery).

7. Ibid., 30–31 (job with Kurt Wolff), 32–33 (Der jüngste Tag series), 33 (writers whom Werfel published in the series), 31 (friends he met at Leipzig), 31–32 (empathy with Goethe and Lessing). On the Der jüngste Tag series, see also Paul Raabe, H. L. Greve, and Ingrid Grüninger, eds., *Expressionismus. Literatur und Kunst, 1910–1923*, Sonderausstellungen des Schiller-Nationalmuseums, 7 (Marbach-am-Neckar: Schiller-Nationalmuseum, 1960), 171–175 (catalogue no. 83).

8. The play was first published in *Herderblätter* [sic] 1, no. 3 (May 1912): 1–13, and is reprinted in Rolf Italiander, ed., *Herder-Blätter. Faksimile-Ausgabe zum 70. Geburtstag von Willy Haas* (Hamburg: Freie Akademie der Künste, 1962). See also Adolf D. Klarmann, "Zu Werfels 'Besuch aus dem Elysium,'" in *Herder-Blätter*, ix–xii. On Werfel's military service tours in Galicia and elsewhere, see Jungk, *Werfel*, 40–55; also 41 (respect shown by superiors), 41–42 (no time spent in trenches), 46 (assignment as telephone operator), 42, 47, 53 (chance to write while on duty).

9. Jungk, *Werfel*, 36 (on *Die Troerinnen*, its timeliness, and on Euripides as "a harbinger, . . . an early dove of Christianity"), 42–43 (reads Dante and other early Christian writers), 36 (on Werfel's "sense of home" at this time).

10. On the story of Werfel's leg injury and of his meeting Gertrud Spirk, see ibid., 42–44, 45–64 passim.

11. Ibid., 53; On Werfel's metaphysically directed luck, see ibid., 54: "He had hardly left Hodóv, traveling west, when the building in which he had lived and worked as a telephone

operator for months suffered a direct hit from Russian artillery and was completely destroyed." Also ibid., 51 (Kessler helping Werfel).

12. Ibid., 58–60; also 56 (comes to Vienna in midsummer heat), 56 (long hours at the Press Bureau), 56–57 (makes new friends at the Café Central), 58 (Franz Blei).

13. See Kokoschka's painting *Die Windsbraut* (The Tempest, 1914), now hanging at the Kunstmuseum, Basel, in which the features of the two lovers are clearly recognizable. Reproduced in color in Ludwig Goldscheider, *Kokoschka* (London: Phaidon, 1963), plate 16, and p. 76 (artist's note); also p. 20. A black-and-white reproduction is in Karen Monson, *Alma Mahler, Muse to Genius: From Fin-de-Siècle Vienna to Hollywood's Heyday* (Boston: Houghton Mifflin, 1983), fourth plate following p. 188. On the tempestuous affair, see Monson, *Alma Mahler,* 142–161. On Alma's background, see Jungk, *Werfel,* 58.

14. Jungk, *Werfel,* 24 (Werfel hears premiere of Mahler's Eighth Symphony), 58 (Alma sets Werfel's "Der Erkennende" to music).

15. Ibid., 86 (Alma divorces Gropius), 122 (marries Werfel in a civil ceremony, July 8, 1929), 60–65 (Alma and Franzl live together), 65–66 (birth of their son), 74 (boy's hydrocephalic condition), 76 (his death), 67 (*Die Mittagsgöttin*), 85–88 (*Bocksgesang*), 67–68 (triangle), 67 (Gropius reads Werfel's work).

16. Ibid., 76.

17. Ibid., 74; cf. 81: Alma had "transplanted him into monkish isolation." See also 70 (Gropius "boring"), 192 (sage advice from Alma on choice of subjects).

18. See Monson, *Alma Mahler,* 279.

19. On November 12, 1918, see Jungk, *Werfel,* 71–72; on Kisch, see ibid., 71.

20. Ibid., 140. The book was *The Forty Days of Musa Dagh.* Werfel's attempt to reach an understanding with the Nazis was in vain; on May 10, 1933, he became a "burned author," along with Freud, Marx, Kisch, Schnitzler, Zweig, and others (ibid., 141). See also ibid., 49–50, 108 (on Brod and Buber).

21. Franz Werfel, *Das Lied von Bernadette* (Stockholm: Bermann-Fischer Verlag, 1941), 9 ("Ein persönliches Vorwort"). On *Barbara oder Die Frömmigkeit,* see the perceptive analysis in Lionel B. Steiman, *Franz Werfel, The Faith of an Exile: From Prague to Beverly Hills* (Waterloo, Ont.: Wilfrid Laurier University Press, 1985), 45–55 (chap. 5, "Alma and Barbara").

22. Jungk, *Werfel,* 150, 152–153 (Manon's illness and death from polio), 89, 104 (Casa Mahler, Venice), 104–105 (Alma's economic expectations), 93 (public, rather than critical, success of *Schweiger*).

23. Ibid., 131.

24. Ibid., 126; also 132–133, 151 (parties at Hohe Warte), 132–133 (envy on the part of Schnitzler's mistress), 131, 151–152 (Werfel not comfortable there), 162 (parting with Hohe Warte). On the last party at Hohe Warte and the move back to Breitenstein, see Monson, *Alma Mahler,* 248.

25. Steiman, *Faith of an Exile,* 65. On Werfel's politics, see also 57–65 (chap. 6, "Alma and Franz: Political Counterpoint"), 67–73 (chap. 7, "Poetry and Politics: Werfel between the Wars").

26. Jungk, *Werfel,* 126–127. See also 106–108 (first trip to Middle East), 109–110 (writing of *Paulus unter den Juden*), 122–123 (meeting with Tina Orchard at Santa Margherita), 123, 130–131 (writing of *Die Geschwister von Neapel*).

27. On the research for and writing of *Die vierzig Tage des Musa Dagh,* see ibid., 127, 128–129, 137–139, 142–143, 144. See also 154–155 (exiled Armenians feting Werfel in New York and Paris), 147, 207 (Turks prevent filming of *Musa Dagh*).

28. On the Werfels' first trip to the United States and on the production of *The Eternal Road* in New York, see ibid., 149–155. See also 154 (success of *Musa Dagh* in the U.S.), 117 (Werfel and Alma meet Hauptmann), 162 (Werfel and Joyce meet in Paris).

29. On the worsening of the political situation since 1934, see ibid., 148–156 (the chapter entitled "Bad Tidings"); on the *Anschluss* and on the arrest of Kurt von Schuschnigg, see 169–170. See also 170–193 (the Werfels' escape), 195–196 (California), 196–198 (Werfel writes *Bernadette*), 201–203 (U.S. publication and sales), 207 (filming), 209–210 (the Werfels' move to Beverly Hills), 206 (writing of *Jakobowsky und der Oberst*), 211–227 passim (*Stern der Ungeborenen*), 228–229 (Werfel's death), 229 (funeral).

30. See Fred Wagner, "'Das herrliche Verhängnis': The Poetry of Franz Werfel," in Lothar Huber, ed., *Franz Werfel: An Austrian Writer Reassessed* (Oxford: Berg Publishers, 1989), pp. 37–54. Wagner does not seem to realize that "to assess the impact of Werfel's early poetry on the audience of his day" (37) is not the same as to assess the quality of the poems as poems.

31. Jungk, *Werfel*, 48.

32. This gift is especially stressed by Paul Stöcklein in his essay "Franz Werfel," in Hermann Friedmann and Otto Mann, eds., *Deutsche Literatur im 20. Jahrhundert. Strukturen und Gestalten*, 2 vols., 4th ed., exp. and rev. (Heidelberg: Wolfgang Rothe Verlag, 1961), 2:226–244, 227–233.

33. Adolf D. Klarmann, "Vorbemerkung," in Franz Werfel, *Gesammelte Werke*, ed. Adolf D. Klarmann, vol. 1, *Die Dramen* (Frankfurt-am-Main: S. Fischer Verlag, 1959), 7.

34. Werfel prepared German translations of *La Forza del Destino, Don Carlo*, and *Simone Boccanegra*; see Jungk, *Werfel*, 115.

35. See R. S. Furness, "A Discussion of *Verdi: Roman der Oper*," in Huber, *Werfel*, 139–151. For a warning on important differences between the Verdi of Werfel's conception and the historical figure, see Walter H. Sokel, *The Writer in Extremis: Expressionism in Twentieth-Century German Literature* (1959; Stanford, Calif.: Stanford University Press, 1968), 228–229.

36. See John Simon, "Loves and Torments of a Man-Child" (review of *Franz Werfel: A Life in Prague, Vienna, and Hollywood*, by Peter Stephan Jungk), *New York Times Book Review*, April 29, 1990, 15.

37. Werfel, *Das Lied von Bernadette*, 13 (silver watch), 19 (postmaster's wisdom). That the postmaster should be given words Werfel deeply believes in seems logical since in a sense the novel is a self-portrait. Sokel states, "By writing a novel in a style as simple, naive, and conventional as that of *Bernadette*, and utilizing a theme made for capturing the imagination of millions of readers, Werfel successfully emulated his ideal of the artist set forth in *Verdi*" (*Writer in Extremis*, 228). For a brief but penetrating discussion of the interfaces between Werfel's personal character and his work, see Heinz Politzer, "Franz Werfel: Reporter of the Sublime," in Lore B. Foltin, ed., *Franz Werfel, 1890–1945* (Pittsburgh: University of Pittsburgh Press, 1961), 19–25. I would like to express my indebtedness to the very helpful primary bibliography of Werfel's work included at the end of that volume: Frank McGowan, "Bibliography, Works Published 1911–1950," 96–102.

Dan Kulka sculpting *Franz Kafka* (1967). Courtesy of Erich Kulka.

# Dan Kulka Remembered

## FRANK MEISSNER

Dan Kulka was born on May 2, 1938, in Zlín, Moravia, to Olga and Milan Kulka. His Jewish father died in a German concentration camp, and Dan, with his mother and his sister Lia, survived World War II hiding in the rough Beskyd Mountains. His paternal uncle Erich and his cousin Otto were among the few who miraculously survived the Auschwitz concentration camp and returned home in May 1945, when Dan was seven years old. Erich later married Olga, his brother's widow, and adopted Dan and Lia.

In 1951 the Kulkas moved to Prague, where Dan finished his secondary education in 1953 to become a mason plasterer apprentice at the State Training Center of Kladno, a steel mill town in Central Bohemia. Between 1955 and 1959 Dan studied at the School for Plastic Art in Prague. His studies were followed by military service from 1959 to 1961. Subsequently he spent six years (1961–1967) at the College for Applied Art in Prague and worked part-time for the State Film Studio in Barandov and for the National Theater in Prague. In 1967 Dan was awarded the degree of academic sculptor (akademický sochař).

In 1962 he made his first trips abroad and visited his older half-brother Otto (Dov) in Israel, with stopovers in Austria, Greece, and Italy. In 1966 he traveled in East Germany.

During the Prague Spring of 1968, when Prime Minister Alexander Dubček attempted to put a "human face" on socialism, many Czechoslovak intellectuals tried to reintegrate culture and art into the life of Czechoslovak society. The fateful year 1968 became a watershed in Kulka's career. That year a first exhibition of his works was arranged at the Academy of Fine Arts in Prague and at the Municipal Museum of Brno; he won a competition for a bust of Franz Kafka, which is now at the Museum of Literature in Prague; he designed the trophy for the best television journalist of the year; and he made visits to Belgium, England, France, and West Germany.

The beautiful dream about socialism with a human face evaporated after the invasion of Czechoslovakia by the "fraternal nations" of the Warsaw Pact. The invasion was followed by persecution and arrests. People called it a "Biafra of the spirit."

Rape (1968). Courtesy of Erich Kulka.

It caused a massive exodus of artists and intellectuals. These events inspired Kulka to sculpt *Rape*, which in its intensity of expression constitutes a peak in his creativity. Two figures—a man raping a woman—are hewn out of wood with a rough ax. Their features are twisted into bitter grimaces. Brute force and fear are expressed with shocking eloquence.

In August 1968 the Kulka family left Czechoslovakia for Israel to join Otto. For a short period Dan worked as a restorer at the Austrian Authority for Preservation of Treasures of Art, in Vienna. But in November 1968 he left for Canada, where

*Yom Kippur War* (1973). Courtesy of Erich Kulka.

he hoped to settle. Together with other Czech artists Dan organized a joint exhibition at Toronto's Pollock Gallery in 1969 and began to teach sculpture at the College of Art in Toronto.

Despite his enormous output during that period, Dan remained troubled by the loss of his homeland and the cultural atmosphere he had been accustomed to. He felt separated from the tradition that had nurtured him and from the security of his large family now living in Israel. Tormented by loneliness, he began to question the purpose of life and suffered clinical depressions.

He recovered gradually and was awarded a commission from the Collingwood Recreation Center in Toronto. There he created abstract colored ceramic reliefs and a series of huge terra-cotta chess figures. Although he seemed to be on the way up, he continued to be plagued by pathological concerns about his ability to survive. From the hospital Dan wrote his father about his difficulty distinguishing dreams from reality and about his fears that his letters were being intercepted and his telephone conversations tapped.

In 1970 Dan decided to leave Canada and join his family in Israel. There he added painting to his artistic repertoire. While the scope of Dan's work expanded considerably, the basic mood did not change. In spite of all his experiments, his emotional as well as artistic zigs and zags, he remained faithful to the humanist tradition

*Franz Kafka* (1967). Courtesy of Erich Kulka.

of Central Europe. In fact, the link became more conscious and articulate. Dan evidently wanted to make a commitment to the values brought to Israel by the many immigrants who had come from Central Europe during the 1930s and 1940s.

Early in 1971 Dan went to Kibbutz Degania, on the shores of the Sea of Galilee, to experience the local atmosphere and landscape. In a letter to friends in Canada Dan wrote, "I spent a week on a kibbutz and then drove to Jerusalem on a newly opened road along the Jordan River. It leads through a very interesting landscape. The rocks are stratified in a way that we used to see in Gothic paintings, and they reminded me too of our chessboard. This stratification changes along the way and is replaced by gigantic boulders and cliffs hanging together with little caves in between."

With the help of his family he tried to establish himself in Jerusalem. In 1972 he had a one-man exhibition at Jerusalem's Artist's House. He began to research biblical themes and Jewish history and sculpted *Samson*. In 1974 he received his first commission for an open-air work. He made a bronze sculpture of a donkey for a kindergarten in the Neve Yaacov District of Jerusalem. This was followed by *Flight* for the Gilo District and by *Germination* for Ramot, works that brought him critical acclaim. The Yom Kippur War of October 1973 inspired Dan to paint and sculpt several works on the theme of tragedy and heroism.

In 1976 Dan married Hanna Engelberg, a professor of biology at the Medical School of the Hebrew University in Jerusalem. On the surface it seemed that Dan had finally "come home," settled, and found himself. These appearances were deceiving, however, and hid restless confusions and doubts. Tormented by the recurrence of mental illness, the remarkably talented Dan Kulka died on August 10, 1979, at the age of forty-one, by taking his own life.

František Langer.

# The Czech-German-Jewish Symbiosis of Prague

## The Langer Brothers

AVIGDOR DAGAN

In the history of Czech literature usually only two pairs of brothers are cited, the brothers Mrštík and Čapek. In the case of a third fraternal pair, František and Jiří Langer, their being brothers has not been especially emphasized. This is due to the fact that in contrast to the Mrštíks and Čapeks, the Langers never wrote in collaboration. Moreover, their paths through life were so antithetical and their contributions to literature so divergent that even on repeated examination we would find nothing betraying some spiritual affinity or suggesting traces of common sources.

In a study written on the occasion of František Langer's sixtieth birthday in 1949 Edmond Konrád stressed the deep cleft created in his work by the First World War.[1] And indeed, this division is truly startling. Nothing that František Langer wrote after 1918 shows any trace of the neoclassical detachment that characterized the theme, structure, and atmosphere of his prewar plays *Svatý Václav* (Saint Wenceslas, 1912), *Noc* (Night, 1914) and *Miliony* (Millions, 1915).

Langer returned from the war a different person. He experienced life in the Austrian trenches in Bukovina, in Russian prisoner-of-war camps, and in T. G. Masaryk's Russian legions, finally returning home in 1920 via China, Japan, and India. The war and the Russian experience erased from his work its former intellectual detachment. It was replaced by human warmth, good-natured simple-heartedness, and a humorous folksiness, qualities that bordered at times on the sunny joviality of Ignat Herrmann or even Vojtěch Rakous, two Czech Jewish writers who appealed to all strata of readers.

The year 1923 marked the premiere of Langer's play *Velbloud uchem jehly* (A Camel through the Needle's Eye), his first work to gain international attention. In essence the play deals with the same subject he had already developed in *Miliony*. Langer's subsequent work was characterized by a simplicity and interest in the everyday life of common people. These qualities are evident in *Předměstské povídky* (Suburban Tales, 1926). They provided the impetus for Langer's most powerful play, *Periferie* (The Periphery), written in 1925. This drama was stimulated by the Russian classics, which Langer enthusiastically read as a prisoner of war and as a soldier in the Czech legions in Russia. The influence of Dostoevsky, particularly *Crime and Punishment,* became especially strong.

*Periferie* was the first of Langer's plays in which the author became preoccupied with the problems of wrongdoing, guilt, conscience, repentance, and redemption. In this first creative struggle with the problems of evil, however, Langer was not capable of arriving at a fully satisfactory solution. It was for that reason that he accepted the suggestion of the famous stage director Max Reinhardt to change the ending. Hence there are two versions of *Periferie:* the second has a conciliatory but ethically questionable ending; the original is perhaps less believable but at the same time more honest. Josef Träger wrote about the original version, "In the very first Prague performance the ending was not entirely convincing. . . . It created a contrived effect that was contrary to the spirit of the drama and left the audience with a sense of dissatisfaction."[2] Commenting on the performance of the second version in Tel Aviv in Hebrew translation, Max Brod remarked, "The new ending is more logical and far more satisfying."[3] By contrast, Alfred Polgar, who saw Reinhardt's production in Vienna, wrote, "The new ending that František Langer gave to the play is more pleasant yet more superficial."[4] The judgment of Josef Kodíček was probably closest to the truth: "It is a pity that the author does not end the play at the point of its poetic and philosophic peak."[5] It is interesting that Langer always insisted on the original version when the play was performed in a Czech theater.

*Periferie* became world-renowned. In fact, František Langer was the only contemporary Czech dramatist other than the Čapeks to win recognition abroad. Yet he himself was aware of a certain unresolved problem in the drama. As early as 1925 he remarked somewhat apologetically, "When I started *Periferie* there was still too much of Russia in me."[6]

But this sense of inadequacy was hardly the only reason why Langer kept returning to the problem of crime and punishment and to the problem of conscience in particular. He did it always in a new way and from a different viewpoint. It is characteristic of Langer's work that he produced pairs of plays on the same theme, whether intentionally or in response to a subconscious motivation. Likewise the tragic drama *Periferie* gave rise four years later, in 1929, to its counterpart, the comedy *Obrácení Ferdiše Pištory* (The Conversion of Ferdiš Pištora). A similar link exists between two of the later plays, *Dvaasedmdesátka* (Number Seventy-Two, 1937) and *Jiskra v popeli* (Spark in the Ashes, written in 1938 but produced only after the Second World War, in 1948). In this pair of plays Langer used the play-within-a-play technique with admirable virtuosity. But he also kept returning to questions of conscience, as in the dramatic legend *Andělé mezi námi* (Angels among us, 1931) or the play about the Czech legionnaires in Russia, *Jízdní hlídka* (Cavalry Patrol, 1935) and in a quite different way in Langer's last and until now unperformed verse drama *Bronzová rap-sodie* (Bronze Rhapsody, published in 1962), set on the eve of the Trojan War.

František Langer was also an outstanding author of children's books. Langer loved children; he was the father of a son and daughter, and the most painful period of his life was when the communists arrested his son and released him only years later, in broken health.

## II

František Langer was a year younger than Josef Čapek and two years older than Karel Čapek. The friendship that bound them together was so intimate, and the paths they traveled were generally so close, that Langer could be considered the third member of this brotherhood. Philosophically, the starting point for Langer as well as for the Čapeks was pragmatism. In the case of the Čapeks it manifested itself in the form of intellectual schematization; Langer, on the other hand, employed a warm, human approach to problems, an approach that transcended cool logic. Yet the parallelism between these authors is in many ways quite far-reaching. It is not limited to the love of children, interest in ordinary people, and the enjoyment of gardens and the small things of life. Nor is the affinity restricted to love of the theater, the virtuoso mastery of theatrical technique, and the mutual fascination with the speech of common people. Sometimes we find characters in the work of Langer and Karel Čapek that are identical, at least conceptually. For example, the judge in *Periferie* speaks the same way as the kindly lord in *Krakatit*. Konrád remarked in this connection, "The development of the whole of Langer's work confirms the view that it is not a question of influence but of congeniality, of a similar disposition and temperament." The two friends would often talk together about themes that interested them and eventually work up the same material, such as Čapek did in *Továrna na absolutno* (Factory for the Absolute) and Langer in *Zázrak v rodině* (Miracle in the Family). Yet each of them would approach the same theme in a different way—Langer more idyllically, so to speak.

Indeed, in spite of the fact that murder is a theme that appeared in his work from the very beginning and to which he returned again and again (*Svatý Václav, Periferie, Dvaasedmdesátka*), Langer is basically an author with an idyllic disposition—or rather, an author who sees a totally unidyllic world around him but longs for the idyll and for peace. The theme of murder is always accompanied by that of repentance and the search for justice, judgment, and purgation, as is already manifest in his first play, *Svatý Václav*. There we find the theme of moral responsibility, to which he returned in various forms in every one of his works down to *Bronzová rapsodie*.

The same is true of another theme, that of the power of love and its ability to fill man with regenerative strength, already present in *Noc*. Vítězslav Nezval correctly identified what most concerned Langer in his life and work when he wrote, "Compassion for man . . . gratitude to man . . . love for man—these are the words pronounced by three of the figures in the play *Andělé mezi námi*. I would like to use them as an epigraph for the collected plays of National Artist František Langer."[7] Those three phrases would provide a fitting motto not only for Langer's work but for his life as well. The life and work of this great humanist was determined by simple warmheartedness and a forbearing optimism, along with the belief that there is a spark of goodness in every person. He cared more for human compassion and love than for his rank of general, his prominent position in the London exile during the Second World War, and the chestful of medals and titles that provoked the envy of others to the very time of his death in 1965.

## III

František Langer had two younger brothers. Josef, younger by two years, chose suicide in preference to transport to the Terezín concentration camp. It is not known whether he too had any literary gifts. But there can be no doubt about the talents of the second brother, Jiří, born six years after František.

Long before he could surprise anyone by the literary gifts that later became so evident, he amazed his family by an act that left no doubt about his unconventional uniqueness. The Langers lived the middle-class life of assimilated, religiously lukewarm Jewish families that attended the synagogue during holidays and contributed to charitable organizations but whose Jewishness was otherwise rather vapid. And yet it was precisely such a family that produced a young man—the healthiest and bravest of three sons, as the oldest was to remark years later—who at the age of fifteen already began to interest himself in mystical Jewish poetry; who immersed himself in religion and secretly learned Hebrew[8]; who freed himself from all worldly interests; and who in 1913, when barely twenty years old, suddenly picked up his valise and left for Galicia and the house of the Hasidic rabbi of Belz. When he returned half a year later, wearing a caftan that reached down to his heels, a black felt hat, and a rusty beard and sideburns, the horror of his family as described by František Langer resembled that of the Samsas in Franz Kafka's *Metamorphosis*, when they learned that Gregor had turned overnight into an enormous cockroach. It should be borne in mind that at this time František Langer had already received his university degree and was recognized as the successful author of *Saint Wenceslas*. It is thus easy to imagine the relief with which Jiří's family greeted his decision to return to Belz.

Shortly thereafter, however, the war broke out, and Belz was near the front. Jiří tried to save himself by fleeing to Hungary, but there he was conscripted and sent to

Jiří Langer.

a regiment in Prague. When František returned in 1915 for a short leave from the eastern front, where he served as a medic, he found Jiří in military prison. Jiří had refused to bear arms on the Sabbath and was awaiting a military court. The results might have been very serious. Fortunately, František managed to convince his fellow military doctors that Jiří belonged neither to prison nor to the army but to the mental hospital. Jiří was subsequently discharged as mentally ill and retired to Belz, where he remained until the end of the war. In 1918 Jiří decided to return to Prague, the capital of the newly established Czechoslovak Republic, of which he was a citizen. This time the circumstances of his return were somewhat different from what they had been five years earlier, but it proved to be no less surprising.[9]

When František Langer came back from Russia with the Czech legionnaires in 1920, he found Jiří "completely Europeanized"—in other words, without caftan or sideburns. And although he still observed dietary laws and other religious precepts and continued to live as a deeply devout Jew, he no longer was preoccupied exclusively with Hebrew writings. Just as he had once been fascinated by mysticism, he now seemed fascinated, even bewitched, by the works of Sigmund Freud and his disciples. František, whose mind was under the influence of his Russian experience and his reading of Dostoevsky, now had a subject he could discuss with his brother. This was so in spite of the fact that for František, Freud was merely an interesting phenomenon and psychoanalysis a "fantastic hypothesis," whereas for Jiří, Freud was the discoverer of a "scientifically valid axiom." Jiří now devoted himself to examining Jewish rites and customs by means of psychoanalytic methods, hoping to explore the subconscious roots of Jewish mysticism.

These studies gave rise to Jiří Langer's first book on the eroticism of the Kabala,[10] written in German and published in 1923. Two subsequent studies dealing with this subject,[11] published in *Imago,* the journal of the Freudian Psychoanalytic Society in Vienna, were also written in German. It should be noted that František Langer was a master of the Czech language, a writer unsurpassed in converting the Czech of common folk into dramatic dialogue, but not proficient in any language other than his beloved Czech. By contrast, his brother Jiří was a polyglot. He wrote and spoke Czech, German, Hebrew, and Yiddish, knew English and French, and insofar as we may rely on František's testimony, he also had excellent command of Aramaic.

Jiří Langer was fascinated by psychoanalysis, but it did not succeed in capturing all of his interest. In his essays based on Freud he "showed how eroticism is relevant even to the most spiritual laws and highest ethical teachings of the Jewish faith" (František's preface to Jiří's book *Nine Gates*). At the same time he wrote Hebrew verse, which he published in the collection *Poems and Songs of Friendship,*[12] the first Hebrew book published in Prague in a hundred years. He also started writing *Hasidic Legends,* which were gradually published from 1930 onward. And that was the beginning of the unique, and certainly most important, work of Jiří Langer.

František recounts how in the year 1935 Jiří brought him a bulky manuscript entitled *Nine Gates*. Jiří asked his older brother, an experienced writer, to take a look at the book and correct any stylistic shortcomings. František began to read the manuscript and was carried away by its originality. Then he read it a second time with an eye to style and found that "those legends exert such magic because they are told in such a magical and legendary way. Alas, the slightest change in tone, rhythm, lightness, simplicity, and turns of speech, in the choice and order of words, would result in a loss of the book's charm. The narrator combines naive sophistication, the basis of all Jewish anecdotes, with sophisticated naiveté, which is the hallmark of the greatest artists, including Heine and Chagall." František Langer characterizes his brother's book as a kind of "Hasidic Thousand and One Nights." *Nine Gates* is indeed quite different from anything else written in the Czech language, and its luster is just as bright as that of any pearl of world literature. In addition, it is probably the best extant literary picture of the captivating world of the Hasidim. Not only does it bear comparison with descriptions of that world by Martin Buber, but from a literary viewpoint it actually surpasses Buber.

After Jiří Langer's return from Belz there was still another turning point in his life. He went to Vienna for half a year, where he studied at the Hebrew pedagogical seminary. He returned as a Zionist—this scion of one of the founders of the Assimilationist Czech-Jewish Union.[13] He then began working part time as a teacher of religion at a Jewish school and as a functionary of the Central Union of the Zionist and Jewish National Fund in Prague. During this period of his life he also spent some time in sub-Carpathian Russia. In the vicinity of Mukačevo he organized a group of young Jews to go to Palestine who were preparing themselves for agricultural work. We know that around 1920 Jiří Langer himself considered emigration to Palestine. The attraction of Western culture was too strong, however; and in the end Jiří remained in Prague. He wrote for various Czech publications and became a regular contributor to *České slovo* (Czech Word), but his friends consisted primarily of a group of Prague Zionists; he was closest to Max Brod, Felix Weltsch, and Franz Kafka. Kafka mentioned him several times in his diaries, where he also recorded several Hasidic narratives that Langer had recounted to him. In fact, Langer and Kafka studied Hebrew together;[14] Felix Weltsch, who edited the German-language Zionist publication *Selbstweher*, published in his weekly Jiří Langer's numerous contributions, and Max Brod remained a close friend to the end of Langer's life.

In 1937, when the first Czech edition of *Nine Gates* appeared, Jiří Langer also published a selection of his Czech translations of Hebrew poetry from the eleventh to the nineteenth century.[15] The scope of the anthology was small; it was limited to a single poem by each of twenty-one poets, including the great Rabbi Loew. Yet it clearly reveals Jiří's poetic talent, whereas his postscript about Hebrew prosody and his remarks about the translated poets testifies to his broad education and profound scholarly knowledge. The small edition of his translations, entitled *Zpěvy zavržených*

(Songs of the rejected), was quickly sold out. A second edition came out in February 1939, hardly a month before Hitler's occupation of Prague.

In the fall of that fateful year Jiří Langer left occupied Prague for Slovakia, and from there he sailed illegally down the Danube to the Black Sea. After a few months of an arduous, adventure-filled journey that undermined his health, he landed in Palestine. He lived there for four years, suffering from ill health, and died of kidney disease in March 1943, at the age of forty-nine. He is buried in Tel Aviv.

During those last difficult years he was helped by his friends, old and new, especially Max Brod and Zalman Shazar, who subsequently became president of Israel. Shazar published Langer's Hebrew poetry in *Davar*, the leading Palestine daily of the time. It was primarily these two friends who were responsible for arranging publication in book form of Langer's last collection of verse, *Meat zori davar* (A Bit of Balm).[16] Shortly before his death Langer was able to see the galley proofs of this work.

Whereas the poems in Langer's first collection, published in Prague 1929, were written in the form of prayers or in the style of the old Spanish masters of Hebrew poetry, those of the later collection were written in the spirit and form of modern European poetry. These poems date from 1940 onward, and their themes are connected either with Palestine or with nostalgic recollections of the past. They clearly reflect Langer's introverted isolation and deep sense of loneliness. In fact, several of these poems disclose his homosexual leaning.

In spite of the effort of his caring friends, Jiří Langer died a bitter, exhausted, and broken man. Yet to the very end he remained a Hasid. According to Dov Sada, professor of Hebrew literature at the University of Jerusalem, who visited the dying poet in the hospital, Langer was firmly convinced that he would get well if only he could shake the hand of the rabbi of Belz.


## IV

The more carefully we follow the life and work of the Langer brothers, the more hopeless seems the task of finding a common denominator between them. Can one imagine a greater distance than the immensity that separates *Saint Wenceslas* from the Jewish mysticism of *Nine Gates*? Or the gap between such purely Czech plays as *A Camel through the Needle's Eye* or *The Conversion of Ferdyš Pištora* and the Jewish melancholy of Jiří Langer's last poems in Hebrew? Between the passionate desire of assimilation on the part of one brother and the Jewish consciousness and ultimate Zionism of the other? Between the agnosticism of František and the devout Jewish faith of Jiří? Between one of the most celebrated of Czech authors, an army general and a National Artist who died in Prague at a ripe age, and an obscure, not particularly successful Hebrew poet, who died at the age of forty-nine in poverty and loneliness in distant Tel Aviv?

Yet it is precisely Prague where the common denominator must be sought, in the unique, unrepeatable circumstances of that city, where three cultures—Czech, German, and Jewish—lived side by side, three peoples living under the constant pressure of symbiosis. The coexistence was not always peaceful; these cultures were often at each other's throat, yet they mutually fructified and enriched each other.[17] Much of the literature that arose in the framework of this symbiosis, whether Czech or German (and in the case of Jiří Langer even Hebrew) could have come into being nowhere else. Only in this unusual soil could the same garden produce such totally different flowers. With the Langer brothers, diversity even bloomed from one and the same stem.

František Langer asserted that the first person to stimulate Jiří Langer's interest in religious mysticism was his best friend, Alfred Fuchs. His family, like that of the Langers, was rather lukewarm in religious outlook, yet Fuchs exhibited a lively interest in religion from his earliest years. He was unusually gifted, and in his high school years he had already begun publishing articles and translations of German poetry in Prague journals. Fuchs and Jiří Langer immersed themselves in the study of Jewish mysticism. Supposedly they had even decided together to join the Hasids of Belz. In the end, however, Jiří Langer went off by himself because, in the meantime, Fuchs had discovered the work of Christian mystics, and their writings apparently influenced him more deeply than the books of the Jewish Kabalists. Subsequently Fuchs converted to Christianity and described the reasons for his spiritual development in his autobiographical novel *Oltář a rotačka* (The altar and the rotary press, 1930). He became a high functionary in the press division of the Czechoslovak government and in Rome was highly regarded as an expert in the field of Vatican diplomacy. He was awarded a number of decorations by the Vatican, yet shortly after the German occupation of Prague Fuchs was arrested as a Jew, taken to Dachau, and in 1941 tortured to death. The life of Fuchs, too, is an instructive chapter in the history of the Czech-German-Jewish symbiosis of Prague.

The unique composition of the Prague cultural soil seemed to have been destined to produce diverse fruit. To mention another example, a pair of writers started as crime and court reporters. One of them, Egon Erwin Kisch, wrote in German, whereas the other, Karel Poláček, wrote in Czech. Nobody surpassed those two in their knowledge of the Prague periphery, the Prague underworld, and the common people of the city in general. Both utilized their knowledge and journalistic experience for literary creation, but each did so in his own way. Kisch, a communist, stressed the social aspects; Poláček, a liberal from the generation of *Tribuna* and *Lidové noviny*, was more concerned with the everyday cares and joys of the average person. And yet there were so many points of contact between the two to the very end. Karel Poláček, who stayed in occupied Prague, was sent to Terezín and then to Auschwitz, where he died in 1944. The fiery Kisch traveled all over the world, spent the war years in Mexico, and then returned to Prague, where he witnessed the execution of some of his best friends condemned in the Prague Slanský trials manipulated by the Soviets.

Another prominent author who grew up in Prague is Max Brod. Brod's *Reubeni* and *Tycho Brahe's Road to God* are surely novels of lasting value. However, Brod often helped others at the expense of his own work. It was he who saved for posterity the work of his close friend Franz Kafka; he was also the first to make the world aware of composer Leoš Janáček and of Jaroslav Hašek, the author of *The Good Soldier Schweik*. Brod went on to live to old age in Israel, as have two of his and Kafka's close Prague friends: Hugo Bergmann, later rector of the Hebrew University in Jerusalem, and Felix Weltsch, a prominent Jewish philosopher.

In contrast to those Zionists who wrote in German, Josef Kodíček wrote in Czech and was fully assimilated in the Czech cultural world; like František Langer and Karel Poláček, he was a member of Karel Čapek's Friday salon, which was often visited by T. G. Masaryk, the first president of Czechoslovakia. Kodíček was an outstanding literary and drama critic, well known for his integrity and courage. He became one of the editors of the now legendary newspaper *Tribuna* and a dramaturgist of the Vinohrady Theater in Prague. During the war years he was in London, mainly active as a commentator in the Czech section of the BBC; he returned to Prague after the war but left again after the communist takeover. Subsequently he became the editor in chief of Radio Free Europe in Munich and died in his second exile.

The list of others who should be mentioned in this connection is long, even if we limit ourselves to the most important figures. For example, Franz Werfel, one of the prominent German poets of this century and an excellent novelist and dramatist, left Prague at the age of twenty. Although he was a young man at that time, there was still so much of the city within him that it was possible to make an accurate guess at which part of Prague was associated in his mind with a particular line of his poetry, even if the indications are not explicit. Much of the action of his novels takes place in Prague, so that Pavel Eisner was able to conclude, "Franz Werfel . . . could have come from no place but Prague. He is marked by Prague and by Czech spirituality even in parts of his work that show no trace of any direct thematic connection." [18] Werfel's "Czech spirituality" became especially meaningful in Werfel's drama about Prokop Holy, *The Kingdom of God in Bohemia*, and is felt even more strongly in *Barbara or Piety*, the apotheosis of an old nurse with whom Werfel remained in touch to the end of her life. In this book, as well as later in the poem "To an Old Servant," Werfel expressed what the simple Czech woman with her wise piety had meant to him, a woman who in real life was more important to Werfel than his own mother.

Pavel Eisner is also a product of the Prague Czech-German-Jewish symbiosis. This perfectly bilingual, unbelievably diligent translator and commentator probably expresses the symbiosis more strikingly than any other Prague author. Although he was born in the German-Jewish environment, this great linguist and lover of the

A broken tablet, with an inscription in Czech and Hebrew, from a Jewish cemetery in northern Bohemia.

Czech language captured the spirit of Czech with profound insight.[19] Hardly anyone has done more for the cause of Czech-German rapprochement than this humble builder of bridges. Still another product of the Prague symbiosis was Johannes (Jan) Urzidil, the son of a Jewish mother from the Czech environment and a Christian, German-speaking father with a Czech name. Urzidil, who wrote in German, was aware as much as anyone in the so-called Prague Circle of this symbiotic phenomenon. He turned to Prague again and again as the most fundamental and powerful experience of his life. In the novella *Prague Triptych*, probably Urzidil's best work of fiction, he portrayed the celebrated group of writers and poets who met regularly at the café Arco. He treated the Prague Circle once again in his book of recollections, *Here Comes Kafka*. Franz Kafka also became the main figure in his last group of stories, *The Abduction and Seven Other Occurrences*.

In fact, Kafka's testimony about the Prague symbiosis is the most eloquent of all. Even though his entire work contains only a single explicit reference to Prague (one nine-stanza poem), Kafka's work unquestionably bears the stamp of his Prague destiny. It is hardly imaginable that his work could have come into being anywhere but in Prague, anywhere but between the Týn Cathedral and Jewish district (Prague Five), between the Stone Bridge and the Street of the Alchemists, anywhere but in this continual religious and ethnic battleground, where Jews acted at times as the pointer of the scales balancing Czechs and Germans—and more often as a piece of paper between the two blades of a scissors. Sensitive Jewish intellectuals searched for a way to come to terms with this constant pressure or to escape it altogether. Some, like Alfred Fuchs, found—or hoped to have found—a solution in religious conversion; others, like Jiří Langer, in the ghetto of Jewish orthodoxy. Some, like Brod and Weltsch, looked for a solution in Zionism; others, like František Langer and Josef Kodíček, in full assimilation; still others, like Werfel, in leaving Prague, or like Kisch, in communism. Franz Kafka, the most deeply tormented of them all, chose a way inward, into himself, instead of a way out. Stumbling against rocks and hurt by their sharp edges, he found the universal truth that the deepest questions of man are beyond the reach of comprehension and that the weak are powerless against the strong.

The soil from which all this evolved was also the common soil of František and Jiří Langer. It was the Prague of the beginning of this century, when these brothers were growing up and when each of them could still choose his own path from tension to reconciliation. True, the brothers ended poles apart from each other. Yet when Jiří Langer, shortly before his death, wrote a mournful poem about the old Jewish cemetery of Prague, and when František Langer provided the postwar edition of his brother's book with a loving preface, it was once again Prague that bridged such almost insurmountable distances and resolved all conflicts and oppositions.

## Notes

1. Edmond Konrád, *Národní umělec František Langer* (Prague, 1949).

2. Josef Träger, postscript to *Periferie* (Prague, 1968).

3. Max Brod, *The Palestine Post* (Jerusalem), July 2, 1944.

4. Alfred Polgar, *Neue Freie Prese* (Vienna), June 2, 1927.

5. Josef Kodíček, *Tribuna* (Prague), February 28, 1925.

6. František Langer, "Jak vznikla Periferie," in *František Langer—divadelníkem z vlastní vůle* (Prague, 1958).

7. František Langer, *Tři vážné hry* (Prague, 1957).

8. Jiří Langer wrote, "I studied Hebrew during religious lessons and then secretly with an old rabbi." This appears in his Hebrew curriculum vitae from the year 1930, stored in the biographical Schwadorn collection in the library of the University of Jerusalem.

9. Preface to Jiří Langer, *Devět bran* (Nine Gates, ELK: Prague, 1937; rpt. Prague, 1937). Also published in German in 1959 and in English in 1961.

10. Georg [Jiří] Langer, *Die Erotik der Kabbala* (Prague, 1923). The second edition was published as *Liebesmystik der Kabbala* (Munich, 1956). Jiří Langer signed his Hebrew publications variously as Mordechai Georg, Mordechai Gergo, or Mordechai Dov Georgo Langer.

11. Georg Langer, "Zur Funktion der jüdischen Turpfortenrolle," *Imago* 14 (Vienna, 1931).

12. Mordechai Georg Langer, *Pijjutim veshirei yedidut* (Prague 1929).

13. See curriculum vitae from the year 1930.

14. Miriam Singer, *Hamoreh leivrit shel Kafka* (Kafka's Hebrew Teacher, Tel Aviv, 1969).

15. Jiří Langer, *Zpěvy zavržených* (Prague, 1937; 2d ed., 1939).

16. Mordechai G. Langer, *Meat Zori Davar* (Tel Aviv, 1943; 2d ed., 1984).

17. A number of authors have written about the peculiarities of this unique symbiosis. For example, Max Brod, *Der Prager Kreis* (Berlin, 1966); Pavel Eisner, *Milenky* (Prague, 1930); Bedřich Rohan, *Kafka wohnte um die Ecke* (Freiburg, 1986); Ernst Pawel, *The Nightmare of Reason: A Life of Franz Kafka* (New York, 1984).

18. Pavel Eisner, postscript to Franz Werfel, *Básně* (Poems), selected and translated by Viktor Fischl (Prague: Václav Petr, 1948).

19. See Pavel Eisner, *Sonety kněžně* (Sonnets to the Princess, 1945); *Chrám i tvrz* (Cathedral and Castle, 1946); *Čeština poklepem i poslechem* (Czech by Percussion and by Listening, 1948).

A demonstration of Czech-American friendship, Prague, July 6, 1948, protesting the recent Communist putsch. Photograph by Jan Lukas.

# T. G. Masaryk

A Radical Feminist

## H. GORDON SKILLING

Tomáš Garrigue Masaryk was preeminent among men in Bohemia in the late nineteenth century as an advocate of women's rights. One scholar has gone so far as to say that he was "the only Czech male intellectual concerned and involved with the woman's question for almost three decades."[1] Certainly Masaryk spoke out boldly and in radical tones against the enslavement of women in all spheres of life, including the home and family. In speeches and articles and in his journal, *Naše doba* (Our Time), he hammered away at what he considered false beliefs about the inequality of women and criticized unjust limitations on women's place in society. In a manner that endorsed the major claims of the contemporary women's movement and anticipated many of the demands of the feminist movement of the future, he called for absolute equality for women in all spheres—equal responsibility of men and women within the family, equal access to education and the professions, equal pay for equal work, the enfranchisement of women, and full participation of women in public affairs. He condemned prostitution and what he called polygyny (*mnoho-ženství*), that is, sexual relations with more than one wife or with several women. He was severely critical of prevalent views about the nature of love and of sex expounded both by official Catholic doctrine and by socialist theory, which, he felt, demeaned women and distorted love and marriage, and condemned ideas expressed in modern literature, which encouraged sexual laxity. Alois Hajn, active in contemporary Czech progressive politics, later described him as "a pioneer of the ideas on the women's question" whose words created "a veritable revolution among Czech youth" at the time.[2]

In the forming of Masaryk's viewpoint on the women's question a number of influences were at work. The first was the position of women in Bohemian society during the latter part of the nineteenth century. Women suffered many liabilities, such as an inferior place in the family, discrimination in the economic sphere, limitations on educational opportunities, denial of the franchise, and discouragement from participation in public affairs, not to mention prevailing opinions that women were inferior to men and should rightly suffer inequality. Nonetheless, from the 1870s on, women's associations were formed, and a strong women's movement came into existence. By 1900 women were able to secure education at all levels, enter the professions, and participate to a limited degree in public life. By 1914 women had already begun to advance toward emancipation to a greater extent than in other parts of the Austrian Empire.[3] At the turn of the century, however, when Masaryk concerned himself with the question, there was still much to be done to achieve genuine equality of men and women.

More direct and personal was the influence exerted by his wife, Charlotte Garrigue Masaryk, who was a strong advocate of women's rights and participated in the women's movement. During their brief courtship, in Leipzig, the couple had often read together and had been greatly attracted by the ideas expressed by John Stuart Mill in *The Subjection of Women* (1869). Charlotte later translated this book into Czech. After their marriage Masaryk adopted Charlotte's maiden name as his middle name and later gave it to each of his children. During their years of life together Charlotte worked in close cooperation with Masaryk in his social and intellectual activities and is said to have left many "traces of her spirit" in his writings and in his plans. Hajn later wrote that Charlotte had been not only "a wife but a helper and collaborator in all his life's work, a close friend and comrade."[4] Masaryk himself later declared that his views on women had been "determined by the living model of my wife; she had been the most decisive influence on the maturing of all my views and on my character." One of his major statements on the women's question, *Mnohoženství a jednoženstyí* (Polygyny and Monogyny), he said was "as a matter of fact my wife's work."[5] He was once quoted as saying that in the women's question "I am only a peddler of my wife's opinions."[6]

Inseparable from this view was the influence on Masaryk of his domestic life and his strong personal beliefs. In one of his earliest writings he stated that the family was "a real school of love for one's fellow man" and of "altruism and work." He laid special stress on the role of the mother: "mother love is actually the basis of all human society."[7] Masaryk himself spoke of the impact on his own life of his mother and of his wife. He told Karel Čapek of the great influence of his mother, a "wise" and "devout" woman; he also said of Charlotte that "our whole marriage was cooperation."[8]

Many witnesses testified that Tomáš and Charlotte's life together was a model of a happy and harmonious marriage. One of his closest friends and admirers, Jan Herben, described the marriage as "rare and beautiful," undisturbed by serious conflict.[9] Their life together was devoted to common intellectual pursuits; they continued to read together and often played music and attended concerts. Charlotte took part in his student seminars at home and in discussions at gatherings of friends. Their apartments were modest, simply furnished and decorated. They usually had household help, but food was frugal and without luxuries. Masaryk himself did not drink or smoke after 1888. He imposed strict rules of dress and behavior on the children but was attentive to them, playing with them in the early years and enjoying social games and singing in the evening at home.[10] Masaryk worked every morning in his study and spent the afternoons walking, reading newspapers in cafés, and visiting his editorial offices. Charlotte looked after the household, devoting much time to the children and assisting her husband in his work.

Masaryk's family life thus seemed to be an embodiment of his own ideas of love, marriage, and the family. It is impossible to be sure how far the reality conformed to the nostalgic reminiscences of friends and Masaryk's personal memories. There is no evidence of serious conflicts within the family or between parents and children. But in 1916, when she was already afflicted by the illness that was to bring about her death a few years later, Charlotte, in a letter to her daughter Alice, then in prison, expressed dissatisfaction with her life in Prague. She had enjoyed a "nice traditional life" but had missed "the ability to think religiously."[11]

Both Alice and Olga, his daughters, devoted much of their lives to him. Alice had studied at the first women's gymnasium in Prague and had been the only woman medical student. During Charlotte's sickness and after her death Alice served as his hostess and support; she remained single. On her deathbed, however, she admitted that she had had a love affair early in life and regretted that she had not married.[12] Olga, who was by his side during the lonely years of exile, spoke of the "rare friendship" she enjoyed with her father and of the feeling of "complete freedom and openness" in her life in the family.[13] Masaryk's relations with his son, Jan, were perhaps less than happy since the latter left home and family as a young man and made a life for himself in America, but there is no evidence as to the cause of his departure.

Masaryk's trip to America in 1893 had a profound effect on his thinking about the place of women in society and in the home. During a visit to the small college town of Oberlin, Ohio, he was greatly impressed by the position of women, who had free access to all schools and studied at all faculties of the university, including even theology. They could act as preachers, could serve on school boards, and in some states had voting rights. He was affected by the general deportment of women, who were "freer, and hence men were freer there." No one would kiss a woman's hand as was the Czech custom at home, and she in return would not address a man with the greeting "my respects" (*má úcta*). Young women could talk with young men about matters of common interest, including politics. "All this is a new world," Masaryk said. This freedom "signified a higher cultural development, a higher moral level, a purer relationship between man and woman." He believed that in Bohemia there should be "greater freedom of thought; the woman would cease to be a slave (cook, housekeeper, wet-nurse, and concubine), and the man would cease to be the lord over the woman."[14]

## "The Women's Question"

Masaryk did not attempt a systematic scholarly study of the women's question. Apart from a few brief references in his works on suicide, the social question, and the Czech question, he expressed his views in several important speeches and articles that reflected not so much empirical research as his own philosophy and ideology as a believer in strict morality in personal and public life and in social justice, national equality, and democracy.[15] As he often stated, he considered the very term "the women's question" inappropriate, since this issue was but a part of broader social, cultural, and national questions.

The question of the place of women in society was, for Masaryk, first and foremost a moral one involving new attitudes on the part of both men and women. In reporting on the first women's congress in Prague in 1897, Masaryk asserted that "it is not enough merely to proclaim oneself a friend of women's emancipation. . . . It is necessary to give practical expression of this opinion in every aspect of life and in the most mundane affairs." This meant "a turning of one's whole life, a completely new way of looking at one's own 'I' and at human society. It meant a real inward revolution by which a person becomes a new person. Emancipation of women is the emancipation of men." It was thus necessary "to correct ideas previously rooted in our education and social atmosphere, both in men and women" and "to struggle inwardly, to learn to be just and thus less egoistic."[16]

Masaryk also expressed his belief that "the women's question and the social problem go hand in hand." If one "admits the principle of justice to woman, one certainly wishes justice in all of human life." In his essay "The Modern View of Women" he stated even more emphatically, "I have not spoken and do not like to speak of a women's question. Since there is not a women's question, there is not a merely men's question. It is a question of society. It is incorrect to pose men and women against each other—society, the nation, is millions of men and women, millions of individuals mutually linked in a single whole; there must be a common concern of man and woman that this should be an organic whole."[17] In the same essay Masaryk argued that the women's question was a part of the national question. He observed, "This modern effort of men and women is a necessary continuation in the work of national revival. Our revival will not be a reality as long as the Czech man, along with the woman, does not undergo revival, a spiritual, moral, and social revival. The modern Czech woman signifies for our small nation a doubling of our strength" (*Masaryk a ženy,* 67, 69).

Masaryk's views on women were intimately related to his belief in democratism. In an appeal to youth in 1906, Masaryk declared, "Democratism is first and foremost the equality of woman and man, mother and father, sister and brother."[18] In an undated statement quoted by Alois Hajn, Masaryk observed, "The women's movement is a product of democratism; women wish to be equal. The woman and the man form an intimate unity; there cannot be any talk of a women's question, just as there cannot be talk of a men's question. The women's question is not only a women's question, but it is also a men's question, a children's question—in a word, it is a cultural and a human question." [19]

## Theories of Inequality Rejected

Masaryk's intention, as he expressed it, was "to formulate in positive terms what seems to me a really modern progressive view of woman" and to express the essence of "this new opinion, this new life, this new world." This required the refutation of old views and prejudices and the destruction of myths about men and women, held equally by both sexes, as to the "enormous difference" between them, especially concerning the inferiority of women to men (*Masaryk a ženy*, 61, 85).

In the first place, women were not "weaker in intellect: our mothers and wives, as to capacity, profundity, and perceptiveness, do not think less nor worse than we men do. The proper care of a poorer household and everything connected therewith demands greater intellectual strain than activity in any office, university chair, or pulpit" (62). "Do you really think," Masaryk asked, "that a woman worker or peasant, professor, or official who brings up perhaps five children by the sweat of her brow, in performing this work, thinks less than her husband, some boring—or perhaps not so boring—scholar? A scholar who knows much, and knows how to make a living with his head, does not think as much as his plain wife, toiling away from morning to night, unseen by anyone" (85–86). Women, he noted, "did better than men at the university, and everywhere else" (72–73).

Women, he asserted, were not physically weaker than men. There *was* a "physiological difference"; by virtue of certain sexual functions (pregnancy, nursing) a woman was excluded for a time from a man's employment. Perhaps women were "muscularly" weaker, but even this condition should not be exaggerated. Yet it was doubtful that she was weaker as far as "nerves" go: "Bringing up several children, especially in poorer, or even straitened circumstances, demands much more nervous strength than a man's work in public service, instruction in schools, or anything else" (87, 62).

Nor did women have more "feeling" than men, who, it is said, were more devoted to cold reason, were rougher and less delicate. "We must especially get used to differentiating oversentimentality in novels from real feeling" (86), wrote Masaryk, even though such wives' tales were repeated in scientific books. "Just as in the case of men, there are women with deeper feeling and women without feeling. It is not true that a woman has in particular some kind of special feeling" (73).[20]

Women were also not morally superior. "A woman is not better, nor is she worse than a man; it all depends on the individual. Men and women develop to-gether from the beginning; they mutually influence each other everywhere and con-stantly, so that is not possible that the moral or the generally spiritual state of one or the other is lower or higher" (62). "Women and men are always together; there is such intimate contact among them that there cannot be such a difference" (86–87).

Nor were women more religious or more devout than men, who were supposed to be more rational. True, more women than men attended church, but this was be-cause the woman was excluded from social life, not because she was more devout. "While the man sits in the tavern, there is nothing else left for the poor soul." If she *is* more devout than man, Masaryk argues, "she, and not the godless man, ought to be a priest or a pastor" (73–74).

Masaryk also felt obliged to dispose of a number of myths concerning women and their role in society and the family, especially that of domesticity, which assumed that the woman in the household was cook and servant. Women were therefore dis-couraged or prevented from taking work outside the home. In Masaryk's view, the household would not suffer if the woman had outside employment. Many tasks, such as washing, ironing, and sewing, did not need to be performed in the house-hold, just as baking bread was no longer a necessity. There was even the possibility of having domestic cooperatives or large family houses with common heating and kitchens. The household was indeed sacred, but that condition did not require the woman to be a "domestic slave" or to be deprived of a career. There should be equal-ity within the household, as outside it. This parity would make the woman "spiri-tually independent" and would require her husband to respect her and treat her as an equal (71, 64, 163).

The opposite side of the coin was the escape of the man from home. Masaryk observed that although the father should share the task of caring for the children, he usually shifted the family responsibilities onto the wife. "Hardly has he come home than he goes out again into nonfamily life—let us say it openly—to the tavern. O, these horrible Czech taverns, which steal the husband and the father and destroy the sacredness of the family" (70–71, 66).

Another myth was that women were not able to compete equally in economic life. Masaryk regarded as totally false the ideas that women should not be forced to compete in the marketplace, since as "delicate creatures" they were not able to com-pete, and that work would destroy family life. If women were to earn a living them-selves, men would to an extent be relieved of responsibility and would have an easier position. Moreover, among peasants men and women worked equally, both in the field and at home; and among workers, too, the problem had been to a considerable degree resolved. Only in the middle class were there still conflicts about certain kinds of employment, such as in medicine, but the exclusion of women was groundless. In literature, there were outstanding women writers in all nations (64, 76, 87–89).

Another view Masaryk held to be erroneous was that the sexual instinct was more powerful and more important for men and that it must be satisfied. Like other instincts, this one, he asserted, should be placed under the control of reason; the more powerful the instinct, the more it must be mastered. It was quite untrue, he proclaimed, that sobriety harmed a person physically and spiritually (90–91).

## Equality for Women

For Masaryk "the inequality of women and men was not natural; it was not derived from the nature of things but developed historically. Just as in history fateful mistakes were often made, so the suppression of women was a mistake—and a very big one" (*Masaryk a ženy*, 63). Emancipation did not mean that the modern woman should conduct herself like a man and do what a man did. Imitating men in smoking and drinking, for example, was nothing but reactionary (67). It did mean, however, that if they *were* equal, "man and woman should and can have completely equal employment, except that women are directed to certain special employment by virtue of their sexual functions—that is, absolute economic equality, or better said, absolute equality of work" (87, 77).

This position demanded equality in other spheres, too. For example, in education women should have equal schooling, including admission to the university, and should be able to study in all disciplines, even medicine (115). Improved education would make women more independent and less likely to conclude unsuitable marriages. They would also make better mothers. Masaryk approved of coeducation, which had shown itself to be effective in the Department of Philosophy. Similarly, he asked why women should not be equally active in religion and the church (89).

A most important need was equality of women in public affairs and in politics, from which they had been more or less completely excluded. Masaryk affirmed that if in the name of domesticity, women are kept distant from public work, "we lower their horizons, deaden their energy, and waste their talents" (130). Absence from public life deprived a woman of ambition and public respect; participation would provide many sources of pleasure and would encourage her energy and strengthen her will. We should not, because there were bad sides to public life, distance women from it, but rather seek to reform it (77).

Women had an important "social task" to perform. "Women must understand the public and political tasks of the time, and like a man, and with him, dedicate themselves to public affairs" (64–65). As far as political life went, facts had shown that women knew how to be politically effective. "This involved much nervous energy because women, being subjected to special attention, had to perform better than men in public activity. Needless to say, every woman will not be active publicly, but would it be harmful to national life or to the family if half of the deputies in Austria were women?" (75–76).

## Love, Marriage, and the Family

Not surprisingly, Masaryk's consideration of the place of women led him to draw conclusions about the more personal side of life—love, marriage, the family, and sexual immorality. Although the concept of love, for Masaryk, referred to humanity in the broadest sense, he admitted that one could not love all equally. One must select the object of love among those closest to us—mother, father, brother, sister, wife, and children. "Closest is the wife to the husband, the husband to the wife. True love must sanctify effectively this most intimate relationship. The wife is completely equal to her husband; only physical difference should be recognized; she is weaker."[21]

Love, Masaryk said, must not be identified with the sexual instinct. "Real love is not a union of bodies, but of souls." He called love and marriage a union of independent souls, of healthy spirits in a healthy body. But today, asserted Masaryk, man finds a slave more pleasant. "Marriage is the beginning of common development and common work for the whole of life, for an eternity" (65). "Pure marriage is the most intimate friendship; it is the apex of association, an association of spirit. There cannot be a more intimate association than between man and woman" (90).

This kind of spiritual unity formed the basis of a moral family life. Family life was a "real school of love for those close to one"; it was a stimulus to altruism of father, mother, brother, and sister, so that "all would love each other equally and equally care for each other." The family was the "basis of character, in which the children learn and are trained." The father embodied authority, requiring obedience from children, but "it is on mother's love that all human society is actually based."[22]

It followed from such a conception of marriage and the family that divorce was not to be encouraged or permitted. Although Masaryk admitted that in some cases divorce was necessary and desirable, it should not be resorted to simply because a married couple were beginning to be bored. Everything should be done to avert divorce (96). He felt that a rise in divorce would simply encourage frivolous marriages. "Not divorce but purity—that must be the slogan of Czech youth. Preserve purity for marriage and you will be happy. Many marriages are unhappy because few men live purely before marriage. Divorce must not become a means of general legalized prostitution."[23]

A marriage of the kind advocated by Masaryk also involved "strict monogamy" of both wife and husband. This meant that "every man should have in his life only one wife and a woman only one man, of course, in a state of matrimony." Even a second marriage was contrary to this ideal. At the present time, Masaryk argued, monogamy existed more on paper than in fact; there was much polygyny, both after marriage in the form of prostitution and before marriage among young people. He called this condition "a social evil." Strict monogamy, he declared, must be the goal of human sexual evolution (79–80).[24]

## Sexual Immorality: Prostitution, Abortion, and Illegitimacy

Masaryk was a strong foe of prostitution, as a form of polygyny, as well as of adultery. In 1884, in one of his earliest writings, he rejected the idea that prostitution was a necessary evil or that it was mainly caused by penury. The primary cause was not physical, but moral, and was the result of failures in training and education, especially of women. The whole of modern life, and the bad moral atmosphere created by novels, the theater, ballet, and illustrated magazines, led to a precocious awakening of the sexual instinct. This trend, he held, was aggravated by alcoholism. Although prostitution was forbidden by law, it was a common sin in civilized society, an "impurity" weakening both the individual and the nation. Prostitution led to the degeneration of women and to an infection of society as a whole. Hand in hand with prostitution, he argued, went adultery, bigamy, lewdness, unmarried sexual relations, and the sexual abuse of children. It was an evil that could be fought against, like other moral evils, by improvement of moral training.[25]

More than twenty years later, in 1906, Masaryk was still fighting against prostitution and urging common action against impurity among the intelligentsia, especially the youth. There would not be *prostitutky* (female prostitutes), he said, if there were not also male prostitutes; the man should be blamed and punished as much as the woman. The main cause of prostitution was "the entire outdated moral opinion about women"; the only way to correct it was to recognize the equality of women.[26]

Masaryk lamented that prostitution was not much talked about and that neither church nor state did much to fight against it. Doctors, he felt, neglected to clarify such sexual issues, nor did politicians pay attention to them. However, he rejected "state prostitution," that is, regulation of prostitution by the state, which he said amounted to "state polygyny." The solution lay in moral self-help (*svépomoc*) by the family, the school, and the individual (92–93).

Masaryk was also firmly opposed to abortion except when recommended by doctors, and he rejected various reasons advanced for permitting it. Although forbidden by law, it was a common practice. Quite apart from the moral aspect, it did great harm to the woman and weakened her and society. Masaryk sought to judge the matter from a high moral standpoint according to the principle, "Even a life scarcely begun is life, and no one is justified in destroying it."[27]

At the same time Masaryk deplored the growing number of illegitimate births, believing that this was a measure of the moral level of society. He thought one should speak of illegitimate parents rather than illegitimate children, and he deplored the fact that the blame was attached only to the woman and not to the man. He recognized the need for the care of such children by state and society and believed that illegitimate children should have legal rights equal to those of legitimate children. He also lamented the number of abandoned children but felt that providing homes for them simply encouraged illegitimate births.[28]

Yet Masaryk was also opposed to the use of contraceptives, which he regarded as another sin of modern society and called "married masturbation."[29] Incidentally, he was also opposed to masturbation by young men, another "evil" leading to premature and immoderate sexual life and to perversion.[30]

Alcoholism, in Masaryk's view, was closely associated with prostitution and had a strong effect on love and marriage and sexual immorality. It was the cause of many economic and social ills. "Drinking and alcoholism harm the relations of man and woman, lowering and coarsening them; animality replaces humanity. Love is pure love; love with alcohol is not love." Alcoholism, he felt, harmed the relationship of parents and children. It deprived children of a father, separated by the tavern from his wife and children; the latter thus missed the happiness of childhood. The drinker neglected his family; money needed for food and medicine was wasted on drink. Alcoholism affected not only the father physically and mentally but also the children, who grew up in an evil atmosphere and learned to drink from the parent. Only abstinence could make family life what it ought to be. After the overcoming of alcoholism "the relationship between husband and wife, families and children, will be different, better, purer, and more spiritual."[31]

## Criticism of the Catholic Viewpoint

In defending what he called "a modern viewpoint," Masaryk, as was his wont, subjected other viewpoints to severe criticism. One of his chief targets was the "old view" that "woman is for man—that woman is a comfort for man, at best for the rearing of his children" and that "woman must be subject to the husband and the father" (*Masaryk a ženy*, 61). This concept was upheld principally by official religion as embodied by the Catholic church, and in Masaryk's view it represented "absolutism or aristocratism of the male" (84). This "Christian ascetic ideal" was based on the false idea that body and spirit were different, the former something impure, not deserving of respect (90). This led to the Catholic idea of the Madonna, representing "physical virginity," and cultivated "a special Jesuitical sensualism, which devalued the ideal by a coarse opinion of a woman's lower value" (66). This position was expressed concretely in the requirement of celibacy for priests and monks, which confirmed "the view that woman was something lower" (74).

In Masaryk's view, contemporary Catholic teachings on women were based on, and justified by, the Old Testament (Proverbs 31 : 10–31) and carried on in the New Testament, especially in the teachings of Paul.[32] This patriarchal view treated woman as virtuous above all as a worker and home provider, one who cared in all things for her husband ("O ženě" [On Woman], in *Masaryk a ženy*, 99–101). Paul's teaching, which became the official doctrine of the church, reasserted the view that women were subordinate and drew the conclusion that they should be excluded from the priesthood. The ideal of the church became the monk or the nun, who did not marry but abandoned family life (105–6). From this practice later developed the rule of celibacy for priests, although it was often more honored in the breach than in observance, and priestly failings were hidden. It also led to the doctrine that marriages were only valid if conducted by priests and to the ban on marriages between Christians and non-Christians. The cult of the Virgin Mary reinforced the view that marriage was somehow impure and the equation of virtue with physical inviolability. This ascetic view, for Masaryk, degraded women and marriage and ignored the fact that a man could be purer in marriage than in virginity, since marriage constituted a relationship of body and spirit. Only Saint Augustine recognized that in marriage both partners were "brothers and fellow servants" and were one in spirit and body (108–9).

Masaryk discerned a significant difference of attitude between Jesus and Paul, although he admitted there were difficulties of interpretation. Jesus also accepted to a significant degree Old Testament views, for instance on divorce, asceticism, and celibacy (80–81). Divorce was permissible only for reason of adultery; yet he was also willing to forgive adultery. Chastity was for him the ideal, better than marriage. Yet in Masaryk's view, Jesus was not an ascetic; chastity involved a great but painful sacrifice for an ideal, such as religion. His disciples must be ready to abandon family for his sake. Jesus himself did not marry, although it was not foreclosed that had he lived, he would have married. Yet for Masaryk, Jesus' religion was a religion of love, whereas official religion had no understanding of the higher union of man and woman (99).

## Criticism of Socialist Views

Masaryk was also extremely critical of Marxist views of women. In his systematic exposition of Marxism in *Otázka sociální* (The Social Question), he subjected to severe criticism Engels's historical interpretation of the rise of the family and private property, not only for its historical inaccuracy but also for its exclusively economic or materialist approach.[33] Under capitalism, according to Engels, women were servants and slaves, and the man was ruler of the family. Under socialism the woman would be liberated; mutual love would be the basis of marriage, the hegemony of man would be abolished, the indissolubility of marriage would end, and prostitution would disappear. Although Masaryk could agree with the desirability of many of these objectives, he did not believe that socialism would liberate the woman merely by removing the economic conditions of monogamy.

Masaryk believed that Engels was in error in considering marriage an overwhelmingly physiological and economic institution. Engels's view led him to "reduce family life and its social significance too much to a sexual union," whereas in fact "family life and sexual relations give expression to the whole morality of society and to a complete view of the world."

Engels's standpoint led to what Masaryk called "the doctrine of free love" and the "decadent" view that the sexual instinct was the center of all life and was of such an absolute character that it could not be controlled. On the contrary, Masaryk held that real love was a union not merely of bodies but also of spirits. "It is not enough to recommend free love; we must first and foremost demand a higher, nobler love" (*Otázka sociální*, 93, 96).

Repeating a favorite theme, Masaryk stated his belief that Engels failed to grasp the fact that the women's question was also the men's question. "It is a question not only of liberating the woman but also of liberating the man. Woman is not to be liberated from the man, nor the man from the woman; both are to be liberated, on the one side from animalism (bestiality), on the other side from decadent corruption (depravity)" (*Otázka sociální*, 93). Moreover, Masaryk could not accept the view that prostitution was something necessary and inevitable:

> Prostitution, adultery, and sexual immorality generally are forms of immorality which arise independently and develop under all conditions, and always independently and in new forms. . . . I do not agree with communism in general, and I reject any kind of sexual communism, in whatever form it presents itself— whether prostitution, polygyny and polyandry, remarriage, free love, and so on. Humanity was moving toward absolute monogamy, but for this to be possible, it was necessary to have, besides the necessary economic reforms, moral and spiritual reforms all along the line.[34]

## Criticism of Modern Literature

A third target of Masaryk's was what he called the "decadent" tendency, presenting itself initially on the eve of the French Revolution (Rousseau) and then in the revolutionary ideas of liberty, freedom of the family, and free love. This agenda was expressed in manifold ways in literature, especially French (Stendhal, Balzac, Zola) but also German (Goethe, Schopenhauer) and English (Byron, Shelley, Wilde). Although there were differences according to period and country, these writers expressed in common "the ideal of modern love"—free love, free union and marriage, and freedom to divorce. Liberalism also applied the slogan of political and economic liberty to the family—"husband, wife, and children have to be free." Socialism too placed the family on a basis of political and economic equality and free love. According to these views, monogamy hindered the full development of the human being, both man and woman, and must be replaced by "a noble, higher form of polygamy" (*Masaryk a ženy*, 82–85).

Masaryk expressed his own opinions more fully in many critical reviews on literature published in his journal, *Naše doba*, from the end of the century on.[35] These reviews showed his wide knowledge of comparative literature, but his sweeping generalizations were polemical, sometimes dogmatic, and often complex and obscure. One can only somewhat arbitrarily select, from among his general arguments, some of Masaryk's thoughts on love, marriage, and sex.

Alfred de Musset wrote of "the disease of the century," which resulted from the instability and uncertainty of the transitional period following the French Revolution. Lack of belief expressed itself in skepticism, egotism, and a decline in all spheres of life and had a damaging effect on men and women and their relationship. There was a "fatal division of love into physical love and spiritual love, into clean and unclean love." Love was reduced to sexual passion, and this led to sensual love and cruelty, licentiousness and unnatural living, faithlessness and prostitution: "Love became egotistical; the prostitute, the courtesan pushed back the dreaming, romantic, gentle, sweet grisette. Man separated himself from woman, for he had begun to disdain her; he threw himself upon wine, and leaving the cosy fireside of love, killed himself in foul places. Love succumbed to the spirit of the times. As they did not believe in the old kings and the old religion, so love also became for them an old illusion" (*Modern Man*, 223–24).

Strangely enough, although religion and the church had been rejected by the new thinking, they continued to exert a profound influence on the new thinking not only in Catholic France but also in Protestant countries, such as Germany. Hence, according to Masaryk, the views of Goethe, as a Protestant, with his doctrine of the Superman and Faust as a titan, bore striking resemblance to those of the Catholic de Musset. There was "the same fight between body and soul, sensual and ideal love, the world and the spirit" (257). Goethe, for instance, "sees a woman's beauty only in her body, and love is for him nothing but a union of bodies; he has not the least idea of the betrothal and marriage of souls." Masaryk asserts that Goethe cannot conceive of an independent woman, or of love and marriage of two loving creatures, who also think and work together. "Goethe's type of woman corresponds to the ideals of the contemporary German bourgeoisie," wrote Masaryk. "The German woman [*Hausfrau*] can always be certain that she will get to the heart of a man most surely through his stomach. On the other hand Goethe looks upon woman as ready at any moment to respond to the advances of a lover" (260–61). "Love is reduced to sexual, sensual love. In the whole of his creative work, Goethe does not deal with children—and yet he wrote so many words about love. How is it possible to love, and yet not to love the little ones?" (284).

Czech literature did not escape Masaryk's criticism, but it also won his praise. Our literature, he wrote, "was penetrated by impurity, and by moral laxity and indifference. As a small nation, however, Czech literature should support the nation by its profound, ethical core and its healthy moral balance" (*Masaryk a ženy*, 154−55). Masaryk valued highly such Czech writers as Karel Mácha, Božena Němcová, Jan Neruda, and Josef S. Machar, who did not perceive women as inferior and maintained a healthy balance in their ethical outlook on male-female relations. Masaryk spoke of these four writers as "pathbreakers for the Czech woman, for the Czech man, and for Czech love" (67−68). It was not without significance that a number of noted Czech women writers, such as Eliška Krásnohorská and Karolina Světlá, were active in the struggle for women's rights.

## Masaryk and the Struggle for Women's Rights

It is not easy to estimate accurately the influence of Masaryk on the women's question. Certainly he gave strong support to the movement for women's rights, corresponding with its leaders and speaking often at women's clubs. In *Naše doba* there were regular columns devoted to the women's question. When the women's journal *Ženská revue* (Women's Review) was established, it took as its slogan Masaryk's phrase, "Let women be placed on a level with men culturally, legally, and politically" (*Masaryk a ženy*, 130). Many women testified to the great influence on their thinking of Charlotte Masaryk's translation of Mill's *Subjection of Women* (122).

Two women active in the movement expressed gratitude for Tomáš Masaryk's contribution to the women's cause. One, a Moravian, wrote in 1905, "The name of Masaryk has and will have in the Czech women's movement a significance rarely accorded by women to men" (126, 129). A leading figure in Bohemia, F. F. Plamínková, writing later in retrospect, spoke of Masaryk as "the strongest support for the political consciousness of Czech women" (125).

Masaryk was a particularly energetic protagonist of the political emancipation of women. By the turn of the century most Czech political parties supported women's emancipation and had joined in the campaign for women's suffrage. Women assumed prominent roles in the Social Democratic and National Socialist parties and in the smaller progressive parties.[36] Masaryk waged an energetic campaign for the extension of the franchise to women. The program of his Realist party in 1900 was, however, not as forthright as might have been expected. Although it advocated full cultural and political equality of the sexes, it expressed uncertainty as to whether there were more substantial fields for the employment of women and pressed for extension of women's opportunities in education by proposing separate technical schools and higher middle schools for women.[37] The Progressive party program of 1905 referred more forcefully to women's state of rightlessness in public and political life and declared that women must be placed on an absolutely equal level with men as to human and civic rights. One could not speak of "a really free people if its greater half is subjugated morally, culturally, politically, and economically."[38]

The 1912 program went further, condemning the medieval view of "woman as a lower creature, unfree, not equal in rights, and designated only for the man, family, and domestic life" and declaring that the woman should be placed on an equal level with man. There should be equal duties, but also equal privileges. There should be equal pay for women's work. The program declared all existing provisions of marriage, family, and inheritance law, and criminal and civil law, which deprived a woman of certain rights only because she was a woman, should be rescinded. Celibacy as a condition of any official post should be abolished. Suffrage should be extended to women, with balloting direct and secret, and with proportionate representation of minorities of both sexes in all representative bodies. The program also included extensive proposals for equal training for women in coeducational schools at all levels, and for special institutions for needy or unmarried mothers, abandoned and orphaned children, and feebleminded and needy children.[39]

When the franchise was broadened in 1907, it did not give women the right to vote. Masaryk himself was reelected to the Reichsrath in 1911, but his Realist party delegation in Parliament remained minuscule. By 1906 women were playing prominent roles in the Progressive party, proportionately more than in other Czech parties, and in 1908 two women were elected to the Diet. The cause of women's political equality still remained to be won.

In his struggle for the rights of women, and in particular in his defense of women's suffrage, Tomáš Masaryk was closer to the mood of the attentive public than he was in his campaign against the Hilsner trial, which he was conducting at almost the same time. Nonetheless, in his advocacy of a wide-ranging and radical conception of women's equality, Masaryk confronted a popular opinion that was largely indifferent and met with prejudices and biases deeply rooted in Czech society. He raised issues that were usually cloaked in silence and was occasionally pilloried for his stand. In 1884, for instance, a Czech "patriot" petitioned several ministries and politicians to strip Masaryk of his academic position for alleged corruption of students. In 1892 Masaryk was prevented by the police from speaking at a rally of working-class women.[40] Although he did not experience the general social obloquy that he suffered in the Hilsner case, he was, as always, a rebel against conformity and a critic of existing beliefs and practices, willing to speak out courageously against what he considered a social evil. As in that case, his success was only partial, but his tireless activity made a significant contribution to public understanding of "the women's question" and helped lay a basis for continuing gains toward women's equality.

## Notes

1. Maria L. Neudorfl, "Masaryk and the Woman's Question," in Stanley B. Winters, *T. G. Masaryk (1850–1937)*, vol. 1 (New York, 1989).

2. Alois Hajn, "Masaryk a ženská otázka" (Masaryk and the Women's Question), *Osvěta lidu*, on the seventieth anniversary of Masaryk's birth, in F. F. Plamínková, *Masaryk a ženy* (Masaryk and Women) (Prague, 1930), 249–250.

3. Bruce N. Garver, "Women and Czech Society, 1848–1914" (Paper read at the T. G. Masaryk Conference, University of London, 1986). See also Tereza Nováková, *Ze ženského hnutí* (On the Women's Movement) (Prague, [1912]), esp. 84–85, 244, 315–320.

4. Hajn, "Masaryk a ženská otázka" (The Women's Question), 254.

5. Letter of January 29, 1910, given in a booklet, *Mnohoženství a jednoženství* (Prague, 1925), 6–7; also published in Plamínková, *Masaryk a ženy*, 78.

6. Milada Veselá, ibid., 188.

7. T. G. Masaryk, *Přednášky o praktické filosofii* (Lectures on Practical Philosophy) (Unpublished ms. circulated in lithograph form, 1884), cited in Zdeněk Franta, ed., *Morální názory* (Moral Opinions), 2d ed. (Prague, 1925), 136–138. For a summary of Masaryk's lectures on practical philosophy, see Zdeněk Nejedlý, *T. G. Masaryk*, 5 vols. (Prague, 1930–1937), vol. 3, chap. 11.

8. Karel Čapek, *Hovory s T. G. Masarykem* (Conversations with T. G. Masaryk) (Prague, 1937), 8, 74.

9. Jan Herben, *Masarykův rodinný život* (Masaryk's Family Life), 7th ed., (Prague, 1937), 23, 64. On Charlotte Masaryk and her relations with Tomáš, see also Nejedlý, *T. G. Masaryk*, 1 (2): 351–382, 2: 26–30; Vojtěch Lev, *Památce Ch. G. Masarykové* (In Memory of Ch. G. Masaryk) (Prague, 1923).

10. Herben, *Rodinný život*; Alice G. Masaryková, *Dětství a mladí* (Childhood and Youth) (Pittsburgh, 1960), 87–97; see also L. Schieszlová, in *Masaryk a ženy*, 177–178.

11. Ruth Crawford Mitchell, *Alice Garrigue Masaryk* (Pittsburgh, 1980), 83–84. See also Charlotte G. Masaryková, *Listy do vězení* (Letters to Prison) (Prague, 1948), 68–69.

12. Mitchell, *Alice Garrigue Masaryk*, 240.

13. Herben, *Rodinný život*, 51.

14. Talk given in October 1893, in Boston, published in *Nová doba* 1, no. 1: 46–49; also in *Masaryk a ženy*, 155–161.

15. Masaryk's four major speeches, all published in *Masaryk a ženy*, were "Mnohoženství a jednoženství" (Polygyny and Monogyny, 1899); "Moderní názor na ženu" (A Modern View of Women, 1904); "Postavení ženy v rodině a ve veřejném životě (The Position of the Woman in the Family and in Public Life, 1907), also published in *Americké přednášky* (American Lectures) (Prague, 1929); "Ženy u Ježíše a Pavla" (Jesus and Paul on Women, 1910), published as *O ženě* (On Women) (Prague, 1929), also in V. S. Skrach, *Masarykův sborník* (Prague, 1926–1927), 2: 241 ff. Henceforth citations from these works in *Masaryk a ženy* are given in the text.

16. T. G. Masaryk, "Ženský sjezd" (Women's Congress), *Nová doba* 4 (1897): 826–829; also in *Masaryk a ženy*, 159–60.

17. See also T. G. Masaryk, *Otázka sociální* (The Social Question) (Prague, 1948), 2:92.

18. Franta, *Morální názory*, 148.

19. Hajn, *Ženská otázka*, 211.

20. In an early study of suicide Masaryk expressed other views, emphasizing the differences between the two sexes as to the motivation for suicide and stating, without offering evidence, that women suffered greater pangs of conscience, shame, and jealousy but were more removed from the worries of politics and business. In their struggle for emancipation, he asserted, women were threatened more than men, as they were not accustomed to the harsher competition of life. See T. G. Masaryk, *Suicide and the Meaning of Civilization* (Chicago, 1970), 25–27. See also Masaryk's lectures on practical philosophy, in which he spoke of women as "having more gentle than reasoning characteristics" and therefore being more suited for work in the family or schools or as nurses. At that time he believed that women would not be successful in politics (Nejedlý, *Masaryk*, 227).

21. T. G. Masaryk, *Humanitní idealy* (The Ideals of Humanity) (Prague, 1968), 57–58.

22. T. G. Masaryk, "Přednášky" (Lectures), lithographed, 1884, cited in Franta, *Morální názory*, 136–139.

23. T. G. Masaryk, *Česká otázka: Naše nynější krise* (The Czech Question: Our Present Crisis) (Prague: 1948), 313–314.

24. In his lectures on practical philosophy Masaryk described monogamy as "a union of two people who marry on the basis of mutual understanding and mutual recognition of one another, and from a noble love and the desire to live together, guided by the moral and reasonable rules of ethics, politics, and sociology (Nejedlý, *Masaryk*, 230). Although Masaryk used the term "polygamy" as well as the Czech word *mnohoženství*, what he really meant was polygyny, that is, sexual relations with more than one person. This applied equally to men and women—polyandry was also taboo. Although he did not refer to homosexuality, there is no doubt that he would have condemned that, too, had it been a matter of public concern at the time.

25. Masaryk, "Přednášky," in Franta, *Morální názory*, 142–144.

26. Speech published in *Čas*, nos. 330 and 332 (1906), cited in Franta, *Morální názory*, 144–148.

27. Dr. V. Bouček, in *Masaryk a ženy*, 306–307.

28. Franta, *Morální názory*, 140–141.

29. Ibid., 142.

30. Karel Čapek, *Hovory s T. G. Masarykem*, 51–52.

31. T. G. Masaryk, *O etice a alkoholismu* (On Ethics and Alcoholism) (Prague, 1912), pp. 18–20; the greater part of this work is also given in Franta, *Morální názory*, 148–156. T. G. Masaryk, *O alkoholismu* (On Alcoholism) (Prague, 1908), pp. 16–18. See also Anna Snižková, in *Masaryk a ženy*, 328–329.

32. "Ženy u Ježíše a Pavla," in *Masaryk a ženy*, 97–111.

33. Masaryk, *Otázka sociální* 2:29 ff., esp. 82–97.

34. Ibid., pp. 96–97. Masaryk also condemned the views of August Bebel, the German Social Democratic leader, for views similar to those of Engels on divorce and free love, the power of the sexual instinct, and the neglect of morality. See Masaryk, *Česká otázka*, 315–319.

35. For a summary of some of these articles, see Kamil Harmach, "Ženská otázka v Masarykově *Naší době*" (The Women's Question in Masaryk's "New time"), in *Masaryk a ženy*,

139–154. For a full discussion by Masaryk of Masset and Goethe, see T. G. Masaryk, *Modern Man and Religion* (London, 1938), 218–255, 256–286 resp. See also B. Prokešová, "Masaryk on Women in Society" (Paper read at the T. G. Masaryk Conference, University of London, 1986).

36. Garver, "Women and Czech Society." See also Bruce N. Garver, "Masaryk and Czech Politics, 1906–1914"; Winters, *Masaryk.*

37. *Ramcový program České strany lidové (realistické)* (Outline Program of the Czech People's Party [Realists]) (Prague, 1900), 11, 34, 54–55.

38. *Ku programu pokrokové strany Českoslovanské* (On the Program of the Czechoslovak Progressive Party (Pardubice, 1905), 58, 62.

39. *Program České strany pokrokové* (Program of the Czech Progressive Party) (Prague, 1912), 70, 112–115, 154–156.

40. Neudorfl, "Masaryk and the Woman's Question"; Winters, *Masaryk.*

# Shall We Dance?

## Reflections on Václav Havel's Plays

MARKETA GOETZ-STANKIEWICZ

*It is an author's job not only to organize existence according to his own lights—
he must at the same time serve it as a medium. Only if he does that can his
work amount to more than its creator and aim further than he himself can see.*
– Václav Havel, "My Temptation"

*In* Temptation *Fistula says: "I don't give concrete advice, and I don't arrange
anything for anyone. At most I stimulate here and there." I could claim this
statement to be my credo as author.*
– Václav Havel, Disturbing the Peace

At fifty-three the Czech playwright Václav Havel has arrived at a cross-road in his life that he hardly could have foreseen. He has been catapulted by the political events in Central Eastern Europe from his writer's desk in a quiet country house in Northern Bohemia to the president's office in Prague's Hradčany Castle, and his life has undergone a change that could hardly have been more drastic. Today his dramatic oeuvre, written over a period of about twenty-five years, comprises nine full-length and four one-act plays (in addition to some early short pieces for stage, television, and radio). When audiences will be able to see a new play by Havel is an open question.

Now, when his name as an important political figure is appearing almost daily in the international press, seems the right time to take stock of his stature as play-wright and determine what he has to tell the waning twentieth century, which has seen the splitting of the atom, the rise of the computer, the mechanization of war, the development of artificial insemination, and the realization of the visions of Orwell and Kafka, on the one hand, and of Bosch and Goya, on the other.

In the postscript to a Czech edition of his plays, Havel provides us, in a typically unpretentious way, with an insight into the first stirrings of playwriting in his life. Equally typically, his statements—never couched in merely informative literal

Václav Havel at the White House, Washington, D.C., holding a portrait of T. G. Masaryk, February 20, 1990. Photograph by Jan Lukas.

prose—also contain a miniature sample of his artistic vision: "In 1956 I was twenty. It was the moment when, for the first time in our part of the world . . . there began that strange dialectic dance of truth and lie, of truth alienated by lie and deceptive manipulation of hopes." [1] Havel feels that this historical moment was felicitous for him as a playwright. Yet despite his claim that he could not have written what he did "without this concrete inspirational background," [2] he was aware that from the moment he started writing, his plays reached beyond the local situation. As he says in a comment for future directors of *Largo Desolato*, written almost a decade later: "Any attempts to localize the play more obviously into the environment where it was conceived . . . would harm it greatly. *Whatever would make it easier for members of the audience to hope that this play did not concern them, is directly opposed to its meaning* [Havel's italics]." [3] Considering the political situation in Czechoslovakia, it is not surprising that Western theater directors and drama critics have tended not to heed the playwright's plea. With interesting and often impressive results Havel's plays have been searched for "clashes between the individual and society," for the deadening influence of "political artificial language" that no longer reflects reality, for rigid power structures and their victims, and for false values and manipulated attitudes, all giving eloquent testimony to an imaginative critic of a totalitarian political regime who was willing to go to prison for his moral convictions. The changed situation today has an odd air of déjà vu about it. In the past there was the "dissident" and "prisoner" obscuring the stature of the writer; now we have the president appearing center stage, and the playwright is literally disappearing in the wings.

When the writer Marie Winn, who translated Havel's latest plays, *Temptation* (1985) and *Slum Clearance* (1987), for the Public Theater in New York, visited Havel in Prague in the spring of 1987, he repeated to her what he had frequently said before in interviews as well as in print, namely that Czech writers "don't really like the word 'dissident.' It makes it seem like a special profession. I'm simply a playwright and it's irrelevant whether I'm a dissident or not." [4] Today one might ironically paraphrase Havel's words: I'm simply a playwright and it's irrelevant whether I'm a *president* or not.

In order briefly to stake out the area of Havel's writings, I would like to bring some other twentieth-century voices into the argument. They are disparate voices from various intellectual disciplines, but they have certain things in common: they reflect postmodern perceptions of the world, and they provide guideposts for orienting ourselves in Havel's dramatic universe—enjoyable and entertaining, yet on a deeper level surprisingly appropriate to contemporary ideas on humanity and its changing views of itself. The voices are drawn from literary theory, sociology, and physics. In his *Physics and Philosophy* the renowned physicist Werner Heisenberg, author of the principle of indeterminacy, raises two points that relate surprisingly to Havel's work. First, there is his discovery that every act of observing alters the object being observed; second, he notes the difficulty of rendering certain phenom-

ena with ordinary words because "the distinction between 'real' and 'apparent' contradiction . . . has simply disappeared."[5] Physics, like philosophy, is faced with "a
world of potentialities or possibilities rather than one of things or facts."[6]

When Eduard Huml, the sociologist in Havel's *The Increased Difficulty of
Concentration* (written in 1968 and, compared with earlier plays, showing a refined
perception of the nature of language) dictates to his secretary a treatise about human
nature, his statements, though not incorrect, are altered by our observing them in the
context in which they are spoken: "Various people have, at various times and in various circumstances, various needs." After pacing about thoughtfully, Huml continues
the dictation: "—and thus attach to various things various values—full stop."[7] The
fact that these statements, hilariously banal tautologies, are undeniably true does not
prevent them from ringing false. Havel has made language transparent and explored
its double nature, though in this play the experiment is still somewhat rudimentary,
and his language has not yet achieved the opaque yet mirrorlike quality of his later
plays—a quality he referred to in his acceptance speech for the Peace Prize of the
German Booksellers in October 1989: "Words are a mysterious, ambiguous, ambivalent, and perfidious phenomenon." They can be "rays of light in the realm of
darkness" or "lethal arrows. Worst of all, at times they can be the one and the other.
And even both at once!"[8]

A cluster of voices pointing in the same direction are concerned with issues of
freedom and constraint, of roles and changed identities, of constellations and interdependencies. They belong to the Russian literary theorist Mikhail Bakhtin and the
American-Spanish philosopher George Santayana. Both have written about the phenomenon of the carnival. Bakhtin sees in it "liberating energy of a world opposed to
all that was ready-made and completed,"[9] whose humor "revives and renews because it is also directed at those who laugh."[10] But carnival can also unleash a sense
of terror because it reveals something frightening in that which seemed "habitual
and secure."[11] The notion of carnival also implies a dance of sorts, a rhythmic sway-
ing controlled by something other than reason. Santayana's lighter but essentially
similar vision of the carnival stresses its salutary aspects, its moment of freedom
when the exchange of the fig leaf for the mask brings release from habitual restraint,
from "custom [that] assimilates expectations."[12] It is here that we touch upon a key
metaphor in Havel's writings—the dance.

Approaching his plays with the theme of the dance in mind, we discover that
another pattern or rhythm, partly a light skipping, partly a dark throbbing beat,
emerges beneath the tightly structured, sober surface of his texts. Occasionally the
playwright lets this mysteriously threatening rhythm burst forth in the final moments
of a play (*The Mountain Resort* [1976] and *Temptation* are cases in point) and calls
into question the obviously cerebral control of the rest of the play. A quick scan of
the metaphor of the dance in Havel's plays is revealing. In his first play, *The Garden
Party* (1963), the dance in its literal meaning is present by implication only: a party

surely includes some dancing. Yet the play is permeated by another kind of dance. The protagonist, Hugo Pludek, spends most of the play learning the forms of new behavior with regard to language. He observes the strictly prescribed steps of the "official language" minuet with precisely measured steps forward and backward, carefully placed silences, and clocked pauses, according to a choreography Hugo learns to master during the course of the play. Whoever joins this dance becomes an integral part of its modulations and precisely measured movements. The whole would not be the same without him. This dance of linguistic patterns, unrelated to reality (although seemingly adhering to logic), causes the incessant merriment of the audience, who come to recognize something vaguely familiar. It is here that we have the beginnings of what Havel later called the "adventure" of theater.

In his next two plays Havel perfects his choreography of patterns and movements (or dance steps and figures). In *The Memorandum* (1965) the characters' professional rise and fall turns on their ability to learn the artificial language Ptydepe. This results in a linguistic dance of power performed by the characters, punctuated by a pattern of familiar daily movements—the common exit to the cafeteria, the icons of cutlery held high and ready for use during the ritual of consumption. These two types of prescribed movements, one new but learnable (Ptydepe), the other reassuringly familiar (the ritual lunch breaks), performed with mind and body respectively, are choreographed by Havel into one interdependent cluster of motions, a perfect artifact that recharges its own mechanism and creates its own momentum.

Havel's next play, *The Increased Difficulty of Concentration,* takes this double dance of mind and body one step further. Its mechanistic nature is brought home to the audience by a dramatic trick: the author jumbles the time sequence. Apologies for attempted seductions precede the attempt at seduction itself; characters who in scene 2 seemed well acquainted with the protagonist introduce themselves to him in scene 5. The comings and goings of a research team collecting "scientific" data to establish a "sample" of human life (Huml's name was chosen at random) alternate with the increasing number of women who, lovingly, are trying to run his life. All this provides a dance of pseudoscientifically and pseudoerotically patterned language that the audience begins to recognize because the patterns reappear at predictable moments. Gradually the audience also realizes that the words remain, but the characters who speak them can be exchanged. In other words, the dance as such remains, but its components, the dancers, change partners and places in the configurations. A kiss on the neck becomes an icon of special devotion; lunch brought in on a tray by wife or woman friend becomes a welcome rest for the hero from the familiar patterns of tearfully extracted declarations of love, linguistic strategies of self-defense, and push-button recall of happy memories.

Before moving on to the most challenging of Havel's plays, his Faust play *Temptation,* I will call on the social scientist among my aiding voices. Since his first major work, the German sociologist Norbert Elias has not only drawn attention to dynamic "figurations" and interdependencies but has also stressed the pervasive tendency to reduce processes conceptually to states. Using the metaphor of the dance, Elias argues against statuary concepts like, say, "the individual" and "society": "One can speak about a dance in general, but no one will imagine a dance as a form outside individuals. . . . Without the plurality of individuals who are . . . dependent on each other, there is no dance." [13] In his well-known essay "The Power of the Powerless" (1978) Havel writes about the greengrocer who puts a political slogan into his shop window not because he wants to express his political opinion but because "everyone does it" and "because these things must be done if one is to get along in life." [14] It is not necessary, Havel argues later in the essay, to believe in these things, but if one behaves as though one did, one has accepted the situation. And "by this very fact, individuals confirm the system, fulfill the system, *are* the system." [15] There are numerous other instances where Havel has made a similar point—explicitly in his prose, implicitly and metaphorically in his plays. The dancers *are* the dance.

In *Temptation* the Tempter and the Tempted (although it is not as clear who is who as my naming them implies) hold three razor-sharp dialogues. The former, a smudgy, non metaphysical but obviously astute fellow, makes a puzzling statement. Revealing his own familiarity with the mechanisms of Foustka's reasoning process, his "intellectual rotation," he comments on how Foustka manages to turn his pet ideas "into a sort of little dance floor on which to perform the ritual celebration of his principles." [16] Principles on a dance floor? An intellectual ritual? Is the tight repartee of the two partners to be understood as a pas de deux of ambiguous ethics? But in a pas de deux each partner repeats in variations the steps of the other. Precisely! They dance with their feet, their bodies, their words, following fixed patterns of entrances and exits, appearing and speaking on cue. *Temptation* teems with variations on dance patterns presented as essential ingredients of human relationships. There are two key "dance" scenes: scene 3, the seduction scene, where Foustka, using his freshly discovered powers of linguistic persuasion, explains to Maggie what life is all about, whereupon she swears eternal love to him. The stage instructions for this scene (Havel's carefully planned, metronomically timed patterns of entrances and exits are, as always, of extreme importance) call for a dance at the back of the stage while the seduction dialogue takes place at the front. Partners are changed, and dancers float in and out, interrupting the wooing process. Repeatedly Maggie is being swept off to the dance floor by other partners, and Foustka's own choreographed linguistic mating dance, his "ritual celebration" (Fistula's perceptive words) of what he knows will appeal and achieve his purpose, suffers lamentable interruptions. While waiting for Maggie to return, however, Foustka is approached by another would-be partner, the Director, who, like a strutting peacock, performs another ritual of seduction, though more banal and obvious than Foustka's own, a stock package of I'd-like-to cliches complete with "home-made cherry brandy," a "collection of miniatures," "a good chat," and the possibility to "stay the night." [17]

In the last scene of the play another dance takes place at the institute's office party, a masked ball with a "magical theme" to the evening, including not only pendants and amulets but also "a profuson of devil's tails, hoofs and chains."[18] During the final minutes "a piece of hard rock, wild and throbbing," gets progressively louder while all figures (Foustka excepted) "succumb to the music"; "an orgiastic carnival" ensues, and the stage goes up in flames and smoke.[19] An atavistic, primitive rhythm is unleashed, obliterating the strategic dance steps by which the rest of the play was controlled on every level. The dark and threatening side of the carnival spills onto the stage. There is, however, another variation on the dance in *Temptation*. A character called only the Dancer (literal and iconic meaning in one) appears intermittently at the flat of Foustka's woman friend and brings her flowers, leaving fits of jealousy and possible (but never proven) lies in his wake. At the end of the play he and Vilma execute some complicated tango steps at the moment when Foustka realizes that his own strategic steps of several levels of deceit had been vain and useless.

Thus Havel works with flexible figurations. His characters are parts or particles of certain groups or systems, yet they make up these systems. In the case of *The Memorandum*, Office Director Josef Gross comes full circle in the system to which he belongs. He loses his leading position, is demoted, and ultimately rises again, having learned to live within the constellation of which he is a part. If he watches his step—the English idiom fits the situation perfectly—in the dance of official dos and don'ts, if he says the right words to the right person at the right moment, if he choreographs his language suitably, he might well be able to remain on top of the bureaucratic pyramid he has climbed again at the end of the play.

Havel has remarked repeatedly that he is interested in the composition of "movements of meanings, motivations, . . . arguments, concepts, theses and words" rather than "the actions of the characters or the progression of the plot."[20] This makes him indeed a "political" playwright in the oldest sense of the adjective. At a performance of *The Memorandum* in 1965, when the protagonist at the end defended the ethical collapse of the world in the jargon of "at that time newly discovered Existentialists," a perturbed member of his audience asked Havel whether he was serious about his defense of this collapse or whether he was trying to criticize this new "Western" philosophy that represented the very opposite of what grimly cheerful official Marxism was teaching. The playwright was delighted because "that particular man was disturbed, and I could not have wished for anything better."[21] The juggling of phrases masquerading as true statements had had the desired effect: it had unsettled a set mind. The playwright had illuminated the mechanism of phrases and revealed their rotating dance within a seemingly closed system.

In one of his letters to his wife from prison, which have now appeared as *Letters to Olga*, Havel writes of "the electrifying atmosphere that attracts me to the theatre," that makes the audience share in "an unexpected and surprising 'probe' beneath the surface of phenomena which, at the same time as it gives them new insight into their situation, does it in a way that is comprehensible, credible and convincing on its own terms." These probes "bear witness, in a 'model' way, to man's general situation in the world. . . . Such theatre inspires us to participate in an adventurous journey toward a new deeper questioning, of ourselves and the world."[22]

What is significant about this passage is that Havel makes it quite clear that as playwright he does not seek answers but rather asks questions; he does not set out to tell us things but invites us to an "adventure." In other words, he puts himself in the same boat with the audience. But what are these adventurous quests that he proposes to us?

Another contemporary playwright might help us out here. The connections between Tom Stoppard and Václav Havel have received some (but not enough) critical attention. Stoppard's recent play *Hapgood* (1988) reveals the artistic kinship of these two playwrights in a new way. Harkening back to Heisenberg, Stoppard's espionage thriller is built around a problem that physics and human beings have in common—their dual natures. As Kerner, the physicist, explains to Blair, the spy catcher: "Every time we look to see how we get a wave pattern, we get a particle pattern. The act of observing determines reality." And later: "Somehow light is particle and wave. The experimenter makes the choice. . . . A double agent is more like a trick of light. . . . You get what you interrogate for."[23] Apply these words to Havel's plays and you have an inkling of what they are about. As his dramatic genius has been refining itself—from the vantage point of today, *The Beggar's Opera, Largo Desolato, Temptation,* and *Slum Clearance* represent his mature period—it has become increasingly difficult to pin down what one might call the meaning of the plays. No wonder, for that is what the playwright is aiming at: "I find it a lot of fun to write various rhetorically adorned speeches in which nonsense is being defended with crystal-clear logic; I find it fun to write monologues in which, believably and suggestively, truths are spoken and which are full of lies from beginning to end."[24] Stoppard's Hapgood is perhaps a double agent, perhaps a triple agent; her identity not only remains an open question but also becomes oddly unimportant when we take up the playwright's challenge and realize that she is "like a trick of light," that her nature changes with our question. When Macheath of Havel's *The Beggar's Opera* (1972) claims to join the general whirl of petty crookedness just because he refuses to pose as a lofty hero, this attitude could well be interpreted as being either good or bad (as wave or particle), depending on the interpretation of the director or—if the latter is particularly astute about Havel's work and keeps its mystery intact—on the frame of mind of the audience. Similarly, Foustka's and architect Bergmann's voluble justifications at the end of *Temptation* and *Slum Clearance* shimmer with ambiguities. We cannot but agree to the single statements, yet we feel that the whole thing comes, uncomfortably, to more than the sum of its parts and that it is somehow false or at least suspect.

If we put the ideas gleaned from other thinkers into formulas, we get something like the following: language and reality, order and chaos, individuals as parts

Souvenir heads of Václav Havel, from a potters' market in Prague.
Photograph by Pavel Štoll.

and initiators of systems, movement and change as constants, questions determining answers. These are obviously vast and complex issues that touch—or mold? determine?—the lives of all of us. I do not think I am stretching a point if I propose that this is the stuff that Václav Havel's plays are made of, though at first encounter they may seem to be primarily a good show, exciting theater. But now, under Havel's guidance, we shelve the abstractions that represent precisely those static intellectual clichés that he has been trying to undermine all along, and we follow him, with open eyes and open minds, into what he calls the adventure of theater.

## Notes

1. Václav Havel, "Dovětek autora," *Hry 1970–1976* (Toronto: Sixty-Eight Publishers, 1977), 302.

2. Ibid., 303.

3. Václav Havel, "Z poznámek Václava Havla, psaných pro inscenátory hry *Largo desolato*," (Samizdat, 1984), 94.

4. Marie Winn, "The Czech's Defiant Playwright," *New York Times Magazine*, October 25, 1987, 80.

5. Werner Heisenberg, *Physics and Philosophy* (New York: Harper & Row, 1958), 175.

6. Ibid., 186.

7. Václav Havel, *The Increased Difficulty of Concentration*, trans. Vera Blackwell (London: Jonathan Cape, 1972), 18.

8. Václav Havel, "Words on Words," trans. A. G. Brain, *The New York Review of Books*, January 18, 1990, 6.

9. Mikhail Bakhtin, *Rabelais and His World*, trans. Hélène Iswolsky (Bloomington: Indiana University Press, 1984), 11.

10. Ibid., 12.

11. Ibid., 39.

12. George Santayana, "Carnival," in *Soliloquies in England* (New York: Scribner's, 1923), 142.

13. Norbert Elias, *Über den Prozess der Zivilisation*, vol. 1 (Frankfurt-am-Main: Suhrkamp, 1976), lxviii.

14. Václav Havel, "The Power of the Powerless," trans. Paul Wilson, in *Václav Havel or Living in Truth*, ed. Jan Vladislav (London: Faber & Faber, 1986), 41.

15. Ibid., 45.

16. Václav Havel, *Temptation, Index on Censorship* 10 (1986): 34.

17. Ibid., 29.

18. Ibid., 40.

19. Ibid., 43.

20. In Karel Hvížd'ala, *Dálkový výslech*, first appeared in German as *Václav Havel, Fernverhör—Ein Gespräch mit Karel Hvížd'ala*, trans. Joachim Bruss (Reinbek: Rowohlt, 1987), 238.

21. Ibid.

22. Václav Havel, *Letters to Olga*, trans. Paul Wilson (New York: Knopf, 1988), 252.

23. Tom Stoppard, *Hapgood* (London: Faber & Faber, 1988), 12.

24. Havel, *Fernverhör*, 237.

# Dada and Structuralism in Chytilova's *Daisies*

## HERBERT EAGLE

Of all the films of the Czechoslovak New Wave, Věra Chytilová's *Daisies* (1966) was the most radical in its structure and, in many ways, the most unsettling in its subject matter. Today, at a distance of twenty-five years, it still appears audacious, absolutely original, and every bit as pertinent thematically for culture worldwide. If two decades of enthusiastic responses from my students at the University of Michigan can be taken as an indication, the path toward avant-garde feature-length films blazed by Chytilová is one that has widespread appeal. Now that the political situation that limited the distribution of her films both domestically and internationally has come to an end, her stature as one of the most important pioneers in the art of film is certain to be recognized, and *Daisies* will take its rightful place among the masterpieces of cinema.

*Daisies*, made in collaboration with film designer and director Ester Krumbachová, evokes Dadaism in its imagery, compositional strategies, and explicitly rebellious attitude. The film frequently quotes Dada directly through its wild spectacles, its parodic visions of technology and bureaucracy, its natural images made abstract through animation, and its combination of words and images within the same frame. The principle of collage, a major source of Dada's radical collision of signs from disparate cultural and artistic orders, is realized in *Daisies* in two respects: within the frame of each shot and as montage between shots. The frequent violation of cinematic conventions, the unpredictability and logical impossibility of the film's spatiotemporal syntax, and the heterogeneous, paradoxical nature of the incorporated signs themselves nonetheless produce a constant awareness of structure. There is a persistent tension between logic and illogic, argument and nonsense, which is characteristic of Dada's attack on nineteenth-century rationalism.

*Daisies* employs a wide span of images and techniques, constantly interrupting and intersecting one kind of practice with another: painterly tableaux become animated with actions, but these actions no sooner begin than their narrativity is interrupted by a new type of formal play. Real-life situations in the lives of two young women evolve into absurd and rowdy spectacles and rituals. Color is foregrounded through costuming and mise-en-scène or through the use of filters. *Fabula* is dis-

Věra Chytilová, with Karel Nepraš's *Please Turn*. Photograph by Meda Mládek.

rupted by abstract collage—of leaves, flowers, butterfly wings, cutouts from magazines, and so on. Images are optically distorted, decomposed, and rearranged. Collage is the dominant constructional method in *Daisies*. We are presented with a
heterogeneous variety of material signs from different systems; the film frustrates our
attempts to structure and give meaning to the syntagmatic connections, but at the
same time it tempts us to do precisely that.

Like Dada, Chytilová's film calls to mind the Russian formalist concept of *os-
tranenie* (making strange). Any artistic canon or code that becomes established suffers a certain loss of dynamism and of creative possibilities for the receiver, as many
elements of the artwork become entirely predictable. By continually initiating and
subsequently violating codes and conventions, the artist heightens perceptions and
the awareness of possible meanings. Dada explicitly evokes structures and codes by
foregrounding them through violations; such art is inherently more critically oriented than works based on accepted canons, which efface their construction as texts
and through their seeming transparency and comprehensibility lay claim to a natural
validity.

Thus in *Daisies*, as in Dadaist art more generally, the principle of anarchy is
balanced by a principle of structure. Yet, although the signs are diverse and the syntax is completely unpredictable, the modes of expression recur and meet one another
across a field of intersecting paradigms. Particular settings, happenings, rituals, color
schemes, and techniques of visual distortion form a grid against which we can sense
differences and similarities—anticipations are fulfilled or meaningfully frustrated.
Formal elements become semanticized through their interaction with denotative
signs from the everyday. Although a single well-defined message is not conveyed, a
field of signification arises with clear relevance to the disruption of society's patriarchal order. The images of patriarchy are parodied or physically destroyed, just as the
logical flow of patriarchal language is frustrated. The text that emerges asserts its
own dazzling creativity at points of disjuncture, exploding its answer at male ma-
chines, wars, courtships, bureaucracies, and narratives.

The opening sequence of *Daisies,* which accompanies the film's credits, consists of an alternating series of images—shots of an enormous, rusty gear, as if from
some giant industrial machine, slowly turning to the sound of drums and trumpets;
and aerial footage of a military bombing run, in bright color, with white puffs of
smoke marking hits on the target, accompanied by silence. Several shots of each kind
are alternated rapidly, and it is unclear to the viewer what the primary signification
of each image should be. The gear wheel has the character of a joke, because we
cannot see what, if anything, the wheel is attached to; the bombing footage recalls a
military documentary, except for its bright colors. The relationship of these two sets
of shots to each other, and to the rest of the film, remains unclear until the finale.

Then what seems to be a narrative begins. Two attractive young women in
bikinis, a brunette and a blonde, are sunning themselves on a riverside boardwalk,

with their backs to a partition. As opposed to the beginning of the film, which is in color, this sequence is in black and white. The two women begin to speak to each other, and as they do, they move their heads and gesture with stiff doll-like or puppetlike movements, accompanied by creaking noises on the sound track. (The names by which these two women address each other change throughout the film; for simplicity's sake I will refer to them by the first names they use in this sequence—Ježinka, the brunette, and Jarmila, the blonde). Thus our expectation that we are watching some modeling of real life (our first impression from the presence of two characters in a plausible combination of costume and mise-en-scene) is replaced by the idea of parody or puppet theater (or both). The dialogue also plays on this tension between real-life banality and satiric artistic convention:

> Ježinka: This doesn't get us anywhere.
> Jarmila: What doesn't get us anywhere?
> Ježinka: Nothing gets us anywhere.
> Jarmila: I look like a virgin. I am a virgin.
> (Jarmila reaches offscreen for a wreath of flowers and puts it on her head.)
> Ježinka: Everything in the world is spoiled.
> Jarmila: If everything in the world is spoiled, let's be spoiled, too.
> Ježinka: Does it matter?
> Jarmila: It doesn't matter.

This is a possible conversation between two bored young women at the beach. But its formulaic repetitiveness, combined with stiff gestures and creaking noises, contradicts realism. The conversation seems to be a string of non sequiturs, but the announced position that everything in the world is spoiled—that nothing matters but still some action, namely *spoiled action,* is called for—has some clear echoes of Dada's position during and immediately after, and in reaction to, rapid industrialization and the First World War. So there appears to be a semantic connection between the opening sequence (the machinery and the bombing run) and this one, but it can only be made by proceeding via several different sorts of codes, and it certainly is not absolute or predictable.

At this point Ježinka slaps Jarmila, and the latter slowly begins to fall over. The next shot shows her landing . . . but in a lush, green, flower-filled meadow in the country! Jarmila is wearing a brown dress and her flower wreath, and the shot is in bright colors. Here Chytilová's editing pointedly frustrates our expectations of cinematic codes. On the narrative level the montage resembles a conventional cut on action: a motion begins in one shot; the next shot, from a different angle, ends the action. Time is thus understood to be continuous according to the classical codes of narrative cinema. Chytilová's changes in setting and costume are only possible, of course, if this is a different time and space in the world of the story. Thus we cannot construct an illusionist reality out of this editing. We are encouraged to recognize the status and priority of the artistic text itself, as a language that plays by its own rules and violates or changes those rules as it pleases. Indeed, Chytilová continues to employ this paradoxical spatiotemporal editing throughout the film.

The artistic space-time of *Daisies* is not that of our Cartesian world. Yet it begins to demonstrate a logic and even a geometry. This is quite literally a *filmic* world, where space can be spliced together smoothly, without gaps in time—just as pieces of a two-dimensional Dada collage on a canvas have a straightforward physical connectedness and a simultaneity of temporal experience, regardless of how puzzling the semantic connections may be.

No sooner is this principle presented then Chytilová embarks on a new departure. The shots that follow Jarmila falling into the meadow have no apparent connection with fictional narrative and proceed with a language more abstract than any heretofore presented—an animated sequence of images of leaves. (Each leaf image is optically printed on only one or a few frames of film; when the sequence is projected, our visual perception cannot register consciously the detailed image of each leaf; instead, our persistence of vision creates the effect of a rapidly, but discontinuously, changing leaf. The technique is frequently referred to as single-frame animation). The sequence is an intriguing, formally beautiful visual display, but one with no ostensible relationship to the preceding sequence. We come to accept these formal asides as part of the language of *Daisies* since Chytilová employs them repeatedly, and, as with all of Chytilová's images, they take on semantic values within the context of the entire film.

After the leaf animation the film returns to the two young women in the meadow, as they hop like bunnies around a tree filled with multicolored fruits of various kinds (the Garden of Eden?). The next shot places them in an apartment, apparently their own; however, they wear the same dresses and heavy eye makeup that they wore in the meadow. When Ježinka throws a handful of apples, they land on a checkerboard mat somewhere else. The flower wreath is then seen falling into a pond—alongside the bobbing apples! We have not seen the place from which the wreath was thrown, but we are shown two places where the apples land. The film thus gives us another lesson about its language: associative relationships will dominate over spatiotemporal continuity.

As the film progresses, we begin to amass recurrences against which to measure difference, enabling us to construct meanings. Jarmila and Ježinka (although the names by which they are called change) remain the principal protagonists. We come to realize that their actions, however they are spliced together, take place in settings that form paradigms—their apartment (the preferred site of symbolic rituals); the riverside boardwalk; a stairway on which the women descend to, or ascend from, a ladies' restroom; the restroom; a restaurant or alternately a nightclub or a banquet hall; the train station; the apartment of a suitor; the outside world of nature. These settings are also interrupted by formal visual displays that have no place but only artistic form. Each of the settings have characteristic actions that evolve in concert with one another; they form a paradigmatic space out of which we begin to make sense.

Let me turn to some of these critical elements and their development in a few selected sequences. One set of recurrent scenes involves dinners that Jarmila and Ježinka have with older men, with the implication that sexual services will also be provided. In the first of these sugar-daddy scenes, Ježinka sits at a table in a fancy restaurant having dessert and wine with a distinguished looking man in his early fifties. Jarmila enters the restaurant wearing her flower wreath and, seeming surprised, spots Ježinka. She sits down with the couple abruptly ("So it's you! I'm her sister.") and proceeds to order, in a commanding tone ("Have you got snails? Jugged hare?"), a sumptuous feast, which she eats in reverse order—beginning with several desserts and a variety of wines, then moving on to an entire roast chicken. Jarmila eats like a barbarian, lifting the whole chicken in her hands, and she talks a mile a minute: "How come you're not eating? Are you on a diet? I have a splendid appetite; I enjoy eating. It's super!" Turning to the older man, she asks, "Have you any kiddies?" Jarmila's attitude and actions are a direct assault on the institution of young mistresses (if one may call it that); Ježinka has these relationships, and Jarmila flaunts the social conventions that accompany them.

In an analogous manner, Chytilová simultaneously flaunts the conventions of narrative cinema (a system developed predominantly by male artists). The dinner scene is presented through a series of jump cuts (moments of time are excised without changing camera angle, whereas in standard narrative cinema, camera angles are changed whenever there is a slight temporal ellipsis in order to mask the cutting out of a segment of time). Furthermore, each of these cuts is punctuated by a change in color of the initially black-and-white scene (to yellow, red, and green) through the use of filters. Jarmila even calls attention to this device in the punning style of Dada, when she says, asking the older man for a cigarette just as the color changes, "Do you have filters?"

The restaurant scenes and the departures of the sugar daddies at the train station (which always follow) consist of an escalating series of pranks at the expense of the older men—and a rising sequence of cinema pranks, violations of normal narrative cinema practice that are visually challenging and exciting. For example, in the first railway station sequence, the women hop off the train as it leaves the yard. As travelogue music begins on the sound track, Jarmila says, "I thought it was the Orient Express"; Ježinka replies, "Bohemia is beautiful, too." Cymbals clash and a time-lapse sequence of a speeding train begins, complete with dazzling color patterns produced through selective solarization of particular areas within the frame of the shots. Later in the film, after the departure of the third sugar-daddy train, a more abstract display shows only a multicolored, elongated flash of light (the train itself is no longer visible in this ultrarapid montage). The prank in the narrative is also more extreme: the women get off the train, the doddering sugar daddy follows, they hop back on, and he is left at the station helplessly chasing the departing train. Over the course of the railway scenes the men grow successively older, weaker, and less in control, and the women manipulate and mock them ever more easily.

From this description we can get some sense of the overall structure of the film as well. The women have a series of adventures, with no other apparent motivation than amusing themselves and being spoiled. Although there is no causal link between the episodes, they are semantically as well as formally interrelated as a result of the recurrence of particular actions, objects, colors, and marked cinematic techniques.

Thus, for example, a sequence interpolated into the sugar-daddy series opens with a red curtain being drawn and cymbals introducing the "act," a tap-dancing couple doing the Charleston (which we may by this time understand as another, more or less sexual, entertainment arranged predominantly for the benefit of men). Jarmila and Ježinka enter in colorful dresses (the tap dancers are shown in black and white) and are ushered to a table that is elevated a bit above the floor and curtained in the manner of a proscenium. They are hardly passive spectators. As the camera alternates in shot-reverse shot between them and the *paid* entertainment, the two women prove to be by far the more inventive and amusing (although their "art" seems to be created for their own pleasure). First they begin to bounce up and down in their chairs in time to the music. They order some drinks, but as the waiter approaches with bottle and glasses, they reach under their table and magically pull out an identical set (a prank that of course involves the collusion of the filmmaker). They pull out straws and begin to blow multicolored bubbles from their drinks. As they get "higher," their part of the sequence is colored with various filters (finally the scene turns green as they begin to overdo it). Not only the music but also whistles and applause on the sound track are matched to the women's entertaining antics. Each time the camera cuts back to the tap dancers, they seem to be working harder to capture the audience's attention, looking more and more discouraged and displeased.

This sequence establishes Jarmila and Ježinka's spontaneous creativity, as opposed to formal entertainment, as a music hall commodity produced for a passive audience. The synchronization of the characters' antics and the filmmakers' antics (both the music and the colorizations) aid in the establishment of a semantic linkage between the spoiled but creative *characters* and the spoiled (in terms of violating norms) and creative female artists (Chytilová and Krumbachová). Official reaction to *Daisies* certainly bore out the validity of this semantic connection. The censure with which the film was met in official quarters is prefigured in this sequence as well, as Jarmila and Ježinka are forcibly evicted from the nightclub. Their vulnerability and the potential for vengeful action by established society—directed against their free-spirited behavior—is thus present here as elsewhere in the film.

In the ritualistic sequences in the women's apartment, the potential for violence, destruction, and self-destruction is expressed more fully. The expulsion from the nightclub is followed by a shot of Jarmila wearing her wreath, lying on the grass—but then the camera pulls back to reveal that Jarmila is actually lying on a turf mat on her own bed. Ježinka enters, sniffs gas and closes the valve ("Whose going to pay for this?"), then walks over to the open window ("You forgot to shut the window"). Jarmila gets up—her legs are loosely tied together at the knees—and begins to shuffle around the room like a mechanical toy. Ježinka eats a pickle from a jar. When the phone rings, Jarmila puppet-walks over to it ("Don't answer it," says Ježinka), picks it up, and announces into the receiver, "Rehabilitation Institute! Die, die, die!" The words "Die, die, die!" are accompanied by a cut to a single-frame animation of roses. The notion of suicide, as well as of murder, are here linked to romantic symbolism expressed ironically in the director's innovative (rebellious) language.

The meaning of the above sequence is greatly amplified by two later sequences involving a suitor who calls himself "your Romeo" and addresses Jarmila as Juliet (we also come to identify him as the telephone caller). The first sequence opens with a single-frame animation of butterflies. A lecherous-looking young man sits down at a piano, murmuring romantic clichés. In the next shot we see Jarmila standing, with rows of mounted butterfly specimens in picture frames behind her, as Romeo's voice offscreen intones: "You are not of this world. Without you, Juliet, life is a torture. I must have fallen in love with you." To the sound of a lively music box tune, we see another butterfly animation, intercut with two quick shots of Jarmila huddled in a corner of the apartment; she is naked—in one shot she holds a picture frame full of mounted butterflies over her genitals, in another over her breasts. The young suitor disappears behind a screen and begins to disrobe. There follow more butterfly collages: shots of butterflies mounted on sheets speed by; then close-ups of butterflies; finally, a sequence of butterfly wings. The animated sequences recall the rose and the leaf animations we have seen earlier (all natural objects that might conventionally be associated with women and with fertility, an association reinforced by Jarmila's placement of butterflies over her sexual parts). On the other hand, the mounted butterflies are explicitly dead in this sequence, and it may occur to us that collages are also made out of dead flowers and leaves. There is a tension between these objects as dead, in the hands of a male collector, and as alive, dynamically animated by a woman filmmaker. A metaphor for the objectification of women by men is thus formally created here.

Jarmila and Ježinka respond to sequences in which they are objectified by men with rituals in which they attempt to exorcize male power and assert their own independent identity. One such sequence is preceded by their announcement that they will "do something terrific." The next shot reveals ribbons of flames in varied hues; the women are burning crepe-paper streamers hung from the ceiling of their apartment. With solemn church music in the background, they are roasting sausages over

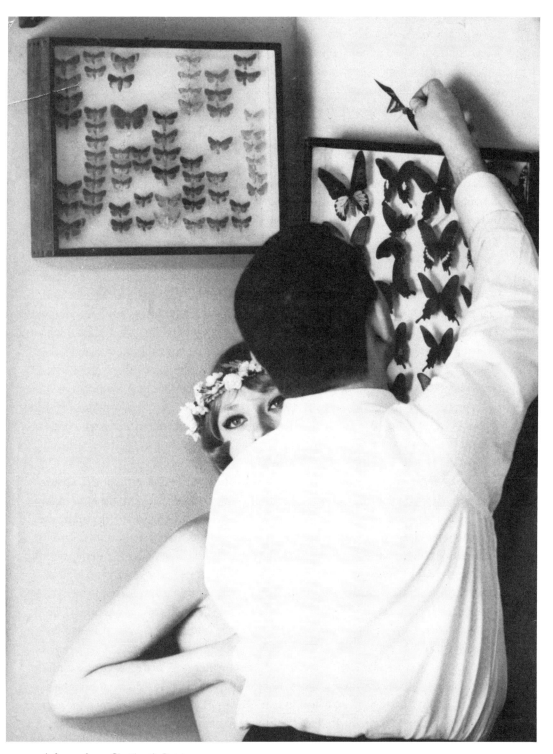

A frame from Chytilová's *Daisies.*

a fire and devouring various "phallic" foods (the sausage, a croissant, a pickle), held by surgical forceps or rings and snipped with scissors. While these symbolic castrations are taking place amidst colorful flames, the voice of Romeo can be heard emanating from a dangling telephone receiver. The obvious relish with which the women bite into their phallic treats while his romantic blabber continues clearly suggests the women's hostility to a system that has turned them into objects, beautiful but dead.

By the end of their last apartment ritual, the women's rebellion against, and ironic attitude toward, patriarchal power has clearly turned self-destructive. They cut each other to pieces with scissors, and Chytilová turns these still battling pieces into an animated collage (through the use of complex matte shots). Although this sequence would appear to be representative of the way oppressed women can turn on one another, the sense of play and artfulness still remains. Jarmila and Ježinka never lose these qualities.

And indeed the film ends not with a sequence of self-doubt, born out of boredom and frustration, but rather with one last burst of outright rebellion. The women return to an industrial building where they previously had tried to assert their identity only to be met by a collage of locks. They find themselves in a dingy subbasement, met by an animated sequence of no-entry signs. They discover a small-goods elevator ("Carrying People Prohibited") and ascend to the top floor, where they find a banquet room with a table laden with sumptuous, expensive, and elegantly displayed foods and furnished with place settings for a dozen or so guests (just the size of a politburo, cabinet, or corporate board of directors). The walls are covered with heavy white curtains, and there are sideboards laden with desserts, wine, and liquor. Hanging over the center of the banquet table is an ornate chandelier made of hundreds of pieces of crystal; its shape is distinctly phallic.

At first the women walk around the table gingerly, tasting some of the sauces with their fingers. Then Jarmila sticks her whole hand into a dish: "Very good sauce. Why don't we take a plate and have a banquet for ourselves?" As the sound track changes from light music to a triumphal military march, the women move from chair to chair along the table, heaping food from the serving dishes onto their plates with their hands and gobbling it down. Ježinka gets up and brings over a tray of liquor; they begin drinking from several glasses at once. Jarmila spots the desserts ("Look! Little cakes!"); Ježinka brings over a giant wedding cake ("This is a proper cake. None of your custard pies"). At the mention of custard pies, the women are simultaneously inspired; they begin throwing large chunks of cream-filled cake at each other, and soon a total food war begins. Wine bottles are knocked over, the china and crystal are smashed, and the beautiful display of food is turned into a shambles.

Jarmila walks over to the white curtains to wipe off her hands on them, but in the process she pulls them down. She wraps herself in a curtain so that she resembles a bride in a veil and climbs up on the table. As the sound track switches to fashion show music, Ježinka (also on the table) begins a striptease. Thus, as bride and whore, the pair dance along the table, grinding with their heels what still remains of the banquet dishes. They meet at the center of the table and climb up onto the chandelier, happily swinging from it.

From symbolic destruction the film has moved us to concrete destruction of shocking proportions (in the spirit of a Dada happening). The destruction of so much food seems gratuitous and horribly wasteful—unless or until we think of the guests for whom it was intended. Could such a small group possibly have eaten all that food? Did they really need it? The characters' (and the director's) gesture of protest against the rich and powerful merely turns elegant conspicuous consumption into the gluttonous spectacle that it actually is.

This expression of rebellion and subversion meets with swift punishment in the film. The women kick over the table with their feet, and as it crashes, we are transported, in the next shot, to a murky river at night. The women are crying out ("Help! Save us! It's only because we are a bit spoiled!") as they grab onto long poles, which, instead of carrying them to safety, dunk them repeatedly into the black waters (as witches were dunked, also for their challenge to patriarchal power). As Jarmila and Ježinka continue to cry for help, a teletype machine clatters out a subtitle: "That's the only way they could have ended up! Could all of that destruction possibly be undone? Even if they had been given a chance, it would have ended up like this."

The next sequence places the women in a purgatory of sorts. They reenter the wrecked banquet hall dressed in wadded newspaper held to their bodies by a fishnet webbing. They walk like marionnettes, taking mincing steps, and talk to one another in barely audible whispers: "We won't be spoiled any more. We'll be diligent. We'll be happy!" They begin to pick up the broken pieces of crockery and wine glasses and reset the table by placing the shards in roughly circular patterns. Then they shovel up food from the floor and heap it onto these "platters": "Everything will be clean again, because we're diligent and good." "We'll polish this." "Everything will be lovely, tidy and clean. Everything will be wonderful again." The women have returned to the puppet behavior that characterized them at the beginning of the film and has haunted them throughout.

Yet the women's deliberately wooden behavior and the comic ridiculousness of their task give the whole scene an air of *parody* of repentance and obedience rather than obedience itself. Jarmila and Ježinka lie down next to each other on the reset banquet table, wrapped in their paper:

> "Are we pretending?"
> "No, we are really and truly happy."
> "Does it matter?"
> "It doesn't matter."

At this point we see a shot of the chandelier above them. In a slow-motion sequence it falls, its plunge made cometlike through selective colorization; it is a blur of color as it hurtles down on the women. But instead of showing it crashing onto their bodies, the film cuts to bombing footage, as in the prologue; only now we see actual buildings destroyed. A staccato message is typed out on the screen to a sound like machine-gun fire: DEDICATION: TO ALL THOSE WHOSE INDIGNATION IS LIMITED TO A SMASHED-UP SALAD.

The representation of the male world in *Daisies* has been built around images of would-be mastery and dominance. In the bombing sequences that frame the film, this dominance is marked as violent and destructive in the extreme. By contrast, the women's rebellion has always been clever, playful, and artistic. We have seen Jarmila and Ježinka cutting out from magazines the very images which have appeared or will later appear in Chytilová's animated collages. Frequently, it is a gesture by one of the women characters which set collages in motion. Even the destruction of the banquet is filled with clever visual devices. These smash-ups cannot be equated to the language of males—the language of the smash-ups of war.

Male mastery has also been represented in the film in the world of work, to which Jarmila and Ježinka fail to gain admittance. The male world houses the large gear, which the two women find standing in a field during one of their forays into the real world. Near this gear, they turn the waste products of industry (metal shavings and wire) into clever apparel (a hat and a shawl). The women have been excluded from productive behavior as defined in the male world, so they have turned instead to art and to play. And as in Dada, this is art and play with hidden political intent. What Chytilová has created in *Daisies* is something much more deliberate and much more effective than a "smashed-up salad," even though it uses smashed-up salads as raw material for its art.

# Second Conversation with René Wellek

## PETER DEMETZ

DEMETZ: When we met last time we discussed the question of *Mitteleuropa*, but in the meantime Europe has changed. It is quite possible that the entire question of *Mitteleuropa* has been transformed or even pushed aside by history itself. I remember that President Havel said Czechoslovakia was returning to Europe. How do you view the events in Czechoslovakia and the Velvet Revolution that has so greatly changed the country?

WELLEK: I am very pleased with the changes, which came so unexpectedly, so peacefully, and even quietly. And as you can imagine, I was in Prague only very briefly during the communist years and was terribly depressed by what I saw. The return of a freer and better government pleases me greatly. I had not even hoped that the communist regime would fall so quickly and, actually, without much noise. To judge at least from the newspapers and from the few reports I hear from others, it all went peacefully in Prague and, apparently, all over the country as well.

DEMETZ: Do you still remember the last days when you were in Prague? Was it in the fifties? Can you remember how the city looked and how people behaved?

WELLEK: I was first in Prague to see my father again after the war in 1957; I was shocked by the changes. There was, at that time, complete darkness, no neon lights, only one sign, "The Soviet Union: Our Model," on the Václavské Náměstí in the main square there. We stayed at the Alcron, which was quite a decent hotel, yet my sister-in-law did not want to come there, even just to have lunch at the hotel, because she said that they would report that she went to this "American," or Western, hotel. All of this was considered forbidden contact with the West. And the concierge in that apartment house where my sister-in-law lived was a *špicl*, a paid informer who didn't even conceal the fact that she spied, noting every visitor, the length of time of the visit, who was joining the group.

DEMETZ: Did you have a chance to meet some of your old colleagues at the univer-

The first conversation with René Wellek is in *Cross Currents* 9 (1990): 135–145.

sity and see them again then? Did they have the same fears as your sister did, or were they more free in their conversation?

WELLEK: They were free only in private. Zdeněk Vančura, who was a professor of English at that time, told me how much he envied his colleague Václav Černý, a professor of comparative literature. And I knew that Černý had been arrested and, without a trial, had been held in prison for about a year and a half; after his release he was not restored to his professorship. He was given a job in the Academy, which only allowed him to file cards and work on a dictionary. He was totally removed from the academic world, from any contact with students, because the authorities feared that students would be infected by Western ideas. I talked to Vančura and said, "Well, it's not very nice, what Černý had to suffer." And he said, "Yes, but he doesn't have to lie, and I have to lie every day. There is a spy sitting in on my lectures and reporting on me, and it's not only that I cannot attack the Marxist interpretation, but I have to interpret everything according to the official line or else get rebuked when I deviate in the slightest way. I find this double life terribly demoralizing, and it weighs on my conscience. Nothing else is that important; I don't mind poverty, little food, bad food, or other things which do not concern me, but this double life of lies is the worst."

DEMETZ: You began to talk about your father, who survived so many years and events in Prague. Would you care to tell me more about your father, who stayed in Prague during your absence from the city?

WELLEK: Luckily, he retired from the civil service just before Munich and therefore drew a pension continued by the government of the Protectorate and later by the newly established Czechoslovak communist regime. It was a small pension but, for his purposes, sufficient. He paid very little rent at the time, but he had to give up part of his apartment and was actually confined to one rather large room. He was able to go out and eat in different taverns and restaurants and listen to music, and of course he read and followed what happened and, I think, carefully kept his opinions on the communists to himself. He had a few friends and was pretty isolated. Yet he was a man who was apparently willing to carry his burdens; he did not complain. When my mother died in 1950, I asked him to join me in the United States, but he did not want to leave and give up his life in Prague.

DEMETZ: Sons and fathers constitute a difficult chapter. Some sons develop in protest, against their fathers, and others take up some of the interests of their fathers and continue them in their own lives. What would you say about yourself?

WELLEK: I was always on good terms with my father. Not a case for psychoanalysis, or one of a generation gap—no conflict at all. If I had any quarrels with my parents, it was with my mother, and those conflicts were practical, about money or behavior toward girlfriends. That kind of thing. My mother often complained about my total lack of interest in many practical matters and always said, "You should have been born with a valet."

DEMETZ: Your father was interested in poetry, in literature, and, I assume, in music as well. Did you live in an atmosphere that had a lasting effect on your own attitudes toward aesthetic experience in general?

WELLEK: I suppose it was enormously important that I grew up in a home with literary and musical interests, even though my own interests deviated from those of my parents. My father, after all, was a student in the 1890s and went to the lectures of Jaroslav Vrchlický and translated poets like Vrchlický, Sládek, and, later, J. S. Machar, whom he knew in Vienna. Machar would be the most modern poet whom my father admired and translated. He did not care for the new generation of Czech poets.

DEMETZ: We have been talking about your father, about his move from Vienna to Prague, and I wonder whether you would like to tell me something about your mother.

WELLEK: My mother, Gabriele Zelewski, was born in Rome, in 1882. Her father was a Prussian officer, but his family was originally of Polish descent. He was the youngest son, who, however, could not serve in the army for long because he had contracted tuberculosis. In accord with the medical ideas of the time, he was sent to Rome, where he became engaged in business; this shocked the family. On a trip to London, he met my grandmother, who was the widow of a Swiss banker in London and already had two children—two sons, Oscar and Albert. He married her, although she was slightly older than he and in greatly reduced circumstances. My grandmother moved to Rome, and my mother grew up in Rome. She went to Italian schools and learned both German and English. English was the business language. They had a strict regimen, which included conducting the conversations at the table in different languages. Mondays, for example, only French was spoken, Wednesdays German, Thursdays English, and so on. So she grew up there in Rome until she was thirteen. Then her father suddenly died; he was not even, or just around, fifty. I think. And my grandmother was, for a second time, a widow, now with four children—a new son, Alexander, and a daughter, Gabriele.

DEMETZ: Did she decide to leave Rome?

WELLEK: My grandmother was extremely restless; she packed up everything and moved to Paris—and with the furniture, so far as I understand. They lived in Paris, and my mother went to what I suppose was high school in Paris, and then they moved to Geneva for a time.

DEMETZ: Your mother had quite an international education. In Rome, in Paris, and in Geneva. But how did she get to Vienna? Or did your father go to Paris where he met her?

WELLEK: My mother went to a French high school in Geneva and even attended some university courses, or something like that. She was certainly interested in getting a teaching position in languages, or maybe one as an interpreter; that was the idea, I think. But then they moved to Zurich, in part because her brother, Alexander, became a student at the Technische Hochschule in Zurich, which had a great international reputation at that time. He became an electrical engineer. They lived several years in Zurich, I think, and when Alexander finished his studies, he was offered a job by the city of Budapest, which at that time wanted to introduce trams, or rather trolleys. He was put in charge of organizing, mapping, and planning the system.

DEMETZ: Did the entire family move to Budapest?

WELLEK: Yes, my grandmother and my mother went to live with him in Budapest, where he apparently had a very good salary. He bought a house in which they could all live and married a woman he met there, a Hungarian of German descent. That went on until about 1900. My mother was not on good terms with Alexander's new wife, and they were discontent and felt isolated in Budapest, so they suddenly decided to move to Vienna, my mother and my grandmother. In Vienna they rented an apartment, which they filled with their own furniture; all this time they had dragged big armoires, beds, and all kinds of things all over Europe. And then my mother, that winter, met my father on the skating rink near the Ringstrasse. There was skating in the park; the rink was not very wide, but it was apparently very popular, and she fell in love with him and got married pretty quickly. My father was a *Finanzrat* in the Ministry of Public Works. They rented an apartment on the Ausstellungsstrasse, where I was born on August 22, 1903.

DEMETZ: Your mother really traveled all over Europe; she lived in big cities, in Rome, Paris, Geneva, Budapest, and Vienna. How did she feel about moving to Prague, where, I take it, she had not been before?

WELLEK: After she married my father, she visited Prague and was introduced to the relatives, to the brothers of my father. But it was merely a courtesy visit, very short. She went again in 1918. Of course, she was much older then, in her forties, or almost in her fifties. It was for her, of course, quite a shock. She had lived all those years in Vienna and was accustomed to Vienna and now had to adjust to completely new conditions. She had had, by then, her last child, my sister Elizabeth, who was born in January 1918, and the family bought a house in Krč, a rather outlying suburb of Prague. It was the only house my father found that seemed a good buy to him, and we lived there. I mean, my mother lived there pretty isolated, taking care of her small child.

DEMETZ: In 1926 you began to travel to do your research in England, and then you came to America and did research and taught there. What were your impressions of America at that time, coming from Prague?

WELLEK: I was very favorably impressed by American universities. This was the first time that I had advanced instruction in literary history in English. Before, in Prague, I had occasionally listened to the lectures of Vilém Mathesius, which were very elementary, descriptive. While at Princeton, I had to compete, for the first time, with students of the same age and the same ambition. You had to write papers there constantly, in the old-fashioned method of positivistic scholarship. For instance, one of the first papers I had to write for Mr. Osgood was about the Irish rivers in the *Faerie Queene*. That meant that you had to study a sixteenth-century map and try to figure out what rivers the poet refers to, often under different names, and you had to guess at the actual location of these rivers. I suppose it was all used by him later in the edition of Spenser's *Faerie Queene* he did for The Johns Hopkins University Press.

DEMETZ: How did you live in America? What was your daily experience when you came suddenly out of Prague to the United States?

WELLEK: The first year I came to Princeton I had what was called a Procter Fellowship, which was at that time very generous because it included lodging, two very good rooms in the graduate college, which you can still see there. The meals were taken in a rather elegant hall, and I was taken care of nicely during the first year. My visa was good for only that year, and I had to find some way of living after that. There was no opening at Princeton, but I finally found a job as an instructor of German at Smith College, which had a very good reputation under President Nielson, a well-known Shakespearean scholar at the time. I wrote to the chairman of the German Department, and he was interested; he was looking for a teacher. He was a German, somebody from Schleswig-Holstein, and he asked me to come up for an interview. I did so and arrived by train. He walked up to me, a man in his early sixties or so, shook my hand, and said, "I see that you are not a Jew." These were the first words I heard from that man. And he took me on a little walk around the campus in Northampton and finally into the office of President Nielson. There, inside, was a prepared contract, which I signed. Immediately Mr. Nielson shook my hand, we exchanged a few polite phrases, and I went back to Princeton. If I had been a Jew, I assume, the chairman would have taken me around the campus and sent me back on the train.

DEMETZ: Did you find, in the late twenties, an atmosphere in which foreign scholars were disadvantaged?

WELLEK: There was no particular resentment against foreign professors in America. I should explain, of course, that my taking the job at Smith was illegal. I had a visa that allowed me to attend school, not teach in one. I had to be a student. I went to Harvard, enrolled in the graduate program of the English Department, introduced myself to John Livingston Lowes, and attended a seminar that met only once a week. My classes at Smith were arranged in such a way that I could also go to Harvard and have a fictional address there as a graduate student. Yet I was teaching at Smith College, which supplied me with the necessary money, two thousand dollars, my salary at that time. It was actually quite an agreeable atmosphere, with some interesting people in the English Department at Harvard.

DEMETZ: Smith is very close to Connecticut and New Haven. Did you ever have a chance to go from Smith College to New Haven, on an excursion perhaps? Or did you pass it by and gravitate toward Harvard?

WELLEK: I looked at New Haven, but since I didn't know anybody there, I only passed through. In the third year I had to teach again because I wanted to stay, and I also had to function as a graduate student. At that time I was offered an assistant professorship in German at Princeton University. And so I went back to Princeton and arranged to attend a graduate seminar at Columbia. John Herman Randall was my teacher there, a man who had written a widely read book, *The Making of the Modern Mind.* He was my supervisor. During this third year my father wrote me and said that I'd better come home because the chance of becoming a *Privatdozent* in English would be lost if I did not return at the right time. And there were other reasons for returning too, I'm afraid, more personal ones. I was, I think, somewhat homesick, and I also had trouble with a difficult relationship with a young woman, and I finally decided to return to Prague. I had saved enough money to pay for my trip back to Prague, but I first stopped in London and studied some manuscripts of Coleridge before going home, where I finally sat down and wrote the *Habilitation,* which was later published under the title *Immanuel Kant in England,* my first book.

DEMETZ: You began to speak of your private problems. Was it because a young woman waited for you in Prague?

WELLEK: On the contrary, that was all American. At Smith College, I had met a young woman, but I had no idea of her background. I fell in love with her and dated her, somewhat awkwardly I might say. And then, after a while, I was introduced to her parents, who came in a great Packard and took us for a luncheon in the country outside of Northampton. I found out that they were very well-to-do people from Buffalo. Her father was a lawyer who had invested in some gold mines in Canada. They had a very fancy house and invited me over; I was there during the Christmas holidays in 1929. I was shocked by the stuffy atmosphere, totally unliterary in some way. The young woman was different, but there was also an attitude of looking down on the poor teacher who earned only two thousand dollars a year. So I didn't like that at all, and, well, I don't want to describe what happened and how things went on.

DEMETZ: It sounds like a chapter from a difficult *Bildungsroman,* but I guess after you closed that chapter you found yourself back in Prague, in 1930. I assume that it was the beginning, after these *Wanderjahre,* of your career at Charles University. Can you tell me something about your life as a *soukromý docent,* or *Privatdozent?* How did you organize your lectures? What did you lecture on? Who were your friends at that time?

WELLEK: I can answer your questions pretty well. When I came home, I had saved some seven hundred dollars, but my parents looked upon me as a *ztro-skotanec.*

DEMETZ: As a man who failed?

WELLEK: As a failure who returned from America with only a vague hope for a university position. Yet I was received well, got my old room back, and stayed with my parents. Of course, I immediately tried to see to it that I fulfilled the requirements for *Privatdozent.* I was interested in Coleridge, and Coleridge led to Kant, and so on. So I sat down and finished the book and handed it in, that is, had it ready for print and offered it to Princeton University Press. They asked for opinions on the book and apparently received very favorable opinions from my teachers at Princeton but demanded a subsidy of some four thousand dollars, which, of course, I could not pay. I arranged to have the Prague State Publishing House print the book, quite nicely I think, although there were quite a few typos and other errors. It was bound the way Princeton University Press does it; it looked like a Princeton University Press book, and the Princeton University Press took it on as one of their own. I think I sent some two hundred copies to Princeton. The Prague publishing house, of course, also wanted some money, but not much, not that much. They only wanted about one thousand dollars, and I asked a friend, an American friend, to lend me the money, and he did so; the book came out in 1931. I lived that entire winter, during 1930–1931, pretty much enclosed in my study room, working very hard to finish the book. But in 1931 something happened to me which was decisive for my later life. I met Olga. An old friend invited me to her house and introduced us to each other. I fell in love with her, and we established an intimate relationship rather soon, certainly by that summer.

DEMETZ: Olga was from Moravia, if I am not mistaken. What did she do in Prague? Did she teach, or was she visiting?

WELLEK: Olga was a schoolteacher in a place called Radotín, which is near Prague. It was very difficult to have a schoolteacher's position in Prague, but her father was the director of a *střední škola,* or middle school, and she at least was employed in a place close to Prague rather than in the city itself.

DEMETZ: Forgive me for asking another question on your daily life. You were young people, intellectuals, in love. What did you do in Prague? Did you walk in the old streets? Did you go on Sundays to Zbraslav? Or did you sit in the Café Slavia? Or in the Café Mánes, as so many other writers did?

WELLEK: During the first summer I went with Olga to her Moravian birthplace, Vsetín, and I lived there with her. We later went to the Tatra Mountains, where my parents had gone. So she met my parents then, and, well, we spent the whole summer outside of Prague. My father always wanted to get away from his office. I managed to earn some money translating; I translated two rather difficult books, D. H. Lawrence's *Sons and Lovers* and then *Chance* by Joseph Conrad.

DEMETZ: Now, when you married and established your own household, where did you move to? Where did you live in Prague?

WELLEK: After we returned from our very modest wedding trip to Špindlerův Mlýn, where we had rented a room in a hotel and actually saw almost nothing because it was so foggy, I rented a small apartment two blocks away from my parents' house. And we furnished it with whatever was in their house.

DEMETZ: What was the name of the street or the neighborhood?

WELLEK: It was in the Ořechovka, a newly built colony of houses for officials, on the hill behind Hradčany Castle. We had a very small garden there, two rooms, and a kitchen. And since I walked over to my parents' for most of my meals, I didn't need much money. My wife, of course, earned an ordinary teacher's salary, and I did translating work and teaching, so we managed to get along.

DEMETZ: I'm very interested in the question of how a *Privatdozent* lived then. Did you actually earn some money for your university teaching, or was that free of charge, forcing you to make your living somewhere else in order to teach?

WELLEK: Well, the Czechoslovak government, after 1918, recognized that these *Privatdozenten* could not be left with absolutely no compensation. The old Austrian joke was *Titel ohne Mittel,* but we were paid a very, very small stipend, which depended partly on the amount of teaching we did. And when Mathesius, the professor of English, fell ill, I actually took over his lectures, and I also had a seminar on English literature. I also began to write for periodicals. In 1924 I had, as a student, already contributed to *Kritika,* founded by F. X. Šalda and Otokar Fischer. I wrote all kinds of reviews or sometimes something more ambitious, for instance, for the periodical of the Club of Modern Philology, and so I came to know some of the members of the Prague Linguistic Circle. It had been founded during my absence in America and was hardly an organized circle. It was just Jakobson and Professor Trnka and a few guests. But later, precisely the year I returned, they decided to organize, and a congress of phonology was held. Today, I think, it would be called phonemics.

DEMETZ: That was in the fall of 1931?

WELLEK: It was in 1930. I attended their meetings, which were of course completely outside of my interests, or at least much of it. I was not very good anyway, I mean as a technical linguist. At least I learned how to distinguish between vowels and consonants.

DEMETZ: Where did the circle usually meet? Was it in a coffeehouse? Or in some university building?

WELLEK: The circle was composed of only a few people, at least when I was there. Of course there was this public congress, but otherwise we met only in cafés and in *vinárny* [wine shops]. Jakobson was the person who made the arrangements. I joined and was invited to give a lecture, and I gave a talk on the concept of literary history. And I was, I don't know, co-opted, made a member of the Prague Linguistic Circle at about the same time I became a *Privatdozent*. I was, I think, attending regularly, and I gave two or three lectures there.

DEMETZ: I would be interested to know how many people attended such evening meetings or lectures. Were there five, six? Jakobson, Trnka, Mukařovský, who else? Or were these meetings open to a wider audience?

WELLEK: They were open to students, and, yes, we met in different coffeehouses, but usually there was only a small group present, often in the Národní ka-várna. I remember there were heated discussions about the book of An-tonín Grund on K. J. Erben. The book was violently, I think much too severely, criticized by Jakobson. He was right, of course, that it was old-fashioned, factual, and without much of a perspective, an international perspective, but I think it was a meritorious book that did not deserve that fierce assault.

DEMETZ: Did you discuss at that time the new books by Shklovsky or Ingarden, or were they known to everybody?

WELLEK: Jakobson, of course, brought his considerable knowledge of the Russian formalists to Prague. He knew them personally. He did not admire Shklov-sky and had many reservations. Jakobson upheld what he considered the line of the Moscow Linguistic Circle, while Shklovsky belonged to the Petersburg Circle. Jakobson, quite rightly, considered Shklovsky often ex-travagant and, I think, often didn't quite see that Shklovsky was a witty man who could not be taken seriously and, in some of his extreme pro-nouncements, didn't want to be taken seriously. I believe I reviewed Shklov-sky's *Theory of Prose* in the *Listy pro umnění a kritiku*, but I'm afraid I occupied myself largely with the translator's absurd translation of English names. Shklovsky was very well known, at least his one book, *Theory of Prose*, the only one of the formalists' books that was translated. You asked about Ingarden; I met him at the International Congress of Philosophy in Prague in 1935 and expressed my interest in his book. I think I was probably the first one ever to mention Ingarden in English, but that was later and not yet in Prague.

DEMETZ: We have been talking about Jakobson, Shklovsky, and Ingarden, but I would like to ask you about what attitudes or ideas of the Prague Linguistic Circle most impressed you and were perhaps useful for your own work.

WELLEK: I think I learned a conception of the totality of the work of art, *Ganzheit, Struktur,* from the Prague Linguistic Circle. The term "structuralism" was brought to Prague then, and of course *struktura* is clearly a foreign word in the Slavic languages; it has no association with a building, as it does in English. And this, I think, is how it was understood in the Prague Linguistic Circle. That is, *struktura* was a totality, not by any means a uniform totality but rather one full of conflicts. I felt that the linguistic circle taught me a far greater consciousness of methodological issues and questions, the semiphilosophical questions—What is a work of art? How does it exist? Why? and finally, of course, Why do *we* care? Why do we study these objects which are works of art? I think that all the Prague linguists firmly believed that out there, certainly outside the personal ego, there were these structures which could be studied and analyzed and that these structures also formed a large community which existed in history and could be traced in history.

DEMETZ: Here in the United States you were often considered the father of the New Critics, and I think you always had some qualms about that. Was it because of your memories of the Prague Linguistic Circle that you saw your position as different here? And how did it differ from the American New Criticism emerging in the 1940s and 1950s?

WELLEK: I think it was within the constellation of the academic situation in America in which I was labeled a New Critic. I came to the University of Iowa, where Norman Foerster was the director of the School of Letters, and he was identified with the whole cause of close reading, with selections from literature that emphasized the great English writers—Shakespeare, Milton, the later nineteenth-century poets. I don't believe that I really agreed with the tenets of the New Criticism as it was expounded, for instance, by Cleanth Brooks. Of course, I always sympathized with it in the context of teaching. This is the idea that you should read texts rather than merely have information about the history of literature, as it was before the 1940s. At a place like Yale, that was apparently a great revolution, that the students were asked to read poems instead of relying on information about the views of, say, Carlyle, Browning, and so on. The change also spread to other universities, although Columbia already had many courses in which the actual texts were analyzed and read rather than just the literary history about them.

DEMETZ: The revolution was possible, or at least partly possible, because scholars still agreed that there should be a number of writers or poets included in a book like *Understanding Poetry*. There was a consensus about who these poets were. Today it would be much more difficult to have such a textbook at all, because the consensus about the canon is missing. Do you have any observation about this problem, very acute for many of us who are teaching now?

WELLEK: I am afraid I still believe in a canon. I believe in the difference between greatness and trash, which is, I think, obvious or can at least be demonstrated to a certain extent. Nobody will deny that there is a difference between the writing of the eminent author, who was considered important, say, in the Victorian era, and the writing of an ordinary newspaper article. There is a gulf between great literature and real trash, which now is often defended and taught because it is supposedly representative or indicative of a certain time and attitude. I think we had a course here at Yale where you were encouraged to read the *Story of O*, which was pornography with, however, some literary skill and not just simply commercial trash.

DEMETZ: Perhaps we should return to the story of your wanderings. Your biography impresses me for long stretches as that of a wandering scholar. America, Great Britain, Prague again, and then Great Britain again; only in your later years did you really settle down in a professorial position. Can we speak about your shift from Prague to London, to the School of Slavonic Languages? On what occasion did this happen, and what were your new duties there?

WELLEK: The School of Slavonic Studies at the University of London was founded by T. G. Masaryk during the First World War and financed in part by the Czechoslovak Ministry of Education. Later, as other nations wanted to have teachers there, others joined in and paid. The Romanians, the Hungarians, and who else?

DEMETZ: The Poles too?

WELLEK: The Poles? No, the Poles did not join, they did not pay. Yes, the Yugoslavs. And of course the Russians did not pay either. All appointments had to be renewed every year, because the British were very anxious to find local British replacements for them. That had the unpleasant implication that you could be recalled at any moment, that the British could produce somebody whom they preferred. There was much reason for uncertainty there. The actual work, in the beginning, when I came in 1935, was negligible. I had to teach elementary Czech, and there was only a small group of people moving from course to course, more often deserting for a time and possibly dropping out altogether. I also had to give public lectures at King's College on the Strand, and there I was left to my own devices. During the first year I chose the topic that seemed natural to me, "Bohemia in English Literature." I gave lectures that I later used in an article, in a long article re-printed in my book *Essays on Czech Literature*. I just gave these lectures without any particular intention or ambition and didn't think anything about them until I got a furious, very rude letter from a professor of history at Charles University, Otokar Odložilík, who chided me, in sharp tones, for interfering in his subject. I felt annoyed by this, and I answered him, I'm afraid, far too mildly and apologetically. He was a full professor at the university, and I was only a *Privatdozent*, and I had to be careful because I was thinking of returning to Prague.

DEMETZ: Who were the people who were attracted to studies of Czech language and literature? Did you have a chance to meet some London or British intellectuals who were friends of Czech or Slovak literature?

WELLEK: The audience was extremely mixed. For a time there was a woman who wanted to write a cookbook and therefore read a cookbook in Czech, from which she would crib recipes. A more interesting person was a man named Allen Pryce Jones, who later became chief editor of the *Times Literary Supplement*. He was an arrogant young man around town, always with a bowler and a furled umbrella. He was married to a Rothschild, and she had estates in Slovakia, and he apparently wanted to understand the legal documents that were sent to them. And I had to help him. There was also a banker; I never understood why he wanted to study Czech in particular, but that was his hobby, and he attended regularly. And then later there was also a Canadian who has since become very well known as a professor of history, Gordon Skilling. That was in 1937 and 1938. He himself went to Prague, and I have since met him again, and he always says that I taught him Czech, but I taught him only the very rudiments of the language.

DEMETZ: I can understand that you felt you had no particular intention to do some of these lectures, but after reading through the essays that you wrote at that time, it becomes quite obvious that they began to fulfill, especially in the late 1930s, an important political function. The position of the Czechoslovak Republic was threatened by Nazi Germany, and it was important to tell the Western world what was going on intellectually and culturally in Czechoslovakia.

WELLEK: What was a purely academic subject soon became quite topical. The lectures at King's College were public and were visited by a sprinkling of what used to be called culture vultures. Well, my few students from different departments were joined by the staff from the Czechoslovak Embassy, which was in some way embarrassing because they of course knew the situation and the names much better, and you felt awkward sometimes, explaining the most elementary things. It was difficult to know the right level for these lectures. I gave a whole series of lectures on nineteenth-century literature and later on T. G. Masaryk.

DEMETZ: I reread some of these articles on Masaryk's philosophy, on the two traditions of Czech literature and the critical panorama of Czech literature in the 1920s and 1930s, and I noticed that you had very distinct sympathies for some particular writers. I also think you didn't like other writers very much. You didn't directly say so, but it's implied, let's say, in the brevity with which you deal with some of these authors. Would it be right to say that you liked Karel Čapek, Ivan Olbracht, and Jaroslav Durych more than others?

WELLEK: I think that's about right. I don't know, but I don't think I really liked Durych. I admired him to a certain extent, but I don't think I particularly liked him. I suppose I was in some way really old-fashioned, not really well informed about the newest developments in Czechoslovakia, in Prague. When I was a student, before I went to London, in the early 1930s, I of course listened to many discussions and met people like A. M. Píša and Jaroslav Seifert and so on, people who later became well-known poets, and I also attended a few meetings at the house of the critic F. X. Šalda.

DEMETZ: I think you had some qualms about Vladislav Vančura. If I read correctly, you believed that he was really an experimentalist of language who could deal with any theme or question, but I think you distrusted Vančura for his ease in handling experimental language.

WELLEK: I did not read everything, nor did I have immediate access to everything. But I tried to. I had some interest in recent poets and writers, for Vítězslav Nezval, who was obviously prominent and generally admired, and for Vančura, whose writings were also widely read. I certainly tried to keep up. But I agree with you that my sympathies were, well, let us say, lukewarm. Yes, lukewarm.

DEMETZ: I was very impressed by the high praise you gave to Olbracht and his book *Nikola Šuhaj*, which I read much later. That's the one author where I think you were not holding back: you called his book almost Homeric. Have you reread the book in recent times, or do you have memories of it?

WELLEK: Yes, memories. I also had some personal acquaintance with Olbracht. His father had a reputation as a regional writer and lived in a house right behind our house in Krč. We were on good terms, mainly nonliterary, or only vaguely literary. And there, in his house, I met Ivan Olbracht, who did not live with his father but had gone off and had even been in prison for a time. It was a sensation of sorts in Czechoslovakia when President Masaryk visited the father while the son was in jail for causing some kind of disturbance, for resisting the police, or so. I met Olbracht then, but of course very superficially. He had no reason to pay attention to me, but I liked him as a person, and he was obviously a very sincere and devoted writer with great ambitions.

DEMETZ: A final question about these literary affairs in the 1930s. I noticed that when you speak about Nezval, again you hesitate. You are not particularly enthusiastic about Seifert, but when it comes to the later work of others like Halas and Zahradníček, you are very much concerned with recommending them to the British reader.

WELLEK: I think I have trouble with Nezval. I liked the poetry of Seifert, what I read. Halas as well. I especially liked the poem about women, what is it called?

DEMETZ: I think it was called "Old Women."

WELLEK: My knowledge of Czech poetry was really very fragmentary and probably slanted in a way, but that's all I could do at that time. I was more and more engaged in my own work on the history of literary history, and then I plunged into the anti-Goebbels propaganda.

DEMETZ: Now we are really approaching an important chapter in your life, or what I would call today your political activism. Many people might not believe me when I speak about your political activism because they think you have been a so-called formalist all your life. But it's quite clear from your essays in London that you were a teacher with a strong political consciousness, with a strong mission. I would like to know more about your meetings with the representatives of the Czechoslovak Republic in London, the foreign minister, President Beneš, and others. Did you talk to them? Did they visit your lectures occasionally?

WELLEK: I met Jan Masaryk, an envoy, not the ambassador. I saw him both socially and on official occasions. Among the employees of the Czechoslovak delegation there was Paul Selver, an Englishman, actually of Polish-Jewish origins, whom I met first in 1924 when I came to London. Otokar Fischer suggested that I meet him; he was the first modern translator of Czech poetry into English. Selver had published an anthology as early as 1920, and he translated Březina and other writers who were then in the limelight, at the beginning of the century. President Beneš came to London only after the Munich disaster. He was either forced out or he thought it wise to leave Prague. He rented a house in Putney, which is a suburb of London near Wimbledon, and Jan Masaryk must have recommended me to him as an English translator, or as one who could help him with English versions of his work. That must have been in late November or early December of 1938, when I called him in Putney, for me a very important occasion.

DEMETZ: Can you perhaps tell me more about this visit? Was it very formal? Or was the president relaxed, and did you have an informal talk instead?

WELLEK: He treated me like a welcome visitor. He sat in an armchair and launched very quickly into a passionate defense of his decision to surrender at Munich. He was disgusted by the policy of Neville Chamberlain and of course with the whole outcome; he saw very clearly that the Germans had occupied the so-called Sudentenland in such a way as to cut off all communications and completely paralyze the rest of Czechoslovakia, which then could not survive without being completely dependent on Germany. But he was so passionate about the need to surrender. He said that if we had not surrendered, the Germans would have invaded us and bombarded Prague. And he said, in possibly a moment of self-praise, that he had saved Prague from destruction. It would have been destroyed by German bombs, and he said there was no question there would have been no chance of resistance. He was particularly disgusted with the French and British governments, which, according to him, would have looked at the invasion of Czechoslovakia without doing more than protesting noisily. I think in some way this interview explained to me why he then went to Russia. He was so disgusted with the behavior of Britain and France; it seemed that only the Russians could offer any concrete help, so he went to Russia. And as many people think, he was there completely deceived by Stalin.

DEMETZ: You said that Jan Masaryk recommended you to Beneš. Did you have many personal encounters with Jan Masaryk? Did you get to know him better than the others?

WELLEK: I met Jan Masaryk often, at the official and not-so-official receptions and also socially with the staff of the Czechoslovak delegation. I was always, or almost always, invited. Jan Masaryk was an extremely congenial person who loved to talk and tell stories and make jokes. He had no inhibitions at all. I became more and more dependent on him, because he asked me to lecture to all kinds of English organizations—the League of Nations, the Rotary Club, the Student Union, and other very local groups. I always explained what I considered the complete falsity of the claims of Goebbels. Some of these trips were very pleasant. I was very well received, but often did not really do more than come into a lecture room, often quite small, with forty or fifty people or even one hundred. I gave my lecture, was entertained by the hostess, had dinner, and was sent back to London; I didn't want to be away from my wife too long. I saw very little of the places to which I went, yet it was still interesting to go to Maidenhead, Brighton, and other places. And I remember Manchester, which was so full of coal dust and so dark, even at noon.

DEMETZ: You discuss your lectures in London and in various British cities, yet you do not say much about your scholarly work on your *History of English Literary History*. When did you begin to write this important book, and what led you to the theoretical issue of English literary history?

WELLEK: The rules for becoming a professor at an Austrian-Hungarian university, which were the same then as in Czechoslovakia, required that after you received your Ph.D. you had to wait three years before you could submit a new thesis; and on the basis of that thesis you became a *Privatdozent*, and I did that. I was in America from 1927 to 1930, came back, sat down, and wrote *Immanuel Kant in England*. I was very ambitious, and so I started to work on the history of literary history, a problem which was partly suggested to me by the debates in the Prague Linguistic Circle and the discussions on literary evolution and literary change. And I thought that I would like to write such a history, and at first I even had the ambition to write it on a completely international scale, but then I thought that that was far too difficult. I looked into the scholarship on English literary history and found that there was practically no information on older books and writings. I was able to work on many unknown, or very little known, books and writings in the British Museum and started, I think, far back in the past but then ended up with Thomas Wharton, who wrote the history of English poetry in the 1780s. That was the foundation book for English literary history far into the nineteenth century, and it was used and imitated all throughout the nineteenth century. I only brought my book up to Wharton and, with some care, studied him, his surroundings, and his context. I wanted to show the rise of historical consciousness and of narrative history, which did not exist before, or hardly so. I worked on steadily when I was in London in 1935–1936. I went every day by the underground. We lived in Hampstead, and I went to the museum and worked there until closing time, which then was at five o'clock.

DEMETZ: Did you have a chance at that time to discuss your intentions or the text of the manuscript with English colleagues, on the spot?

WELLEK: Yes, but it was not very profitable. This topic was foreign to them, at least to most of them. I talked with R. W. Chambers, who was professor of English at University College and was famous for his book on Thomas More at that time. I knew a few others. Bruce Pattison, who wrote on music in the British Renaissance, a very intelligent young man, was interested in my topic, as were a few others as well. But I think I was fairly isolated. I mean, I had my Czech lecture and then I was in the museum; I worked steadily and rarely talked with anybody as far as I remember.

DEMETZ: Perhaps we could talk a little about your last months or weeks in London, when Munich was approaching, or when Munich was already part of world history. Czechoslovakia was divided, and you were there without a job, without income.

WELLEK: You see, this is a little too compressed. I went to Prague during the Munich days, and we were in Switzerland, Olga and I, during the actual crisis. Then I went back to London and taught as usual, and I saw the actual Munich business from there. I mean I saw the surrender there, the fake business with the digging of trenches and the distribution of gas masks, and so on. All of that was very repulsive and depressing. Yet I still received my usual salary from Prague, actually. At Christmas in 1938, after Munich, I wanted to see my parents again and what happened in Prague. We took the train, and we visited my parents and Prague and had, I'm afraid, a very gloomy, depressing experience. Everybody was extremely nervous and apprehensive; they had every right to be. It was strictly a family visit, and I don't believe I saw anybody else. I was as ignorant as everybody else—as apprehensive too. I returned to London on January 11, 1939, and that was the last time I crossed the Channel for a long time. Then I taught my classes as usual, my lectures. I still remember, of course, so much of the morning of March 15, 1939, when very early, I think it was six o'clock, the phone rang, and the embassy told me that Hitler had invaded Czechoslovakia, that the Germans were entering Prague. It was horrible but not quite unforseen. We had tried very hard to save some money, and I had written letters to America, for I knew that I would have to emigrate. I hated the Nazis; I had no illusions about what they would do in Czechoslovakia; I knew that they would easily find out that I had lectured and what I had said. We simply decided to emigrate to the United States. I had no illusions about the British keeping me, and after April 1 no money came from Prague anymore. I talked to the director of the school, Sir Bernard Pares, and he promised to find some English source of money. He actually found it, much later, in June. So I carried out my assignment for the year, but I think it was useless in many ways. I was preparing to move to America; I had written letters, above all to my Princeton professors. Mr. Root told me, "You go back to Prague." Only Mr. Parrott, who was professor of English and taught a course on Shakespeare there and whom I knew also socially, a man who was extremely anti-Hitler, had some help to offer. He sat down and wrote a letter to Professor Foerster at Iowa. Foerster looked at my writings, and by April I already had an offer from the United States, from the University of Iowa.

DEMETZ: Perhaps we should discuss your move to the United States, to the University of Iowa and to Yale, another time, and I will be looking forward to this third conversation with you.

# Contributors

MARIANNA D. BIRNBAUM is professor of Hungarian studies at the University of California, Los Angeles. Her books include *Janus Pannonius: Poet and Politician; Miklós Radnóti: A Bibliography of His Poetry;* and *Humanists in a Shattered World: Croatian and Hungarian Latinity in the Sixteenth Century.* Her forthcoming book, *Esterhazy-kalauz,* will appear in Hungary.

THOMAS BUTLER, professor of Slavic languages and literatures, taught at the University of Wisconsin, Harvard, and Oxford. The list of his publications includes *The Origins of the War for a Serbian Language and Literature; Bulgaria: Past and Present, Monumenta Serbocroatica;* and *Memory: History, Culture and the Mind.*

ALINA CLEJ is associate professor of Romance Languages at the University of Michigan. She has been a frequent contributor to *Modern Languages Notes, Romance Philology,* and *The Romanic Review.* At present she is completing a two-volume work on the limits of confessional discourse and the invention of modernity, *Fables of Transgression.*

AMY COLIN is associate professor of Germanic languages at the University of Pittsburgh. Her publications include essays on contemporary German literature, Holocaust poetry, and fin-de-siècle Austrian writing, as well as *Paul Celan: Holograms of Darkness* and a compendium, *Argumentum e Silentio: Internationale Paul Celan-Symposium.*

AVIGDOR DAGAN (born Viktor Fischl) emigrated from Czechoslovakia to Israel and for several years served as Israeli ambassador in Vienna and in other European cities. He lives in Jerusalem and writes belles-lettres as well as books on political subjects. His publications include *Conversation with Jan Masaryk* and *Moscow and Jerusalem.*

PETER DEMETZ is Sterling Professor of German at Yale University and former president of the Modern Language Association of America. The list of his publications includes essays and books on eighteenth- and twentieth-century literature. He has translated into German a number of Czech poets, including Jiří Orten, Jaroslav Seifert, and František Halas.

HERBERT EAGLE, editor of *Russian Formalist Film Theory* and *Russian Futurism through Its Manifestoes,* has written on verse and film theory and on Russian and Central European literature. He is Director of the Residential College at the University of Michigan.

EMERY GEORGE is professor emeritus of German at the University of Michigan. Among his recent books is *The Poetry of Miklós Radnóti: A Comparative Study.* At present he is completing a study on the late poetry of Hölderlin.

MARKETA GOETZ-STANKIEWICZ is professor of Germanic studies and comparative literature at the University of British Columbia. She is the author of *The Silenced Theatre: Czech Playwrights without a Stage,* editor of *DRAMACONTEMPORARY: Czechoslovakia* and *The Vanek Plays: Four Authors, One Character,* and has written essays on contemporary Central European literature.

JOHN-PAUL HIMKA is professor of history at the University of Edmonton and is the author of *Galician Villagers and the Ukrainian National Movement in the Nineteenth Century.*

FRANK MEISSNER (†1990) was an officer at the Inter-American Development Bank (IDB) in Washington. In addition to his numerous books in the field of business administration and management, he frequently wrote about cultural contributions of the Czech Jews.

VICTOR H. MIESEL is professor of art history at the University of Michigan. His teaching and research concentrate on Central European expressionism, Italian futurism, and cubism. He is the author of *Voices of German Expressionism.*

CZESLAW MILOSZ, Polish poet and Nobel Prize laureate, has recently published a comprehensive volume of his poetry in English, *Collected Poems: 1931–1987.*

DASHA ČULIĆ NISULA teaches Russian language, literature, and culture at Western Michigan University. She has been translating poetry from Yugoslavia for several years.

JAROSLAV PELIKAN, Sterling Professor of History at Yale University, has held numerous national offices, including the chairmanship of the U.S.-Czechoslovak Commission on the Humanities and Social Sciences. His latest books are *Imago Dei* and *Eternal Feminines.*

FRANK R. SILBAJORIS, born in Lithuania in 1926, teaches Russian literature at Ohio State University. He has written on Pasternak, Dostoevsky, and Tolstoy. Much of Silbajoris's research and publications has been devoted to various aspects of Lithuanian literature.

H. GORDON SKILLING, a historian and political scientist specializing in Central and Eastern Europe, is professor emeritus of political science at the University of Toronto. His books include *Czechoslovakia's Interrupted Revolution; Charter 77 and Human Rights in Czechoslovakia;* and *Samizdat and an Independent Society in Central and Eastern Europe.* He has received medals of honor from Charles University, Prague, and Komenský University, Bratislava.

JINDŘICH TOMAN, Professor of Slavic Languages and Literatures at the University of Michigan, specializes in grammatical theories and the history of linguistics. He is preparing a monograph on the cultural history of the Prague Linguistic Circle.

KONRAD WEISS is an East German filmmaker. Since the 1960s he has worked in the section for documentary films at the State Film Studios. His interest has centered on German relations with Poles and Jews and on the history of German intolerance and aggression against minorities. He has frequently written for East German samizdat publications.

JOHN WILLETT specializes in East German culture. His books include *Art and Politics in the Weimar Period: The New Sobriety, 1917–1936; Brecht on Theatre; Expressionism; The Theatre of Erwin Piscator: Half a Century of Politics in the Theatre; The Weimar Years: A Culture Cut Short;* and *The Theatre of the Weimar Republic.*

# Cross Currents 1–10

## Author Index

# Cross Currents 1–10

## Subject Index

# Order Form

Yale University Press, 92A Yale Station, New Haven, CT 06520

Customers in the United States and Canada may photocopy this form and use it for ordering additional copies of number 10 of *Cross Currents*. Individuals are asked to pay in advance. We honor both MasterCard and VISA. Checks should be made payable to Yale University Press.

The prices given are 1991 prices for the United States and are subject to change. A shipping charge of $3.00 is to be added to each order, and Connecticut residents must pay a sales tax of 8 percent.

Quantity                                    Price                          Total amount

_____ *Cross Currents*, 10              $19.95                         _____

Payment of $ _____ is enclosed (including sales tax if applicable).

MasterCard no. _____

4-digit bank no. _____ Expiration date _____

VISA no. _____ Expiration date _____

Signature _____

SHIP TO _____

_____

_____

See the next page for ordering issues from Yale University Press, London.

Numbers 1–9 of *Cross Currents* can be obtained from the University of Michigan, Department of Slavic Languages and Literatures, MLB 3040, Ann Arbor, Mich. 48109.

# Order Form

Yale University Press, 23 Pond Street, Hampstead, London NW3 2PN, England

Customers in the United Kingdom, Europe, Africa, and Asia (except Japan, Korea, and Taiwan) may photocopy this form and use it for ordering additional copies of number 10 of *Cross Currents*. Individuals are asked to pay in advance. We honour Access, VISA, and American Express accounts. Cheques should be made payable to Yale University Press.

The prices given are 1991 prices and are subject to change. A post and packing charge of £1.95/$3.00 is to be added to each order.

---

| Quantity | Price | Total amount |
|---|---|---|
| _____ *Cross Currents*, 10 | £10.95/$19.95 | _____ |

Payment of _____is enclosed.

Please debit my Access/VISA/American Express a/c no. _____

Expiration date _____

Signature _____ Name _____

Address _____

See the preceding page for ordering issues from Yale University Press, New Haven.

Numbers 1–9 of *Cross Currents* can be obtained from the University of Michigan, Department of Slavic Languages and Literatures, MLB 3040, Ann Arbor, Mich. 48109.